Daughters of Saturn

DAUGHTERS OF SATURN

From Father's Daughter to Creative Woman

PATRICIA REIS

CONTINUUM • NEW YORK

1995

The Continuum Publishing Company
370 Lexington Avenue
New York, NY 10017

Printed in the United States of America

Library of Congress Cataloging-in-Publication Data

Reis, Patricia.
    Daughters of Saturn : from father's daughter to creative woman /
Patricia Reis
      p.   cm.
    Includes bibliographical references and index.
    ISBN 0-8264-0812-5 (hardcover : acid-free paper)
    1. Fathers and daughters.   2. Archetype (Psychology)   3. Women-
-Psychology. I. Title
HQ755.85.R444   1995
306.874'2—dc20   94-42832
                                            CIP

To John G. Reis,
in grief and gratitude.

To Hendrika de Vries,
who asked the right question.

Contents

List of Illustrations and Plates

Acknowledgments

As anyone who writes books knows, the writing life can oftentimes be a lonely one. The hours, days, months, even years that it takes to read, research, digest, and integrate one's own dreams, ideas, and information is time necessarily spent in creative solitude. I do not mean to resuscitate the dead notion of the artist as lonely hero, but I do mean to acknowledge that writing is often done at the expense of other things—simple, lovely, human things—like going to the movies, having friends for dinner, spending a morning in bed or a Saturday afternoon on a hike in the mountains. And so I wish to acknowledge all of those women in my circle of friends who knew I was writing and honored my efforts. They did so by inquiring often and attentively how the work was going, by not taking my inability to meet for lunch as any comment on my love for them, by respecting my need for long periods of withdrawal from social activities, by not making demands on our friendship or distancing from me. Indeed, I have felt held in an invisible yet palpable net of caring. Although writing can only be done alone, I was not truly alone. I was continually encircled by the many women whose voices are heard in this work and to them I wish to express my thanks.

My first gratitude goes out to all the women who shared their stories, dreams, psychological, and creative processes with me. Your contribution helped shape and inform my thinking and understanding, your courage and commitment inspired me. Without you this book would probably have taken a much different direction, or maybe it would not have been done at all. Along with those who desire to remain anonymous, I wish to thank Susan Amons, Maureen Booth, Gayle Briggs, Ann Carroll, Susan Doughty, Happy Dunn, Lisa Foley, Patty Gray, Mary Cash Gillies, Charli Griffin, Ginny Keegan, Nancy Lowell, Christine Peirano, Kathryn Phoebe Simon, Kaye Redford, Cora Ellen Weaver, and Lise Weil.

To the "Witches of Ojai," my small circle of wild women who meet together whenever we can to passionately plot and craft our lives, I offer my deepest gratitude. To William E. Wolf, who has provided us with the gift of a safe and beautiful space in which this meeting can take place, I bow in thanks to his quiet knowing.

My gratefulness goes to wisdom woman Hendrika de Vries, who intuitively asked the right question at the right time and then graciously supported me to answer it as fully as I could, and to Kate Smith Hansen, who gave me her fearless example as a wise and wild woman. To Mary Wolf Leibman, a true high priestess, who has offered unstintingly of her great wisdom, abundant love, and generous support, I offer my profound gratitude.

I wish to acknowledge two women who gave their time and energy to reading this manuscript when it was sprawling and misshapen. Especially do I wish to thank Linda Trichter Metcalf, whose friendship is a treasure and whose mind is truly a wonder. Without her critical reading of the manuscript at the right moment, I would have stumbled on in darkness and confusion for a longer time. My thanks also goes to Lise Weil whose reading and appreciation of the manuscript midway encouraged me to continue.

For conversations that excited and inspired, I wish to thank Louie Galloway, Apara Borrowes Toabe, and Joan Marler, as well as astrologer Wendy Ashley. To body-worker and performer, Karin Spitfire, who engaged with me in spirited and hilarious conversations on the wonders of the body, I offer my laughter. To my friend of over fifty years, Pat Reinke Mepham, I offer my continuing gratitude for her memory and her humor. Thanks also to Ann Furan Spartz, the Reis family genealogist and to Barbara Reis Barnes for their help with family history. I wish to also acknowledge the wild wisdom of Anne Dellenbaugh and "Her Wild Song: Wilderness Trips for Women" for some of the best times of my life in the wilderness. A deep bow to analyst Eleanor Mattern, who remained a faithful and steadfast partner as I made my way through the sometimes bewildering places my psyche took me while I was writing. Without women like these, my life would be infinitely smaller and less interesting.

I wish to thank my family for their love and interest—to my mother, Sylvia Reis, who lived with endurance and dignity for almost fifty years with the man who was my father, and to my sisters and brothers, Elizabeth Johnson, Virginia Reis, J. T., Willy, and Doug Reis, who encouraged me to write my version of the struggle with the man we shared as a father, I offer my gratitude. I realize that each of them could tell a different story and I thank them for supporting me to tell mine.

On another note, I wish to acknowledge the tremendous gift that feminism has given me. The rebirth of feminism in this country has provided me with both a personal *raison d'être* as well as a paradigm through which I can re-vision not only texts but contexts, the written canon, the lives of women, and my own life. It is clear to me that I would not have my work as psychotherapist with women nor be able to express my passionate interests through my written work without the guiding principles of feminist theory and praxis. Feminism has also given me connection to a vast community of women whose works stimulate, support, and nourish me. I have drawn strength from their labors as the text of this book will testify and I thank them all for their efforts.

In that light, it is clear to me that no work on father-daughter relationships can appear without acknowledging the pioneering work of two Jungian analysts— Linda Schierse Leonard and Marion Woodman. Their writings on the father-daughter relationship broke new ground on this most difficult subject and we are all indebted to them for their labors.

To Justus George Lawler, my editor at Continuum, I offer my continued thanks for his unwavering belief in feminism and my work. My gratitude extends to Evander Lomke, who shepherded the book to completion, and to Rob Baker of Watersign Resources. I also wish to acknowledge the women at the Maine State Interlibrary Loan Department, who worked tirelessly and cheerfully to meet even the most obscure requests. My thanks also goes to Tami Kennedy, wizard of detail, who provided grounded, practical assistance throughout the production of this work, and to Sudie Rakusin, artist extraordinaire, who so generously gave her work for the cover.

Finally, close to home, to James Harrod, who has shared the gifts of his creative imagination and rare intelligence as I struggled to find the form for this book, and whose deep commitment to me has been a continual source of wonder, pleasure, and inspiration, I offer this book as one of the fruits of our relationship. My thanks also goes to Ruckus, our fifteen-pound tiger cat, who keeps me in touch with cross-species wisdom by sitting on my lap while I work at the word processor.

This was a hard book to write. I understand now that taking up the theme of Saturn was a daunting project. Saturn, notorious for delays, blockage, depression, the dominator of my astrological chart, can be transformed only through the application of hard work and devotion and it is my hope that my efforts have succeeded.

The author and her father

Preface

Memories are not history. They are fragments of things and feelings that were, tinted and sifted through varying prisms of present time and disposition.

—*Yael Dayan*[1]

One evening after dinner, a friend of mine from California called me on the telephone. She works as a psychotherapist and periodically we have long, intense phone calls sharing the events in our outer lives but mostly sharing our dreams, and whatever burning questions we are currently dealing with. During this particular call, she was talking about her father, long since dead, and her need to get out from under a weight she felt she still carried related to him. She asked, "Patricia, are there any myths about the daughter and the depressed father?" I felt this question drop into my ear and begin to quicken. I said I would think about it and call her back, although already my mind was racing and my body felt electrified. My first thought was about my father and the complicated relationship I had with him.

I have in my study a small black-and-white photograph taken with an old box camera in late summer in 1944 before my fourth birthday. In this photograph, probably taken by my mother, my father and I are standing in his garden, surrounded by tomato plants and pole bean "teepees." My father is wearing a pair of baggy shorts. The rest of his bare body is relaxed and shows the musculature of a natural athlete; one hand holds onto the handle of a rake, the other arm akimbo at his hip. He has a slight smile on his face. I am standing next to him about a foot away, as erect as a newly sprouted plant. I am waist-high to him, in a one-piece swimming suit. My whole torso is thrust out and my knees are locked; I am standing as "proud and tall" as I possibly can and I have an enormous grin of delight on my face. I love this picture. I can still feel what a great pleasure it must have been for me, a first-born daughter, to be in my father's garden with him.

I have another image, this one from forty years later. It is a dream that I had while visiting my parents in the house my father built, the house we had moved into when I was thirteen. I am sleeping in my old room in my childhood bed, and I dream that I am in this room, although I am now forty-four. The dream begins as

I hear a great swelling sound of music, which I identify in the dream as "the music of the spheres." In the dream I get up out of my bed to find the source of this music and look out the second-story window onto the garden below. There I see my father, with flowing white hair and a great long white beard. He is sitting in some piece of farm equipment that looks like a thresher; his head is tilted back and his eyes are closed; his look is utterly beatific. The music is coming from the thresher; he is playing it like a harp. I am transfixed by this vision and the music emanating from it.

What transpired in the forty years between the photo and the dream is a long and painful daughter-father story, one filled with love and passion, rage and revenge, oppression, separation, liberation and, much later, a sense of peace and reconciliation. My father died when I was almost forty-seven. Now I feel his presence daily, encouraging, supporting, watching. This was not so for most of our years together in real life. I find it much more gratifying to commune with his soul in the spirit world than I ever did when he was alive and I had to continually confront the many aspects of our complex and difficult relationship.

It is often said that in order to understand one's own background, one must go back at least three generations. I believe this is true. In undertaking the writing of this book I began to investigate more deeply my own father's history, including that of my paternal grandfather and his family.

My father had always spoken fondly of his father, Jacob. I have a small black-and-white photograph taken of them standing together one early spring day outside the family home in Iowa. My father, returning home on vacation from the university, is wearing a stylish belted coat and muffler, his hat held in his hand at his side. Next to him, his father is wearing what looks like a well-worn, matching wool vest and pants; his hat is held in his hand like an offering. He has a big white mustache and a pipe in his mouth. His stance is strong and proud.

I remember my father telling me many times about his father's hard work as a laborer, his love for music, his passion for growing flowers, and his periodic trips to Illinois to stock up on liquor, which was difficult to come by in the dry state of Iowa. Only later did I learn that his father had periodic spells of depression, that he would sometimes sit at the kitchen table weeping. Nor was it ever said to me that my grandfather, due to the circumstances of his growing up on a farm, could barely read or write: there are hints that his wife had felt grossly misled when she married him, believing her husband to be more educated and literate than he really was. It was generally acknowledged that this wife's intellectual ambition had spurred her three sons on to becoming so well educated and that she had enlisted her seven daughters into the pedagogic program for her sons. Some of the daughters were expected to stay home and help, both financially and as caretakers, so the boys were free to go off to school. How my grandfather must have felt to have each of his three sons complete advanced degrees remains a mystery.

My father, it seems, was the least able to bear the burden of his mother's ambition. He became what in those days was called a "perennial student," making his way from university to university during the Depression years, working his way through school, getting football scholarships. He did not complete his bachelor's degree until he was thirty-two, after I was born.

Unlike many men, my father did not "go to war" in the 1940s. Between my birth and the beginning of World War II, he developed what I believe was a psychosomatic illness which kept him from active service. This lack of military service did not make him a better person, but it did eliminate the possibility of war trauma from his personality. After World War II he began to build houses, and that became his work throughout my growing-up years. In his later life my father liked to compare himself to his own father—and the comparison held in more ways than one. He, too, began to sit in the rocking chair for long hours listening to music; he, too, spent most of the Wisconsin growing season outside in his garden; he, too had a great white mustache; he, too, distanced himself in many ways from his large family; and he, too, would experience bouts of deep melancholy exacerbated by occasional episodes of drinking. The major difference between my father and his father was my father's ability to read, which was one of his primary joys. But the weight of paternal melancholy had been inexorably passed on from father to son. As I took up the writing of this book, I began to search for its origin.

How a family can so quickly lose its history in the mists and fog of time and silence is illustrated by my search for the emotional realities at the core of my father and his family. In two generations the sources are all but gone. My own father is dead. Now, I can guess that he himself did not know what I found out. And I do not know nearly enough to satisfy my own desire for understanding the profound and tragic underpinnings that are at the foundation of this family history. I am really sure only of the impact that my father's history had on me, his first-born daughter, the first granddaughter of Jacob. At times this family story seems deeper then I will ever be able to plumb. But even in my limited uncovering, I feel a resonance. Susan Griffin gives the feeling words: "I am beginning to believe that we know everything, that all history, including the history of each family, is part of us, such that, when we hear any secret revealed . . . our lives are made suddenly clearer to us, as the unnatural heaviness of unspoken truth is dispersed."[2] It is the "unnatural heaviness of unspoken truth" that seems to me to be at the core of my father's melancholy. It is this weight which I want to redistribute—the only way that I can, through words.

My father was thirty-two when he married my mother, who was already pregnant with me. This marriage put an end to his life as a student, that "other" life I would hear about as a child in his bedtime stories. He mythologized those early years, telling heroic tales of his youthful travels, his love for literature, his football scholarships, the friends he made on different campuses, and the one mysterious woman whom he wanted to marry. Her presence sat like a ghost at our family table; his unrequited love for her a constant reminder of the life that could have been. In the photo album from his college years, I saw pictures of this woman, the woman who never came on the promised train to meet him. She was Southern, small, dark, intense, and intellectual looking—the opposite of my mother. The woman my father married was high-school educated, hard-working, a healthy young woman from a small German Catholic town in Wisconsin.

In many ways, my parents were mismatched. My father always said, as if in explanation, that he married her because he knew she would make a good mother. Whether this was foresight on his part or hindsight and six children later, the truth was that my mother turned out to be a very steady, reliable, predictable, energetic mother who spent her life caring well for her large family. She was not prone to illness or moods. She was a good cook. She managed the household and all of its endless chores with an invisible strength and vitality. She had married my father because he was very handsome and college educated, a "good catch" for her. She talked about him proudly in terms of how he looked, what he wore, the image he projected. Little did she know then that she would live for almost fifty years with a man who was completely out of her range emotionally and intellectu-ally, a man who felt terribly caught by his life circumstances, a man who was fre-quently beset by melancholy.

My mother never questioned the terms of her life. She never deviated from her role as a traditional wife and mother. She followed the script with cheerful deter-mination and expected to be well thought of because of that. In many ways the arrangement seemed to suit her. The price she paid—lack of decision-making power and economic independence—were offset by the fact that her social status was guaranteed and she had her children. Her devout adherence to Catholicism no doubt helped to reinforce her position as did the times. Only later was I, as her oldest daughter, able to ascertain what was lost.

At some point very early on, my father took me over as his companion, and my mother relinquished me to him. He became my primary emotional resource—all of my feelings of attachment, almost all of my earliest conscious childhood mem-ories are of him; telling stories and playing outdoor games; riding on his shoulders on a moonlit night; lying out in the yard on an old army blanket watching an approaching storm and counting the seconds between lightning and thunder; tak-ing a long train ride with him to visit his parents, a trip he affectionately recorded in my Baby Book. I remember his body, the warmth and broad expanse of his sun-browned back. I remember him teaching me how to read and telling me his own made-up bedtime stories. I remember him teaching me how to throw a pass with a football and how to jump the hurdles. I remember him pulling me up out of the lake when I had dived in to show off and hit bottom and knocked myself out. He had his work clothes on, his carpenter overalls and boots.

As Adrienne Rich has so rightfully said, "It is a painful fact that a nurturing father, who replaces rather than complements a mother, must be loved at the mother's expense, whatever the reasons for the mother's absence."[3] My first book, *Through the Goddess: A Woman's Way of Healing* documented in many ways my search for and recollection of my personal mother, along with the Great Mother and her wisdom. Standing on my own female ground, I am now ready to face my relationship with this man who was my father. This man whose burden of pain so influenced the direction of my life—my relational life as well as my creative life.

It is not merely my personal father with whom I have struggled, however. Through my relationship with him, I have been forced to confront the larger impact of the culture of patriarchy in which I live. The hold that my father had on me as a daughter and that which my society had on me as a woman have frequently felt one and the same. The process of extricating myself psychologically, creatively, and spiritually from the tenacious grip of personal and cultural father-rule demanded that I take radical action. One of my last strategies was to undertake a seven-year period of deliberately chosen separation from men when I was in my late thirties to my mid-forties. My father was still living when I did this. It is to his credit that he did not interfere. He stayed at a respectful distance, not needing to take center stage as was his usual place. He must have sensed my fierce determination, if not my desperate need, to separate. Only when I unplugged from my craving for love and approval from him and the men who represented him, could I find within myself, with the help of other women, my own woman-centered sense of authority. Only then could I find work that fulfilled me, creative expression, and a partnership that is enduring. Only then could I begin to bring what I have learned and am still learning back into the world. Although I still struggle at times, I know who my people are and where my battles need to be fought. I know, too, where my spiritual resources are and how to replenish myself. This book is grounded in part on the story of my own struggle, but it is also an attempt to understand the cultural context within which those conflicts took place.

Many of us have turned our attention toward understanding and deconstructing the collective father, that organized rule of the fathers and its institutionalized power structures that we call the patriarchy. It seems easier somehow to name, confront and, as Adrienne Rich says, "dispose" of the system and ideology that has oppressed us. What is more difficult, less thrilling, tinged with ambivalence, fear, sorrow and guilt, is coming face to face with the relationship that has set the tone for all our later confrontations. Understanding the interconnections between the personal father and the cultural father is imperative if we are to free our bodies, minds, and souls and claim our power to live a creative life. The personal daughter-father relationship is one that shapes all women. It may, in fact, be the last stronghold of attachment, the hand at the ankle, holding us back as we work to liberate ourselves.

Introduction:
The Personal and Cultural Father

With the exception of the incesting father, there has been surprisingly little written by women about the particular impact of the father relationship on our lives. Outside of the critical investigations into the trauma of the abusive father, explorations of the daughter-father story are few. There seems to exist a kind of uneasy ambivalence in most daughter's accounts of fathers—a certain kind of love and yearning mixed with frustration, anger, and sadness. Whenever I mentioned to women that I was working on a father-daughter book I could count on hearing a groan, which soon became familiar to me: it was the sound made up of a woman's inarticulated, mixed, and complex feelings for her father—part sigh, part growl, its tone ranging from painful to poignant. What is it in this relationship, I wondered, that causes us to feel such a strange and powerful mix of emotions?

When they have bothered to look, conventional wisdom and popular psychology have acknowledged that the relationship is an important one. For a daughter, the woman she will become is thought to be shaped in essential ways by the nature of her relationship with her father. And a father is known to affect his daughter in decisive ways throughout the different stages of her life cycle. A father's influence is commonly understood to be implicated in a woman's feelings of self, sexuality, and competency. Her deep patterns of trust, autonomy, ambition, initiative, creativity, and intimacy are believed to be developed in part by how her father has responded to her—if he has been there for her physically, emotionally, and spiritually, a woman will easily find these positive qualities in herself. If he has abandoned her, not protected her, mistreated her, abused her, made her dependent on him, withheld approval, or merely hidden himself from her, a woman will have to contend with the results. She will struggle during her life with issues around mistrust, dependency, lack of ambition, inability to initiate, problems with intimacy.

As noted in all accounts, a father's influence on his daughter becomes most apparent in women's experiences of work and love. Despite the changes occurring in gender roles, fathers are still experienced by daughters as a symbolic link to the outside world. It is well understood, both objectively and subjectively, that a daughter's relationship to her father can make or break her feelings of self-esteem and self-confidence, her understanding of herself as a woman, her belief in herself and her own authority as she enters into the world. If a father has failed to live up to the expected paternal image, if he has defaulted, disappeared, abandoned, or abdicated his power, a woman may feel diminished in some way. If he has hoarded his power and approval, kept her dependent on him or misused his power and abused her in any way, a woman may feel herself to be defective, missing some crucial part necessary for full functioning in the world. A father is thought to be most influential in the areas of financial stability and work. A daughter's feelings of mastery and competency in her work, and her capacity to make and handle money, are thought to be directly related to her father and his own abilities in these areas.

Given the interests of our culture, much attention has been paid to the heterosexual nature of the daughter-father bond and how that influences a daughter's later response to men. A father's attitude toward his daughter's sexuality begins at birth. How he handles her physically, his comfort with holding, feeding, playing with his daughter is highly influenced by a father's own attitudes toward her gender. When she becomes an adolescent, a father's comfort, or more usually discomfort, with the woman the daughter is becoming will register on the daughter and feed into her own comfort or discomfort with herself as female. His view of women will color and shade her perceptions of herself. It is at this vulnerable point that a father's unexpressed emotions and unexamined sexism can easily enter into a woman's psychology.

Most women still retain great quantities of desire for a father's approval, for feeling chosen and cherished. A father who is characteristically distant, absent, emotionally and otherwise unavailable, will leave an enormous chasm in the daughter's psyche, one that she will yearn to bridge. Sometimes the absence of an emotionally engaged father leads a woman to fill in the psychic spaces with false god-like idealizations of men and she may become susceptible to the domination and authority of father figures that she tries to please. If a daughter has not gotten the love and approval she needs from her personal father, she may, as an adult, seek it elsewhere, in teachers, priests, gurus, therapists, doctors, bosses, and other men of authority. Or she may expect her lover or husband to provide her with the missing relationship. If she has been the recipient of an abusive father's anger or sexual transgressions, she may become revengeful and retaliatory. If she has not undertaken her own healing, her relationships with men will tend to be self-destructive and she may find herself in a protracted process of mourning the loss of vital connection. Compensatory relationships will be colored by rebellion or depression.

Turning to Freud

While doing the research for this book, I read various popular versions of daughters and fathers which left me deeply dissatisfied. They all seemed too facile, too superficial, lacking in the kind of charged visceral struggle I had experienced and knew to be at the crux of many other women's experience with their fathers. I found myself coincidentally (I thought at first) immersing myself in a study of Freud, reading different accounts of his life and work by feminists and non-feminists alike. I began to see that Freud had, in a strange way, come closer to the molten core of the daughter-father story than the more currently popular diluted versions.

In *Through the Goddess: A Woman's Way of Healing*, I was occupied with looking to the goddesses as a way of reclaiming the wisdom of our lost and silenced mothers. I was also concerned with a feminist revisioning of some of Carl Jung's concepts about the female psyche, particularly his debilitating notion of the animus. Now, working on the daughter-father relationship, I found myself turning to the quintessential father of psychology. It was Freud, the proclaimer of the primacy of the father in psychological development, who drew my attention. The power of Freud to influence was clearly illustrated to me during my one attempt to discard his material from the manuscript. I dreamed:

> I am at an important party with lots of people. Freud is here. He is an old, frail, and kindly man. He comes over and places his white-bearded cheek against mine in a fatherly embrace.

I am acutely aware of my own susceptibility for wanting this kind of paternal blessing and I am also aware of the other side of Freud that is not so benevolent, particularly to women. But I took the dream as a sign to include Freud in my daughter-father story, for better and for worse.

Daughters and Fathers According to Freud

There is something extremely compelling about Freud that still engages many women at the deepest level. I think this is because Freud's investigation into psychic life and its interactions with the culture are so monumentally comprehensive, yet his waverings, doubts, and fears about women appear as fault lines at every juncture of his thought. His eventual disavowal of women's childhood "seduction" stories, his reluctance to revise and reformulate his thinking about female psychology, as he did most every other aspect of his work, indicate that he felt himself in deep water when it came to women. His very bewilderment and uncertainty reflect a recognizable fatherly attitude.

Although Freud's thought came out of a profoundly patriarchal bourgeois environment and seems terribly dated by now, he still exercises an enormous influence on popular culture. Certainly his thinking and theorizing about female development are contradictory at best and outrageous at worst. But it was Freud's understanding of the daughter-father relationship that set the stage for his psychology and much of our popular understanding of this relationship still rests on his perceptions.

Ever since Freud asked the fateful question, "What do women want?," feminists have been formulating their answers. The Freudian revisionist, Juliet Mitchell, once said about Freud's psychoanalysis: "However it may have been used, psychoanalysis is not a recommendation *for* a patriarchal society, but an analysis of one. If we are interested in understanding and challenging the oppression of women, we cannot afford to neglect it."[1] So, too, I approach Freud, not for guidance, authority, or approval, but for an examination of how women's psychology has been understood by the society in which we live. Freudian psychoanalysis does, as Mitchell says, analyze how a daughter, situated within the paradigm of the patriarchal family, develops. For this reason, I find Freud's interpretations to be illuminating, especially his theories of female psychosexual development and "femininity" with their particular focus on the daughter-father relationship.

Freud was really the first to begin theorizing about female psychology and, in particular, female sexual development. From his earliest observations and experiences in treating women who were called "hysterics," he learned that the father was of primary importance in a daughter's life. It now seems no surprise to us that his earliest findings were based on women's experience of and response to childhood sexual abuse. In his first work, "Studies on Hysteria" (1893–95)[2] he studied the case histories of four women, two of whom had been sexually abused as children by their fathers. (In his first report Freud obscured this fact by stating it had been their uncles!) A year later, after studying the cases of thirteen women with hysteria, he noted that each had had what he called "a passive sexual experience" before puberty. What he discovered was that later events in these women's lives triggered memories of their early childhood trauma and these memories were then translated into physical symptoms. Freud rightfully concluded that hysterical symptoms such as partial paralyses, nonorganic blindness, muteness, and other medically unexplainable symptoms had symbolic meaning—that is, they were an encoded communication about a real traumatic event, or, as he began to call it, a "seduction." And it was, he thought, this "seduction" which formed the core of the woman's illness, or neuroses. Although Freud originally tried to pass these cases of "seduction" off onto early events in the nursery with governesses and nursemaids, he later, in private communications, divulged that a significant number of these women had been "seduced" by their fathers.

Ten years after his work on hysteria, it became increasingly difficult for Freud to comprehend the scope and magnitude of the sexual abuse he was hearing about. In a by now (in)famous revision, he abandoned what he called his "seduction theories" in favor of the notion that these women's memories were primarily comprised of their repressed fantasies and unconscious wishes and desires. This move immediately shifted the burden off and away from the father and placed it squarely on the daughter, where it has been ever since. As feminist psychologist Ellyn Kashack says, "The fathers of psychology have all but ignored the psychology of the father."[3]

Freud's so-called abandonment of his seduction theory led him to his most famous formulation—the Oedipus complex. The myth Freud chose to represent the great challenge of childhood, the centerpiece for his psychoanalysis, is the myth of Oedipus.

What is at the core of this myth, as Freud tells it, is the essential story of the son's secret desire to kill off his father, an act which would then allow him unimpeded access to an exclusive relationship with his mother. The guilt and castration fear that accompanies the son's desire for unshared maternal love, Freud determined, is at the heart of male psychosexual development—all other important psychological events proceed from it. In order to quell his intense castration fears, a boy soon learns how to positively identify with his father. In this identificatory process, he renounces his mother as a love object, repudiates her values, disidentifies with her, switches his allegiance to the father and his phallus, and later, as an adult, goes on to make his own sexual object choice of another woman. This is the culmination of a "healthy" resolution to his oedipal conflict. All other attempts are unsatisfactory and leave the boy unresolved and neurotic. Not an easy thing to accomplish for a boy, Freud thought, but generally realizable. For the daughter, however, the switch of love from mother to father was, Freud came to appreciate, an extremely difficult one.

Although over the years Freud expressed his befuddlement about female psychosexual development by referring to it as a "riddle," and "the dark continent," this did not stop him from theorizing about how this momentous shift of desire from mother to father takes place. Initially Freud was mystified, sensing only gaps and obscurities in girl's sexual development. Then he formulated the notion that a girl's castration complex differs dramatically from that of a boy. Whereas a boy fears castration by the father as retaliation for his incestuous desire for the mother, girls do not fear castration or the loss of their penis since they obviously do not have one. Rather they experience "penis envy." And it is this envy that fuels the little girl's desire for her father. Behind "penis envy" is the supposedly devastating realization that the mother does not have a penis and is herself castrated and therefore inferior, while the father who manifestly does have a penis becomes *ipso facto* the more desirable parent. When the girl realizes that she cannot in fact have her father's penis, she begins to substitute a wish for a baby from him as a substitute. Freud describes what follows for the girl—a very difficult process of negotiating an extremely tricky path.

> Quite different are the effects of the castration complex in the female. She acknowledges the fact of her castration, and with it, too the superiority of

the male and her own inferiority; but she rebels against this unwelcome state of affairs. From this divided attitude three lines of development open up. The first leads to a general revulsion from sexuality. . . . The second line leads her to cling with defiant self-assertiveness to her threatened masculinity . . . and the phantasy of being a man in spite of everything often persists as a formative factor over long periods. . . . Only if her development follows the third, very circuitous, path does she reach the final normal female attitude, in which she takes her father as her object and so finds her way to the feminine form of the Oedipus complex.[4]

Although he was never completely satisfied with his answers, in his later years Freud began to acknowledge that a daughter's relationship with her mother was the earlier and more intense attachment while the relationship with her father only assumes major significance in relation to the daughter's later "acquisition of femininity." Fathers were important to this acquisition in that they became objects of love, admiration, respect, protection, and, most important, authority. But the daughter's turn toward the father was, Freud finally thought, a secondary formation growing out of an initial rivalry with him for the mother's love. He noted that for a girl this switch from mother to father was, at best, difficult to achieve if she managed it at all.

I have included this detailed section on Freud's theories of female psychosexual development because I think it is important for us to hear how Freud gained his conceptualizations. Despite how outdated these ideas may seem to us today, they still operate subliminally within much of psychology's thinking about the daughter-father story.

Daughters and Fathers in Modern Psychology

After Freud, there was very little study on the daughter-father relationship. Only in the 1970s did the impact of this relationship come under new scrutiny. The new interest in fathers followed along two divergent lines. One focused on the father's influence on infant development—as an important attachment object and as a facilitator of ego development. The phenomenon of the "absent" father grew out of these investigations.[5] The other line appeared as a kind of return of the repressed, a resurfacing of what Freud had hoped to bury—the incestuous father.[6]

It is clear from his theories that Freud never critically examined his own assumptions about female sex and gender roles, assuming they were one and the same. It is only recently that modern psychology in general has begun questioning the cultural beliefs embedded in theories about women's development. The few examinations of fathers and daughters that we do have seem to me to be missing this very important and critical perspective.

Although more currently popular books that look at this relationship understand that feminism has made an impact, they are sorely lacking in a basic feminist analysis of our sex and gender system. One researcher in the field of daughter-father psychology, Suzanne Fields, claims her most important finding was that "the two values most strongly influenced by a father are a women's femininity—her sense of herself as a woman; and her competency—her sense of herself as an accomplisher."[7] Fields assumes that we all know what these two value-words describe. She does not undertake an analysis of who is defining "femininity" and "accomplishment," nor does she indicate how these definitions have been constructed to fit the culture's requirements for women. Like Freud, she too, assumes that sex and gender are one and the same and that the culture's definition of "femininity" and "accomplishment" is the one we all agree to and want for ourselves. Fortunately, some feminists have succeeded in examining the depth and power the daughter-father relationship exerts on a woman's understanding of herself as a female living in a father-oriented world. Their insights broaden and extend our knowledge of this still largely unmapped terrain.

Two notable works both by Jungian analysts, both published in 1982, began the process of opening this frontier. Linda Schierse Leonard's groundbreaking book, *The Wounded Woman: Healing the Father-Daughter Relationship*, explores the various manifestations of psychological and spiritual wounding that occurs when a woman's relationship with her father and the cultural fathers is damaged. Marion Woodman's *Addiction to Perfection: The Still Unravished Bride*, a psychological study of women's relationship to their bodies and their creative and spiritual potential, also looks at the father-daughter relationship as well as the patriarchal context in which this relationship takes place. Over ten years later, Leonard's and Woodman's pioneering works still stand as beacons of light for women wishing to travel through the dark continent of their relationships with the father.

"Under a Powerful Womanly Lens"

Only when she was in her fifties did Adrienne Rich begin writing about her father, an enterprise filled with fear and shame, an undertaking both necessary and dangerous.[8] As a major poet and feminist theorizer, Rich presented thinking which has been of deep significance in helping us all to understand the impact of the patriarchal system we are living in. In her earlier work, with the benefit of a far-reaching visionary lens, she looked past and through the figure of her personal father and saw the patriarchal system, its powerful effects, its destructive agenda. When, for the first time, she brought all her capacities for passionate critical thinking to bear on her relationship with her personal father, she saw him only as her personal representative of the patriarchy. "After your death," she says, "I met you again as the face of patriarchy, could name you at last precisely, the principle you embodied, there was an ideology at last which let me dispose of you, identify the suffering you caused, hate you righteously as part of a system, the kingdom of the fathers." Then she blames him for not allowing her to see his vulnerable humanity: "I saw the power and arrogance of the male as your true watermark; I did not see beneath it the suffering of the Jew, the alien stamp you bore, because you had deliberately arranged that it should be invisible to me." Only much later is she able to focus on the complex personhood of this man who was her father and comprehend his struggle and its influence on her, his daughter. She says, "It is only now, under a powerful womanly lens, that I can decipher your suffering and deny no part of my own."⁹

I believe that Rich's process is deeply instructive. Her womanly search for the vulnerable man hiding behind his role as father, and supported in that hiding by the institution of fatherhood and the culture of patriarchy, is one that touches us all.

Our rage at the limits placed upon us from the patriarchal culture often get easily mixed with our desire for the only confirmation of our being that we are taught has merit—paternal love and cherishing. This confusion creates conditions of hatred or a paralyzing ambivalence that prevent us from taking the steps that would truly break us free as women. The task of sorting out the daughter-father relationship includes both an inner and an outer work. We can understand it only if we include an interrogation of the culture along with our psychological investigations.

Patriarchy and the Power of the Fathers

As Rich and other feminists have noted, it is telling that of all the possible variations on parent-child relationships inscribed in our mythic, historical, literary, and psychoanalytic texts, the daughter's relationship to her father is the least told story.¹⁰ Part of the reason is due to the fact that the rule of the father, the reign of patriarchy, has subsumed the daughter's story into its own history.

While the daughter remains eclipsed, the most silent member within the patriarchal family institution, the father as patriarch emerges as one of our strongest mythic figures. Seated in the center of our ideas about family, the authoritarian father, as *pater familias*, is the acknowledged head of the household. This is the notion of father that has been, until very recently, completely supported by our legal institutions and deeply reinforced by our Jewish and Christian religious traditions. Even though changes have occurred in our gender relations—changes both voluntary and as a result of economic upheavals—this kind of father still remains in our minds, if not our experience, as the upholder of patriarchal values.

If we are ever to change this image of father, women will have to relinquish their need for men to fit this paternal pattern and men will have to work hard to achieve a new kind of fatherhood, one defined by partnership, mutuality, and reciprocity.

The deconstruction of patriarchy is far from an accomplished fact. Contrary to what some say, we have not yet achieved a "post-patriarchal" world. Patriarchy in Western civilization has been with us for millennia. Adrienne Rich has given us a sweeping definition, one that maps the vastness of its terrain.

> Patriarchy is the power of the fathers: a familial-social, ideological, political system in which men—by force, direct pressure, or through ritual, tradition, law, and language, customs, etiquette, education, and the division of labour, determine what part women shall or shall not play, and in which the female is everywhere subsumed under the male. . . .[11]

Rich goes on to acknowledge how problematic it is to articulate our experiences as women within this kind of system. She says: "The power of the fathers has been difficult to grasp because it permeates everything, even the language in which we try to describe it. It is diffuse and concrete; symbolic and literal; universal, and expressed with local variations which obscure its universality."[12]

Despite its persuasiveness, patriarchy as a system is historical, not "natural." In its most narrow definition, patriarchy refers to an historically derived system drawn from Greek and Roman law, in which the male head of the household retained absolute legal and economic power over his dependent female and male family members. As Gerda Lerner has pointed out, this narrow definition distorts in several important ways.[13] First it gives the impression that patriarchy began with the Greeks, when in fact it began much earlier. That it began in Europe during the Bronze Age with the takeover of the goddess-worshipping civilizations of Old Europe is something we have only recently known about in detail.[14] The second misconception is that patriarchy ended in the West in the nineteenth century with the granting of civil rights to women. This demise, of course, did not occur. Even to this day we are trying to convince ourselves that we live in a "post-patriarchal" world.

The Institution of Fatherhood

What Lerner suggests is that we adopt a wider definition of patriarchy, one that recognizes patriarchy as "the manifestation and institutionalization of male dominance over women and children in the family and the extension of male dominance over women in society in general. It implies that men hold power in all the important institutions of society and that women are deprived of access to such power."[15] But, Lerner goes on to say, "this wider definition should not imply that women have been or are totally powerless victims, oppressed and deprived of all rights, influence, and resources. Women have and do make up over half the population and are positioned into society in such a way that they are both subjects and agents."[16] Because we are not simply victims, women "have collaborated in their own subordination through their acceptance of the sex-gender system. They have internalized the values that subordinate them to such an extent that they voluntarily pass them on to their children."[17] In her discussion, Lerner makes another important distinction between patriarchy as the institutionalized system of male dominance and a subset of patriarchal relationships she calls "Paternalistic Dominance" where "the dominated exchange submission for protection, unpaid labor for maintenance."[18] What she is describing is the root of the cultural institution of fatherhood:

> In it historical origins, the concept comes from family relations as they developed under patriarchy, in which the father held absolute power over all the members of his household. In exchange, he owed them the obligation of economic support and protection.[19]

As Lerner points out, although male children's subordination to the father's dominance is temporary, "the subordination of female children and of wives is lifelong. Daughters can escape it only if they place themselves as wives under the dominance/protection of another man."[20] And this is clearly no "escape." It is within this extensive context of patriarchy and paternalistic dominance that the daughter-father story takes place, and for that reason it is a story that has been and remains to this day conspicuously absent or at least difficult to tell.

Culture, more than biology, determines the role of father, making the institution of fatherhood more inherently fragile for the individual man and more strongly reinforced by cultural expectations. According to the institution of fatherhood, a father can feel he has fulfilled his role with his daughter if he has successfully negotiated the taboo of incest, usually through the tactic of distancing himself from her when she approaches puberty, and has ensured her virgin status through his safekeeping and protection.[21] The culmination of his responsibility toward her takes place when he "gives her away" (as a virgin) in marriage to another man. (In the past he was paid a "bride's price" for her.) A daughter thus dependent moves from the "safety" of her father's house into the "security" of her husband's home. Upon marriage a woman traditionally leaves her father's name behind and takes her husband's name as her own, and that man's name is passed on to her children. The acceptable variations on this daughter-father plot throughout history have been few and a woman's worthiness has been easily judged according to her ability (or lack thereof) to eventually find her way into this scenario.

In talking about the father's role in a woman's life, Suzanne Fields states: "The parent of the opposite sex carries a special responsibility: the child's first guide to dealing with the opposite half of the human race is the crucial one. How carefully a little girl is taught by her father, and how thoroughly she learns his lessons, may well determine how she enjoys the rewards of bedroom and, for the women who reach it, boardroom."[22] But, how does a woman grow into herself if she has been thus "carefully taught?" How does she learn her own name? Is the complexity of her connection to her father so easily translated into student and teacher? Is this relationship the one that gets transferred onto the man who will be her husband? Is this a good idea? Will it bode well for the woman? for the relationships and work she undertakes? And what happens to the woman who is not interested in the traditional "rewards of the bedroom," what if she does not marry, chooses other women, or herself, or an unconventional partnership, does she escape the pressure of this story? What if the woman has no desire to enter the father's "boardroom?" What happens to the woman who chooses to pursue her desire to be creative?

The Father and Women's Power to Create

Creativity is generally thought of as the work of discovering and bringing to form something new—new symbols, patterns, stories, myths, movements. Through the creative process, the symbols and images that give an enlarged meaning to our lives are made. In this way all art has as its imperative the creation and expansion of consciousness. In his famous work on the subject, Rollo May states that authentic creativity takes courage because it "provokes the jealousy of the gods" and therefore becomes "an active battle with the gods."[23] The Judaeo-Christian tradition is predicated on a male creator god. According to May, human creativity and consciousness are born in rebellion against this omnipotent force and represent man's desire for immortality, to be like god. The creative drive, he says, arises out of man's rage against death, and his creative works are made in defiant compensation against the fact of his mortality. Writing in the mid-1970s, May had no concept for what the courage to create meant for women. In fact, women are barely mentioned in his work. If, as May states, "We express our being by creating" and "Creativity is a necessary sequel to being,"[24] then how women engage in this "necessary" act of expression seems to be an important question. If the goal of creativity is to make new forms and symbols, to transcend traditional ideas, rules, interpretations, it seems certain that it will require nothing less than courage from women.[25]

Women who create do not seem to be in the death-defying, god-defying business. Rather, it seems that women are constantly working not against death per se, but against a living death, a cultural mummification that works to stifle their thought, silence their voice, confuse their mind, and halt their speech. The seemingly simple human act of self-becoming, for which creativity is the pre-eminent emblem, is problematic if the human happens to be a woman. The courage, vision, will, determination, and power necessary to name one's experience and say what one thinks, does not come as a right or a given for women as a class. Women have not had the benefit of historically sanctioned female creative traditions, no community of women writers and artists upon which to model themselves. Only recently has the question "Why are there are no great women artists?" been debunked for its sexist premise. But being a woman and an artist is still not a culturally recognized or ratified condition. Often the requirements of one identity run into conflict with the other. A woman can only resolve the equation "woman and artist" if she is able to re-vision and re-define each of these cultural definitions.

There are other questions besides identity that arise for the "woman artist": How does a woman gain access to her creative life? What are the circumstances under which a woman can take up her creativity? And if she does, what conditions conspire to drive her creative process? What kind of struggles does she undergo, what are the strategies she must devise to live a creative life?

Virginia Woolf once wrote, "We think back through our mothers if we are writers." That thought has led to a great deal of inquiry into the mother-daughter relationship and its impact on women's creative process. With Woolf's observation in mind, one of the questions I wish to ask in this book is "What happens when we think back through our fathers?" What role does the personal and cultural father play in women's creativity?

If there has been little written about the daughter-father relationship in general, there has been mostly blank space when it comes to the father's influence on a woman's creativity. Only recently has the question been raised and this is not because fathers haven't been influential.[26] The effect of fathers on women who wish to undertake creative pursuits is particularly critical. The process of thinking for oneself, finding one's voice, creating authentic work, is usually a complicated one for women. The internalized influence of the personal father can exert a powerful pressure on us, affecting our sense of mastery, our belief in ourselves, in the accuracy and trustworthiness of our thinking and perceptions. The personal father we internalize may frequently be backed up and supported by the cultural, institutional, and spiritual father giving the figure of the father, in general, an unnaturally inflated importance and exaggerated significance in our inner and outer lives.

Learning the Language

Because my focus in this book is on women who use language as a means of creative expression, it is important to understand how language operates. As many feminists have shown, language itself is not just a neutral means of communicating. Language structures how we think and speak, so the language of our culture predetermines not only *what* we can think and speak about, but *how* we must think and speak. Although we seldom think about it, the rights to using language are owned. The myth that predominates in our culture is the one that says God gave Adam the right to name the world. Thus the use of language for speaking and naming is a God-given power—for some.

Sometimes fathers use their male entitlement to language to instruct their daughters. When Yael Dayan was fourteen, she received a pedagogical lesson from her famous father, Moshe Dayan. A bright and avid student, Yael was expected to make her parents proud. When she was given a "cheap, vulgar, and rather violent" book by a student friend, she read it although she did not take it seriously. But her father did. Spying it next to her bed, he picked it up and then slapped her face. She was shocked at his strong reaction. He had never slapped her before and she screamed "Why?" at him. He replied, "This is trash, and I forbid you to read it." She made another approach, this time resistant, "I will read whatever I want. It's a nonsense book, but it's thrilling and fun. All my friends read it." She was slapped again.[27] This is a dramatic example of the way a father will attempt to influence and control a daughter's mind. There are many other ways in which we learn what is good, acceptable, worthy from our fathers.

My father was a certain kind of teaching father. He taught me not only how to read and write but also how to love words. Like many other daughters, I associated words, reading, and writing with him. Mastering these skills at an early age allowed me to enter kindergarten eager and well-equipped. I was four years old when I left my mother's world of domesticity and happily headed for the exciting new domain of school. Later my father would make me do vocabulary exercises in the *Reader's Digest* as a way to increase my verbal knowledge. He insisted that I take Latin in high school so that I would know word derivations. He introduced me to the novels of Thomas Hardy, whose bleak and melancholic landscapes and characters gave us a kind of private language in which we could communicate to each other. But he expressed great disdain for my reading Brian Moore's *The Lonely Passion of Judith Hearne*, which gave me some access to a woman's sexual desire. The book was outside his purview and he wanted to censor my reading by his distaste.

Despite all my father's guidance, I found it difficult to accomplish the kind of education my father envisioned for me. What he was able to do as a young man in the 1920s and '30s was impossible for me as a young woman in the late 1950s. His stories of riding railroad cars to various university destinations, getting football scholarships, and living in fraternities was a script that was totally unavailable for me. Nor did I find any inspiration in those great institutions of higher education. Mostly what I found there was confusion—about my ability to think and learn and about my future role as a woman. It would take me until I was in my forties before I understood my own intelligence and could use it. Until then I was basically silent.

Except for his notations in my Baby Book and some letters, I never saw anything that my father ever wrote. Yet I knew the idea of writing was important to him. As were books. At some level he always seemed to "know" that I would write. But it took me over forty years to realize that the tools he provided were useless to me until I learned my "mother tongue," that is, until I learned to think and speak as a woman. Although my father "knew" I would write books, he had no way of knowing how I would use the language or what my subject matter would be. My first book was published after he died.

Muted Women

Given the power of language to name and claim, it comes as no surprise that a notion commonly held by those who study cultures is that "women do not speak," that is, women are not available, do not make themselves available, as translators of culture.[28] And so interpreters of culture invariably turn to the men of the particular society they are studying for information about the culture. Thus, models of culture are usually derived from what the men in the society say, about themselves and about the women they live with. (Until recently this has been true about women's psychology as well. Women are only observed while it is the men who talk about and define these observations.) Following this perception, social anthropologists suggest that women constitute a *"muted"* group. This muted condition implies that the powers of language and speaking are problematic ones for women. Thus it is that cultural history has more or less effaced much of women's experience because there has been little or no speech or language to name our experiences or because our experiences did not fit in with accepted forms of discourse and so we have remained silenced. Part of the tremendous power of the movie, *The Piano*, was the muteness of the woman, Ada, set against the passionate eroticism of her piano playing. The movie gives a brilliant example of how acceptable language constricts women's emotional and erotic access and fails to provide expression for their deepest feelings. If this is true for speech, it is most certainly true for writing.

Historically, men's writing has been made into public discourse. But much of women's writing has stayed in the private sphere. Many women continued (and still do) to encode their knowledge, understanding, and perceptions in their journals, letters, and diaries. Writing is one important way in which women were and are able to break through their muted condition.

A woman who wishes to write must learn first how to think for herself, then how to use the language of the father's culture and institutions, and finally how to turn it toward her own ends. Often a woman will develop her creative skills to a highly tuned place only to find herself paralyzed as she thinks about putting her work out into the world: fears of not being heard or seen at all combine with fears of what the public will make of her work; fears of drawing forth envy or retaliation lead to desires for hoarding one's "gold"; fears of mocking and humiliation and other kinds of early woundings around the display of one's talents come to the fore. Feelings of being "found out" or of "not good enough" are raised by jeering internal questioners who ask: "Just who do you think you are?" "What makes you think you are so special?" "Are you crazy?" A woman may find that she is afraid of the actual content of her work. Sometimes a woman will be able to say in a poem something she has never been able to verbalize to anyone. The power in the work may unconsciously scare her or, if she is aware of it, she may not be up to standing behind the work as it enters the public domain.

Oftentimes a woman will have created her work out of personal pain. If the work has developed to the level of art she is then faced with having to expose both herself and usually her family members or other loved ones if she wishes her work to be published. Although there are strategies to be employed (Carolyn Heilbrun adopted a pseudonym), this fear of exposure may be a major stumbling block. One woman working to understand her father's influence on her intimate relationships with men writes: "I can allow myself these words and thoughts since my father is dead. If he were alive, he would be outraged."[29] Another woman, whose deepest subject is the incest that ran rampant through several generations of her extended family, argues incessantly with herself about whether or not she can ever allow her poetry to be seen. She does not stop writing, but she does hesitate at the threshold of publishing.

If a woman has achieved the difficult tasks of thinking for herself, expressing her own vision, voicing her own subjectivity, and getting that work out into the world, she has usually worked against great odds. It is the influence of the father in this process, the woman's relationship to her personal father, the institution of fatherhood, as well as the culture of the fathers, that I wish to address in this book.

* * *

In general, the daughter-father story has remained an almost uncharted territory. The landscape is formed of thickly layered strata where experiences of our personal fathers are laid onto the social and historical context in which we live. This book is an exploration into this unmapped geography, noting the dense and complex elements that compose the ground we stand on as women. Ancient myths and images are combined with the works of contemporary writers who are working to articulate the new mythology; literary works are joined with stories from women's lives, dreams, and works, including my own. Feminist analysis provides what Rich has called the "powerful womanly lens" which makes it possible to perceive the diversity and intricacies of influence; women's poetry is the divining rod that locates the sweet subterranean stream of women's speech that runs, deep and refreshing as an artesian well, under all.

This book is divided into four parts: "In the Belly of the Father," "The Battlezone of Culture," "The Wildzone," and "The New Earth." There are four Gates which open out of each section: "The Awakening," "The Threshold," "The Return," and "Possibility."

Living in the Belly of the Father is living completely within the structures of the dominant culture of patriarchy. Using the Greek mythos of Saturn as the archetypal devouring and melancholic father, I explore ways in which women are swallowed and silenced by paternal melancholy. I show how women who sit in the Belly of the Father, attached to the father's umbilicus, are in a state of captivity and basically speechless. I explore what it takes for a woman to awaken out of her muted condition.

After she has gone through the first gate of Awakening, a woman will find herself in the Battlezone of Culture. In this place, a woman learns to break her silence and find her voice. Here she struggles with the defining dynamics of her family of origin and the definitions placed on her by society. This is where she meets the culture of patriarchy head on: the academic, medical, juridical, and religious institutions which dictate and promulgate control of women by limiting our educational, reproductive, marital, sexual, creative, and spiritual choices. The Battlezone is a reality as well as a metaphor. It exists for a woman as an external place of conflict and an internal place of struggle. Here a woman works to distinguish between her culturally defined and constructed self and her self-defined authenticity.

At some point a woman will find herself standing at the second gate of the Threshold. She will have found a doorway, however small, which will take her to another possibility, another way of being. She will have to consciously choose to go through this gate knowing she will never be the same—she cannot go back to the ways she was. This is the threshold of consciousness. A woman's decision to cross the Threshold may come out of desperation, but it is always an act of courage. What lies on the other side is the Wildzone.

The Wildzone is strictly female space, woman-centered, woman-defined, woman-loving space. It is where women find each other as support and resource. It is where women's culture is formed. In this Wildzone, or female space, women leave patriarchal thought behind and get busy giving symbolic weight to female consciousness, making the invisible lives and works of women visible, and helping the silent speak. Here women find their community of sisters, and the Wild Mother. It is where they learn to speak their Mother Tongue. By tracking women's creative process into the Wildzone, we can find out about where and how we raise and shift our consciousness. It is in the Wildzone where women begin the process of constructing our power to create and re-constructing our spiritual lives.

Once she has found the Wildzone, her woman-centered ground, a woman can make it through the third gate of Return. Armed with insight and female wisdom, a belief in the authority of her own and other women's experience, a woman can bring her knowledge back into the culture. She can speak. All her relationships will be subject to change as she makes her way onto the New Earth.

In Part Four, a woman opens to the Possibility of making her own myth. She can now face her personal father and the cultural fathers from the solid ground of her own knowing. She can claim her inheritance. She may be a visionary, a prophet, or just a hard-working woman. But she will not be tamed, nor will she participate in her own subordination or collude in the subordination of other women. She will bring back with her the courage to stand alone, as well as the courage to stand together with other women. Although she will still struggle with aspects of the culture that attempt to limit and control her and other women, she will have gained ownership over her own thinking, her own speech, her own creative and spiritual life. She will be able to make her contribution to the culture. She will be able to make and sustain relationships that nurture and support her. She will be able to create what she wishes. She will be able to bring her own authority to bear on her decisions. She will not be a victim, she will continue to struggle but she will be responsible for her own life.

Throughout this work I make a psychic mapping of women's movement from silence to speech. This metaphor winds its way into the text marking women's passage towards a creative life. I do not imagine this journey as a linear one or a circular one, but a continuously spiraling one whereby women will be constantly on the move, gaining strength, respite, recognition, and affirmation in the Wildzone, bringing knowledge, wisdom and speech back into the cultural Battlezone, helping to give voice to the muted women in the Belly of the Father, working to create new possibilities into which women can venture.

It is the purpose of this book to bring women out of our muted condition; to give voice to the ones silenced in the Belly of the Father; to tell the stories of women's struggles to find their voices within the Battlezone of Culture; to hear the visionaries who are singing from the Wildzone; and to bring women's speech back into the culture as inspiration and an agent for change. The book is a trail-guide telling women how to find their way.

Part One

In the Belly of the Father

The Devouring Father

He lay on the couch night after night,
mouth open, the darkness of the room
filling his mouth, and no one knew
my father was eating his children. He seemed to
rest so quietly, vast body
inert on the sofa, big hand
fallen away from the glass.
What could be more passive than a man
passed out every night—and yet as he lay
on his back, snoring, our lives slowly
disappeared down the hole of his life . . .

—*Sharon Olds*[1]

Saturn

When I was asked the question about which daughter-father myths would shed light on the daughter's experience of the depressed father, I immediately thought of Sharon Olds' poem, "Saturn." Saturn, I remembered, is the Roman name for the Greek god, Kronos, and his story was part of the ancient Greek myth of origins.

Myths have tremendous power to shape our thinking. Greek mythology, in particular, actively permeates our thought not only socially in the sense that our supposed democracy is based on Greek ideals, but also because our systems of psychology are also locked into Greek mythology—Freudian psychoanalysis made the Greek Oedipus into its charter myth, and Jung predicated his analytic psychology on the whole idea of archetypes taken from the Greek idea of formless forms. The new archetypal psychology is particularly enmeshed in Greek mythology. In order to be helpful, however, I believe Greek myth and thought, as well as any depth psychology based on Greek mythology, must first be looked at as systems which privilege and reproduce male power structures. Nowhere is this more clear than in the Greek myth of genesis and the saga of Saturn.

Many of us are somewhat familiar with Hesiod's story of genesis and how Saturn swallowed his children. If we are not inclined toward the Greek classics, our familiarity may come from an image of Kronos, depicted by Goya, which shows a ravaged old man in the process of devouring one of his children. In most renditions of this myth, it is the sons who are said to be swallowed and so the image has traditionally encoded the primal struggle between father and son, the competition between male generations for the privileges of power. But as I looked to Hesiod's version, I saw that Saturn had also swallowed his daughters, the goddesses Hestia, Demeter, and Hera. I wondered whether their mythologies could tell me something of the effects of this trauma on them as daughters. In my investigations I discovered that Aphrodite, although she was not swallowed, was also born out of this myth, and so I have included her as an important other daughter.

Many people look to Greek goddess myths as models, finding in them typologies for the varieties of womanhood. There is a tendency to idealize the Greek goddesses. Ten years ago, in her book, *Goddesses in Everywoman*, Jean Shinoda Bolen offered the opinion that goddess stories provide women with a new way of understanding their inner selves, life-roles, and relationships as well as giving men revealing insights into the important women in their lives. It is true that the goddess myths are potentially transformative tales for women. But we cannot reach their deepest meaning until we push through the patriarchal overlay that keeps us from knowing their core. The Greek myth of genesis is a recording of how the goddesses came to lose their power, and for that reason it stands as an important cautionary tale. The goddesses and their mythic stories as they come to us from the Greek classics are relevant only insofar as they are emblematic of women's attempts to recover and survive in a patriarchal culture. As this work shows, it is only by way of passing through the gates of the father-told stories that women are able to enter into the deeper mystery of these goddesses' meaning.

As I have pointed out earlier, it is a well-known maxim in understanding the roots of one's personal psychology that one has to go back at least three generations to find the ancestral family pattern. And so looking to Hesiod's *Theogony*, we find a recording of the Greek founding myth that tells the story of three generations of gods and goddesses:

In the beginning was Gaia who was capable of creation all by herself. As the mother of all creation, she birthed the natural world as well as all the gods and goddesses and she took her first born, starry Ouranos, as her lover. Together they became the first world parents.

But Gaia's increasing productivity began to threaten Ouranos. She was giving birth (he thought) to monsters. So, Ouranos began to block the birth of Gaia's children. Every time one was beginning to come out, he would push it back again, deep inside Gaia. These attempts to suppress Gaia's creativity caused her great stress and she groaned within for pressure of pain.

Out of her extremity she devised a plan. Creating the element of grey flint, she made a great sickle. Complaining to her children, who hated their father, she began to rouse in them the idea of revenge. Only her youngest born, Kronos/Saturn, took courage and together they planned the ambush. Gaia put the sickle in his hand and Kronos/Saturn hid awaiting the right moment.

When huge Ouranos came, bringing night with him, he embraced Gaia, completely laying over her. From his hiding place Kronos/Saturn reached with his left hand and seized him by the testicles. Holding the enormous sickle with its long blade edged like teeth in his right hand, he swung it sharply, lopping off the genitals of his own father and throwing them over his shoulder to fall where they would.[2]

Following this genesis we can see how the whole of Greek mythology was launched with the monumental act of castration of the first father by his son. In this mythic moment, overthrow as the means to power was put into motion for millennia. Mythologically, the repercussions reverberated throughout the heavens, touching on all the gods and goddesses to follow. But the story does not end there.

After he banished his father, Kronos/Saturn took Rhea, his sister, to wife and she bore glorious children, Hestia, Demeter, Hera, as well as Hades, Poseidon and Zeus. But as Rhea gave birth to each of their children, great Kronos/Saturn swallowed down each one. He knew he needed to protect his lineage, having heard that it had been ordained for him, for all his great strength, to be beaten by his son. Therefore he kept watch, and did not sleep, but waited for his children to emerge and swallowed them (both sons and daughters). And Rhea's sorrow was beyond forgetting.

There are two versions as to how the children were delivered out of the Belly of the Father. Although Zeus is credited with the release, it is really the mothers who accomplish it. One version shows the trickery of Rhea.

Pregnant with her last child, Rhea consulted her parents, Gaia and Ouranos, as to how to save him. Gaia offered to shelter the baby, Zeus, in a cave in Crete. At this point Hesiod's version concludes with how Rhea wrapped a great stone in swaddling clothes and presented it to Kronos whereupon he immediately took it in his hands and crammed it down his belly, not even realizing what he had done. Finding the stone indigestible, Kronos/Saturn then vomited up his progeny—first the stone, then the children.

What we learn from this version is how the mother goddess, Rhea, with her own mother's help, uses deceit to keep her husband from swallowing her baby. Although her only intention is to save her son, Zeus, her actions result in liberation of her other children as well.

Other versions of the myth say that Zeus had earlier consulted Metis, the ancient Titaness, the one "who knew more than all the gods or man." Metis, an ancient woman of wisdom, concocted an emetic that caused Kronos/Saturn to vomit. Later, because he wanted to own her wisdom and because he too feared the paternal legacy of overthrow by his sons, Zeus continued the tradition and, like his power-hungry father, swallowed Metis up as his first wife. Thus the inheritance of a devouring tendency continued on into the Olympian pantheon. The new ruler, Zeus, did not do the one thing that would have stopped the paternal pattern; rather he replicated it in himself.

In his telling, Hesiod does not talk specifically about the release of the goddesses, Hestia, Hera, and Demeter, out of the belly of their father nor what effect being swallowed by him had on them; we are led to assume that, through their brother Zeus's agency, they were freed to join his pantheon. What it looks like from the goddess's point of view is some version of "out of the frying pan into the fire"—out of the Belly of the Father into their brother's patriarchal system, the Battlezone of Culture.

Nor does Hesiod say much about the birth of Aphrodite. When Saturn castrated Ouranos and threw the severed phallus over his left shoulder, he was ridding himself and his mother of something intrusive, oppressive, unwanted. The idea that Aphrodite grew out of this cast-away phallus of the father lends a very deep mystery to who she is and her place in the scheme of things. In the Zeus religion, she is thought to have come from very far away in order to join with the Greek pantheon. The circumstances of her birth, however, seem to linger in the Greek imagination. Although she is greatly respected, Aphrodite and her worship are always tinged with a certain kind of dread. Her appearance is like the return of the repressed, she is the "other" daughter, the daughter of otherness.

The Missing Mother of Power

In Hesiod's version of the Greek creation myth, we can see how, through the successive generations, the initially all powerful mother goddesses are steadily stripped of their creative force as the process of creation continues. Although the great goddesses began as self-fulfilling and self-creating, by Hesiod's telling of the myth of genesis, the mothers, Gaia and Rhea, cannot prohibit their husbands from usurping all their creative powers. They cannot stop the destructive behavior of their husbands, but they are able to scheme against them. By now, the influence of the mother, already caught in the power dynamic of patriarchy, is used for protection of her favored son. Rhea can muster some effort to hide Zeus, but she does not save her daughters. So, too, the daughters swallowed by the father, whether it be the personal father or the collective father of patriarchal culture, lack the necessary nurturing and agency of a strong mother and thus they are left vulnerable and unprotected. This is a story that plays itself out again and again in the myths of the Daughters of Saturn and in the lives of their mortal sisters.

Because this lack of courageous mothering has gone on for so many centuries, the women who became our mothers suffered from this lack as well. One of the hardest realizations for us to accept is that our mothers have been damaged by the culture we live in, as much, if not more, than we have, since often our mothers may seem to be the actual embodiment and executors of the repressive patriarchal system. A woman poet recalls to me that her mother, who had aspired to become a lawyer, became a housewife instead, in part because just as she entered law school her lawyer father died. But, she thinks, her mother's profound unhappiness (which she, the daughter, had absorbed throughout her growing up) had deeper roots. "I think it was this being in the father's belly that was a large factor in Mom's deep unhappiness—the cultural father's belly kept her from law, and her personal and cultural father's belly taught her to devalue her 'feminine' characteristics, to value only the 'masculine' sharpened intellect." In an effort to come to terms with her mother's disempowering legacy she wrote a poem addressed to her mother entitled "Final Judgment:"

> I cannot make you love yourself.
> I cannot depose the damning judge
> lodged in your soul.
> Daily he decrees
> that you prove your woman's worth,
> and daily you fail,
> as do I,
> to meet his standards.
> For all of that I am not guilty,
> but I'm sorry, so sorry for you.
> And what's more I'm through
> pleading my case.
> I've found better things to do.

As often happens, in the Greek version of the myth of the devouring father there is another kind of mother who is hiding in the margins. She is Metis, with her subversive nature, her cunning wisdom, and her willingness to overthrow the devouring father. She once concocted an emetic that released the children out of Saturn's belly. Even though classical Greek myth was content to have Metis swallowed up by Zeus, Metis is a well-known shape-shifter and it is hard to believe that she was so easily conquered. I like to think that she purposely sat in Zeus's belly as an indigestible woman. I imagine she still operates with her wild wisdom ever ready to help awaken women out of their condition of captivity. Her presence may not always be obvious, but she is there.

Saturn and Melancholy

Ever since it was recorded, the myth of Saturn swallowing his children has retained its power as a compelling archetypal image. There is a centuries-old discourse, beginning with Aristotle, that relates how the planet Saturn and his influence came to be associated with the mental condition of Melancholia. Perhaps melancholy was the first body-mind disease to be described in such exacting detail.[3]

Each successive era has had its own assessment of Saturn and his afflictions. Around the fourth century B.C. in Greece, Saturnian melancholy was regarded as the "disease of heros," while in the Middle Ages anyone born under the planet Saturn was considered evil and unlucky. During the Renaissance, Saturn underwent a positive resuscitation. As the acknowledged patron of a certain kind of contemplation and melancholy, Saturn was understood as a particularly masculine intellectual and spiritual force, giving individuals under his sway special creative powers until finally it was understood that "modern genius" could "only take place under the sign of Saturn and melancholy."[4] This set the stage for the grand tradition of Saturn and melancholy. Melancholy soon became identified as an elite illness, one that afflicted men "precisely as the sign of their exceptionality, as the inscription of genius within them."[5] As a sign of spiritual greatness and a condition for creative brilliance, melancholy became an "accredited pathology"[6]—for men.

In this work I wish to add a new dimension to this long mythic, historic, and literary grand tradition of Saturn and melancholy. I want to extend it to include the understanding that all fathers in a patriarchal culture are melancholic in some way and all daughters have to contend with the many manifestations of this melancholic condition in their relationship with them.

Paternal Melancholy: The Burden of the Father

In the myth, Saturn overthrows his father for the sake of gaining his power. This dynamic is imagined in the male psyche as a transformational process whereby the son is born out of the father—the old king dies so the son may take his place— the man outdoes his father and that, by definition, is progress. Our ideas of betterment, growth, development, all the forward-looking values that our culture holds so dear, are predicated on this patriarchal pattern. From the Puritans and their revolt to Willy Loman and *Death of a Salesman*, father-son dynamics have always provided the foundation stone of our culture. Although the depression and sadness that accompany the ouster of the father by son is carefully hidden behind the glittering facade of cultural prosperity, the American Dream is solidly built on paternal melancholy.[7]

All of our fathers stagger under the weight of this patriarchal pattern. Even now, in our supposedly post-patriarchal world, the expectations placed on men as they become fathers cause particular strains that make relationships with their children difficult at best, permanently distorted at worst. All fathers labor under the requirements placed upon them by the patriarchal culture. Some fathers outwardly benefit and succeed in fitting the culture's prescriptions while others are obviously crushed and broken by impossible expectations, but no one fully escapes the burden of carrying the culture's patriarchal ideal. Whether they subscribe to it or not, all fathers participate in some way and to some degree in the culture's institution of fatherhood. In this way, all fathers are implicated and their struggle and its toll are eventually passed on and carried by their children. How the father's story affects the son is more evident in our mythic and literary traditions, while the impact on the daughter remains a more hidden drama.

How our personal fathers have thrived or suffered within the patriarchal culture, how they have succeeded or failed, what they have gained or lost by living in a culture based on father-rule has a direct impact on us, their daughters. Whether they have been caring, protective, and encouraging, emotionally absent, lost, or dead, overly present, domineering, or abusive deeply affects us as daughters and influences the kind of women we become.

Because our personal fathers bear the brunt of patriarchal arrangements, they also carry some element of depression in their lives. This condition, which I call paternal melancholy, may be overtly manifest as clinical depression or alcoholism; it may be acted out in violent or abusive ways; or it may only be felt as emotional absence, an elusive yet pervasive sadness, a vague nostalgia for something missing or lost. Paternal melancholy has a particularly polarizing effect on the father, making him either too remote or too close. The daughter never gets enough of him or she gets too much. He may be retentive and withholding of emotional intimacy, incorporative in his power relations, and implicitly if not explicitly, incestuous. Whatever its manifestations, individual men pay a price for living in a culture that is predicated upon father-rule, and this general condition of paternal melancholy is sensed and experienced in particular ways by their daughters.

As I was researching my father's history to locate the source of his melancholy, I had a tiny fragment of memory. When I was three years old, my father took me on a long train trip to Iowa to see his parents. I have a detailed description of this excursion written in my Baby Book by my father. When I look now at the picture of my old grandfather, Jacob, and my father it stimulates my sense-memory of that trip—a smell of pipe tobacco, the rough feel of wool, a slight odor of urine. Who was this man, Jacob, I wonder? What was his story? What did he pass on to my father? I push back into the next generation.

I am certainly not the first nor the last one to engage in genealogical quests. Although many people seem to undertake this pursuit in the spirit of pride and heritage, I suspect that what we are all looking for really is the answer to some unnamed sorrow, some event that would explain the involutional turn of this one, or the quirky twist of that one. Something that would testify to the pressures of pain and suffering that cause the particular torque of a family pattern.

I have in my possession another family photograph. It is a formal portrait of my great-grandparents, Adam and Elizabeth, and their eight children. But something is strange. In this picture Jacob, the supposed first-born son, is a full-grown man whereas the rest of the children are noticeably younger. As I begin to query about this, I run into a mystery. As I explore more fully, I run into horror.

Adam Reis came to the United States from Heidesheim near Mainz, Germany, in 1865 along with his sister, Catherine, and his elderly parents, George and Anna Marie. Adam was twenty-three when he arrived in America, his sister Catherine was about thirty-six. Their mother was in her late sixties, their father probably older. It is not known why this portion of the Reis family decided to leave for America, nor exactly how many children they left behind in Germany.

This family settled in Sublette, Illinois, where Adam met and married Elizabeth Becker. Adam was thirty-one and Elizabeth was seventeen when they married in February of 1873. Jacob, their supposed oldest son, however, was born in 1869, four years before this marriage ever took place. He could have been their son only if Elizabeth had gotten pregnant at age thirteen. Not likely. Questions arise. If Adam and Elizabeth are not Jacob's parents, then who are they? Who are my father's grandparents? Who are my great-grandparents?

There is a strong possibility that Jacob had been born as an "illegitimate" child of Adam's older sister Catherine, or "Tanta" as I heard my father call her, my great-aunt, Catherine. "Tanta" lived with Adam and Elizabeth, so incorporating her infant son into their family was probably taken for granted. Certainly it was not unheard of for families to foster children that were not their own or "illegitimate." Pioneering family units needed as many hands as possible. When the family moved to Iowa to farm, Jacob was already claimed, according to the census, as Adam and Elizabeth's oldest child. All in all this is not remarkable. It merely raises the question of paternity a few generations back. It amuses me to think that maybe this unknown great-grandfather was a Native American or a Chinese. There is a peculiar Mongolian look, an epicanthic fold, in the eyes of my father, my sister, and my nephew, there are the distinctive high cheekbones and full lips that run throughout our family that I imagine came from this great-grandfather. All of this speculation is amusement, light entertainment. Where it becomes traumatic and horrifying is in the violent deaths of Jacob's surrogate parents, Adam and his wife Elizabeth, and the aftermath.

In mid-life, Adam was killed in a runaway accident. The horses pulling his hay wagon were panicked by barking dogs and the wagon overturned. Adam died three days later, leaving his wife Elizabeth with five of their children still living at home. At some point after this Elizabeth went mad. She was placed in St. Joseph's asylum in Dubuque, Iowa. Jacob, now a grown man, had worked to have her released from the asylum in a supposedly "improved condition" and placed her in the home of her married son. Why he did this is unclear. There is some question about property: the deed to the family farm was in her name. If she was declared "insane," she could not sign the property over to her children— it would go instead into the hands of a questionable trustee. Maybe Jacob thought that by proving Elizabeth capable of living outside the institution, he could get the farm back into his own hands. He was thought to be the oldest son. Yet questions of his legitimacy might arise if he went to the courts to prove his rights of primogeniture.

What followed shortly after Elizabeth's release from the asylum is reported most graphically by the local newspaper record announced by the headline "Suicides While Insane."

> Pouring kerosene oil over her clothing and touching a match to it, Mrs. Elizabeth Reis, a pioneer resident of Odebolt, literally cooked herself at an hour shortly after three o'clock yesterday morning. She lived only a few minutes, but suffered the most intense agony while the flames were eating her body away.

How Jacob responded to this traumatic event, what depth of grief and responsibility he bore for the rest of his life, I can only speculate. I can imagine now that his weeping spells, his quiet drinking, were symptoms of an unbearable trauma. The burden of his anguish and remorse must have passed through to his sons like a silent river of sorrow and pain.

Despite his great gift for storytelling, my father never told me the story of Elizabeth Reis. Only once did he vaguely allude to the fact that maybe her nightgown accidentally caught on fire. Did he know and then forget? Was the story so easily submerged in the family pattern of silence and shame? Was the tragedy beyond speaking? My own father's life, his fear of responsibility, the dread of some unnamed failure, his hypochondria, his over-determined emphasis on health and hard work as purgative, all seem haunted by the specters of these tragedies, the depth of his melancholy harrowed before he was born.

What the Daughter Carries

The daughter often carries things for the father, some part of his life that is not allowed him by the culture or his own personality, some qualities he cannot express, some activity that he cannot participate in, some unlived creative aspect, some emotional softness, receptivity, playfulness, sweetness, vulnerability that is disapproved of by the cultural prescriptions for masculine behavior. Sometimes the father may be a gentle, non-aggressive, even passive man, which leads the daughter to take up her armor and became a warrior for her father, compensating for his softness with her own combativeness. Qualities not permitted to or assumed by a father are easily distributed onto his daughter and she may unconsciously sense this and take up their burden.

One way that fathers become burdened by the institution of fatherhood is by being providers. One woman who believed that her father abandoned his creativity in order to become a financially successful lawyer wrote a poem called "Sugar Daddy." Her father had died quite young of cancer and she was convinced that his quest for money had sickened him. Still feeling the weight of his death as she struggled to find her own relationship to work and money, she writes: "No, I never saw the body. / Is that why I carry you in my dreams? / Your dead weight drapes and drags / over my fine square shoulders. / Daddy, did you know? / I'm still looking / for the place to put you down."

When I was seven years old and delirious from a high fever, I hallucinated a scene that has always stayed vivid in my mind.

> I am trying to walk up some stairs but I am carrying an enormous stack of books that weigh me down, I am sweating from the effort and I complain "Daddy, Daddy! These books are too heavy!"

What was I, at that early age, being asked to carry? Was it the burden of my own creative life? Or was I aware at that moment of having to carry my father's unfulfilled desire to write, to speak the hidden truths? Was I being given an image of what would be an important part of my life—books, writing, the search for knowledge—or was I being impeded, held down by the weight of my father's expectations and the cultural father's artifacts? The answer is not simple, the possibilities have often been entangled in my mind. The effort to distinguish between what I felt were his expectations placed on me as a child, the standards for education and learning, and my own adult desires for creativity, has taken years. Undoubtedly I benefited in some way from my father's early perception that I would do something creative, but sometimes I am suspicious. Was his perception accurate or merely the projection of his own need? In any case, I have had to struggle for years under the burden of his unlived ambitions to find my own chosen path. I still feel that seven-year-old girl at times and work to redistribute the weight she carries. The writing of this book is one of the ways I am unburdening her.

Melancholic Fathers and Their Daughters

Since all fathers stand somewhere in the shadow of the great edifice of patriarchal culture, our individual fathers become our personal representatives of the patriarchal system. It is through the experiences with our fathers that we come to understand in an intimate way how the culture works, what the power differentials are between men and women, how gender role prescriptions are taken up and carried out. This is how fathers become our stand-ins for the culture's power structures. Thus the personal father easily becomes conflated with the patriarchal man and our struggles with him gain an overdetermined and impersonal force and momentum.

Despite the fact that many fathers today may benefit from their entitlements as men in the culture, they pay a price. A father's inability to speak about certain things, particularly his emotional realities, can later become a woman's silence. A daughter may learn early on that her father's condition is somehow "special," that allowances must be made for his moods, for his work schedule, his need for quiet, his emotional distance, his alcoholic temper. No matter how successful in the outer world, at home he may exude a vacuous sadness, a sadness that exerts a primal pull on her, secretly devouring and stealing her energy.

One of the more identifiable manifestations of paternal melancholy is a profound sense of loss or lack, which leads to certain feelings of nostalgia. It may appear as a kind of homesickness which focuses on the past, a past which was a time of happiness, a Golden Age that is no more. For the nostalgic, the present can never be enough or right. Melancholic reminiscences on what once has been have a ruminating and obsessive quality. Memory becomes suffused with a certain eroticised regret or guilt about the past along with a harsh contempt for the imperfections of the present. German romanticism is rooted in this kind of melancholic nostalgia—as is fascism.

My own father certainly demonstrated this kind of nostalgia. He was continually telling me stories from his glorified past when he was a student, a young man traveling on the rails during the Great Depression, heroic tales, full of beautiful and intelligent women he had met at the various universities he attended, tales of athletic prowess and moments of deep thought and awareness, books he had read and poems that had moved him. Later in his life these memories would become suffused with a sense of loss, of what might have been but was not now in the present, where he had a wife and six children to support. He kept these memories alive however by telling them to me, his first child, his oldest daughter. I hungrily absorbed them: they fed my own imagination in ways that my mother's conventional life could never do, and when it came time for me to leave home, I thought I too would live these stories out, thereby giving my father the pleasure of seeing his life recreated in me. The fact that I was female, that I would never be part of a group of energetic and youthful men, that I would never be on a football team or be allowed into a fraternity of philosophically minded peers, never occurred to me. Until I began to actually try to live his life. Then I was sorely confronted with the differences—in gender and in generation. My father had given me a romantic legacy that was useless to me as a woman.

At the time, I felt myself a rather dismal failure. Not only did I not find any romanticism in trying to live out my father's life, it was ridiculously impossible. When I entered the university as a young woman in the late 1950s,[8] I had none of the entitlements and privileges granted a handsome and bright young man of the 1930s. Not only that, my effort was totally unsupported. He had always led me to believe I could accomplish anything I set out to do, and yet my education was then totally left up to me to figure out. There was no money from him, nor any psychological support, only expectation and his example. He did it; so could I. When I failed to live up to his standards, his disappointment in me merely served to fuel his pessimism and my depression.

The pessimistic point of view is endemic to paternal melancholy. It is the perspective concealed in all bleak philosophical treatises as well as religious attitudes that focus on damnation and contempt for the world, in all religious attitudes born out of despair, guilt, and meaninglessness. It is Jonathan Edwards' "Sinners in the hands of an angry God." But, enfolded in the gloom of a man possessed by melancholia is the secret longing for a union with the beloved that would reverse the situation by creating a life filled with meaning and love. Oftentimes a daughter will sense this secret longing in her father and try to fulfill it with her own feminine energies.

A melancholic father can permeate all of his relationships with a certain kind of scrutinizing negativity. The introspection of the melancholic father, when turned out onto the world, is like a microscopic gaze that perceives only flaws, weaknesses, defects, the imperfections, the one rotten spot. This tendency of the melancholic to project his own torpor outward distorts all his perceptions. Seeing only the inevitability of misfortune, his visions of failure inhibit his own potential for psychological growth. The daughter may feel this same psychic paralysis permeating her own life.

In the myth of Saturn, the devouring father swallows his daughters. In fairy tales, the old king locks his daughter up, he hoards her as he hoards his gold. His relationship to her is one dominated by the fear of loss and so he attempts to keep her and her riches under his control. Fathers who hoard their power, who will not share it with their daughters, keep their daughters bound to them, especially when the daughter becomes an adolescent.

A father's response to his daughter's burgeoning sexuality is frequently primitive. In his attempt to meet the cultural requirement of paternal protection, he may become highly controlling. He may unconsciously project his own sexual lust onto the boys the adolescent daughter is dating and see his own uncontrolled appetite in the young men. He may react in highly irrational ways if he suspects her sexual activity, even attacking his once precious daughter as a "slut" or a "whore." Men's general inability to distinguish only two archetypes for females— madonna and whore—becomes an enormous handicap for the relationship as the daughter makes the difficult transition from girl to woman. A father's sexual demons tend to appear in full force at this time.

My own father had the usual fear of my getting pregnant, even when he had no reason to worry about it. His way of handling his fear was to mention at the family dinner table that he hoped there were no "zygotes" at the table. Since I was the only one at the table who understood what this word meant, I knew it was aimed in my direction. I would respond with anger and humiliation. Only later did I realize that his concern undoubtedly grew out of his own experience. My mother was three months pregnant with me when they married.

A woman with a sexually controlling, hoarding, incorporative father may dream of making love to her husband in her own marital bed, but as she turns her head she sees her father sitting on a chair watching her. His inspecting gaze works effectively to stop her own erotic flow. This internalized vigilant father may also curtail a daughter's creative energies, especially if they are in conflict with his wishes or belief system.

A woman in her early thirties on the brink of making major educational and career decisions for herself realized that she was still incredibly bound to her father. From her earliest memory, her father had worked to make sure that they would be psychically merged. She described an early childhood experience of going to hypnosis sessions with her father. As a result of these sessions, she felt like her father had permanently hypnotized her. Her desire to re-enter school as an artist/therapist was repeatedly affirmed by him. He praised her talents and successes by stating that she was a "natural" with issues of the psyche as she was *crazy*, too! He warned her that as an intern she'd be mistaken as a client and kept in the hospital. Her decisions to proceed were tantamount to breaking the psychic binding between them. As she began to make her plans for the future she had overwhelming feelings of being enchanted, put under by his spell. She would feel paralyzed at times, unable to make phone calls or venture out of the house. Her attempts to write resumés would end in debilitating lassitude. Oftentimes her father would telephone her just as she was about to put a plan into action, reinforcing the uncanny feelings that he somehow still controlled her life. It took tremendous determination for her to stay on track with the call from her own creative life and not succumb to the deep sleep of psychic merger.

There are many ways that a daughter and her energies can be swallowed by the father and his needs. It may be that her father is naive, a simple, gentle man without much worldly knowledge who finds it difficult to cope and longs for an earlier time of childhood and innocence. Whatever the manifestation, the daughter will experience her father's paternal melancholy, his aura of sadness and loss. She will sense that he is surrounded with a veil of longing, lost in the mists of unfulfilled promise. And she will make many attempts to find him and fulfill his life for him. Later, as a woman she will bring this quest into all her other relationships. As Sharon Olds' poem clearly says, it is the black hole of paternal melancholy that feels so devouring for a daughter.

The Daughter Divided

Many women express a deep emotional ambivalence when it comes to remembering their fathers. Childhood desires for love and a need for feeling a father's protection are usually mixed with sadness over the father's emotional distance or recollections of his failures. Many women I talked to say their fondest early memories are of their father in his role of protector and provider. Even a father who was regularly drunk was remembered with great admiration because he had gone out in a winter storm to get the family bread and milk. This event was held like a precious jewel in this woman's memory, one she brought out at times for comfort because she had so few other positive recollections of her father.

Another woman expressed a more complicated reaction to her father in his role of protector and provider. When she was eight years old, Nancy's family moved from a beloved home her parents had rented for eleven years into a house that was in the process of being built. For the following three and a half years her family lived in two rooms with no plumbing or running water. Her father was an outdoorsman who loved to hunt and was especially skilled at rabbit hunting. This poem surfaced several years after his death and Nancy remembered how often this scene repeated itself throughout her childhood. She recalls, "My father was a big powerful man who I thought would protect me and love me forever. As a small child I adored him, but I hated the guns and the killing." Years later, for a complex variety of reasons, her adoration turned to a mixture of love, hate, and fear. The poem recalls, in sensory detail, a time of trust and innocence, when she felt great love for her father, the provider. But it also contains her childhood struggle with this man, her deep ambivalence born out of his double capacity for providing and predation.

The Provider

He laces his high boots over his grey socks,
buttons his red and black plaid jacket tightly over
his tattered sweatshirt,
and snaps the earflaps down on his woolen cap.
He takes the hunting mittens from the drying rack
beside the kitchen stove,
the red mittens Mother made for him
with the trigger finger carefully knit in.

The beagles dance with delight around the kitchen,
their sharp toenails clattering on the linoleum floor,
creating the sound of castanets to accompany their baying crys.
Father and the dogs leave the warmth of the kitchen,
eager to hunt the white snowshoe rabbits
in the woods behind our house.

Late in the afternoon, Mother cuts vegetables
into a huge pot on the stove.
The steam coats the windows and my small fingers
trace my name on the glass.
I watch the drops of moisture cry down the pane.

As dusk draws in, I watch for Father, and at last glimpse
his form crossing the snow-crusted field.
He carries three snowshoe rabbits,
Frozen blood coating their thick, white fur.

He carries the carcasses to the cellar and skins them,
cuts the meat into small pieces,

then takes the pan of meat up to the kitchen.
Mother cooks a wonderful rabbit stew,
enough to feed all six of us.
The tasty stew fills me with warmth.

Later that night I settle into my bed,
In the room I share with my parents, two sisters and brother.
I draw the rough blanket up around me and try to forget the sight of
the dead, bloody rabbits,
held feet first in my father's right hand,
nearly as long as I am tall.

Bruno Bettelheim has commented on how the hunter-father frequently figures in fairy tales as a strong and protective rescuer of young daughters, as in Little Red Cap and Snow White:

> Hence the hunter of fairy tales is not a figure who kills friendly creatures, but one who dominates, controls, and subdues wild, ferocious beasts. On a deeper level, he represents the subjugation of the animal, asocial, violent tendencies in man. Since he seeks out, tracks down, and defeats what are viewed as lower aspects of man. . . .[9]

Bettelheim is here referring to "the wolf" as that pre-eminent and unfortunate projection for man's violent tendencies. He forgets that the hunter, himself, is not only the protector and provider, but also the predator. This woman's poem recalls her childhood perception of the father-hunter's predatory aspect.

The poem also captures the intense emotional ambivalence at the core of the poet's relationship with her father. It describes how the daughter perceives the father's power to provide for his family, the ritual of hunting for food, the feelings of warmth and satisfaction in the family meal. While she tries to forget the violence entailed, her identification with the soft, vulnerable rabbit and its bloody death is registered as clearly as the feelings of fullness and well-being. These two opposing feelings form the rudiments of love and hate, strength and fear, safety and danger, each living, as surely as the rabbit stew, inside her body. It comes as no surprise that her approach to life often feels divided.

·II·

The Silent Daughters of Saturn

Lie down an hour after each meal. Have but two hours intellectual life a day. And never touch pen, brush or pencil as long as you live.

A nineteenth-century doctor's instruction to a woman suffering from depression.[1]

When she becomes a woman, a Daughter of Saturn may find herself living out her legacy as a swallowed daughter. The trauma of devourment may not be overtly evident, but she will feel it manifest in her difficulties with love and work. Satisfying relationships will be hard to achieve. She will be preoccupied with issues of space and voice. She will experience the powerful emotional affects of depression and rage which grow out of her isolation and captivity. She will feel herself incapable of finding either the kind of love relationships that truly nurture her or a work that fulfills her. She will be unable to hear her own true voice, or know her own name; she will hear only muffled sounds: all the rest is silenced. Women who reside in the Belly of the Father in their adult lives are either trying desperately to feed off the father's umbilicus or are strangled by it.

Captivity

A woman in the Belly of the Father is a woman in a state of captivity. Deep down she will feel herself in bondage, hostage to some unknown power. She may have suffered a sexually and/or physically abusive childhood. But sometimes she is merely a woman who has been trained from infancy to conform to the dictates of a society that would keep her subservient. Many of us recognize our own mothers as women in captivity. Susan Griffin writes about her mother:

Over time, as many women do, my mother became inseparable from her confinement. She was defined by all she could not do, and then never did and then feared doing. She lost the capacity to imagine any other life, until finally the life she had began to be her choice, as she remained inside her house, unemployed and unengaged in public life, private and shy in her manner. At last, it seemed as if this choice *were* she. Herself then interior, indecipherable, uncommunicative, forever turned away, a person inaccessible behind her private doors.[2]

Women who remain in the Belly of the Father are women held as hostages to the demands of a culture that would use them for its own purposes, to serve itself. As Griffin writes about her mother, it begins to appear that this condition of captivity is natural to women. A woman who continues in the Belly of the Father into adulthood cannot create anything in her life that feels authentically hers. Instead, she will find herself reproducing over and over again the gender role prescriptions for women. A woman in the Belly of the Father will not necessarily know where she is living, but she will experience a certain kind of infertility, depression, and rage, and she will engage in a wide range of ever-increasing self-defeating behaviors.

Oftentimes a woman's condition of captivity is not evident in her outer life. Mary, a woman in her early forties, dreams:

> I am watching a brick building complex being demolished from across the street. Big balls hit into rooms above, almost crushing the people underneath. G. and I decide not to watch. Then we go into a garage that has been shut up. Animals are kept there. Strays. German shepherds with puppies. Others are penned up. There is a man in charge and one or two women. One [woman] is muzzled because she would make so much noise while this man grooms her. G. and I talk about the animals. The man growls at us like we might offend them. We tiptoe out. I think to myself, "Children shouldn't come here."

The woman who dreamed this dream had no conscious awareness that she had been harboring a muzzled woman in her psyche. By all outward appearances Mary was "well-off." She had been doing a lot of inner psychological work, and she and her husband were determined to make changes in their relationship that would free both of them from unhealthy patterns, so the appearance of the chained-up animal/woman was shocking.

This image of a woman under the control of a cruel and dominating masculine force led Mary to a great deal of feeling and childhood memories of her domineering, alcoholic father. The notion that some part of her psyche was still in bondage to this man was revolting to her and yet the image of this captive woman was now, due to the dream, indelibly engraved in her imagination and demanded that she take notice. As she looked more closely at the dream, she saw deeply into this captive woman.

> The man holds her by a leash at the front of the muzzle while he grooms her, brushing her but somehow not touching or cleaning, more like reinforcing. I look at her. Our eyes meet. I see her and she knows it. Her eyes dart away and down. She is hunched over, elbows held close to her breasts. Shamed. So long abused she rarely pulls into being human. She has long matted hair, dirty, with thick body hair. She is shamed that I saw her this way. I feel like I have seen my shame.

Through the process of active imagination, she began a dialogue with this woman. She began by asking her, "What can you tell me?" The dream woman responds: "I can tell you that I have been here for a long time. He does this to purify me." Mary notes, "She has a hard time talking. Her eyes are darting and her brow is furrowed. The man says to me: 'Just go on past. This is normal.' He won't talk to me beyond this."

This scene from a woman's imagination puts us immediately in touch with the same feelings evoked by stories of the Holocaust. The similarity of conditions and psychological response between prisoners taken captive by totalitarian regimes like the Nazis—political hostages—and ordinary women and children who are battered and abused within their own homes is striking. It is not unusual for a woman to internalize oppression and feel like a hostage even when her outer circumstances would give no clue as to her inner state. Similarly, "Political captivity is generally recognized, whereas the domestic captivity of women and children is often unseen. A man's home is his castle; rarely is it understood that the same home may be a prison for women and children."[3] Sometimes, as Mary's dream shows, dreams are the only place where a woman's psychological condition of incarceration becomes evident, where the muzzle is acknowledged.

After further reflection Mary writes in her journal about her connection to the woman in the dream:

> I have been thinking about my perfectionism, how I feel pressured by it, how it keeps me from pleasure, fulfillment, its abuse of me—always finding fault, feeling imperfect, undone. Then the dream of the woman in the muzzle: abused to the brink of her humanity because she must be "purified." She believes she should be there. She colludes with her abuser.

Encouraged to make some gesture towards the muzzled woman, Mary continues with her process of active imagination:

I take her leash from the man and carefully remove the muzzle. I seat her, touch her and gradually look in her eyes to communicate that she is safe, protected. I will need to say something to the man. I know the first steps with the woman and will let the rest unfold. I will check on her like I do my inner child. I will stroke her, cleanse her, look at her lovingly. She has believed in the rightness of her abuse. She has believed she deserved the treatment, like my mother, tolerating my father's abuse, atoning always for imagined sins.

I see how my perfectionism is a muzzle. I am her protector now. I will see that the abuse stops. I will see what she needs.

The day that Mary made these notes in her journal, she also wrote, "This morning I read in the newspaper about an Iranian official threatening the death penalty to women who break the rules of dress." The realization of how brutality in the outer world reinforces a woman's internalization of that brutality made itself vividly clear. Later in her process she will begin to confront the man with the leash.

The Madwoman: Silencing the Mind

The muzzled woman Mary met in her dream life belongs to the tradition of "madwomen" who have inhabited women's dreams and imaginations for centuries. In women's literature she is called the "madwoman in the attic." The "madwoman" is a compelling and haunting female archetype and was frequently used by women writers in the nineteenth century to give voice to their own sense of incarcerated creative aspirations.[4] The madwoman is such a terrifying image because she represents a woman whose mind has been silenced.

In 1884, a young woman who was to become a fervent, life-long feminist gave birth to her first child. This birth was followed by a severe and debilitating postpartum depression. Determined to get better, Charlotte Perkins Gilman sought out the best known physician of her day for treatment of her condition, Dr. S. Weir Mitchell. Mitchell was a "female specialist, part-time novelist, and member of Philadelphia's high society."[5] He was also making a fortune on advising women. His advice to Gilman?

Live as domestic a life as possible. Have your child with you all the time." (Be it remarked that if I did but dress the baby it left me shaking and crying—certainly far from a healthy companionship for her, to say nothing of the effect on me.) "Lie down an hour after each meal. Have but two hours intellectual life a day. *And never touch pen, brush or pencil as long as you live.*"[6]

Following this advice, Gilman nearly lost her mind. It is her descent into madness she records five years later in a short story called "The Yellow Wallpaper."[7]

In Gilman's story the nameless woman narrator has been confined by her patronizing and controlling physician husband to a bedroom in an isolated country house. She is to undergo the standard nineteenth-century treatment for nervous women—a rest cure. Her doctor, in tandem with her physician husband, has outlined a strict regimen of rest and diet. Separated from her child, she is forbidden to put pen to paper since her "imagination" is thought to be part of her instability—all, of course, for her own good. The child, she senses, is being well taken care of by someone else. What tortures her most is the sanction against writing—"never touch pen, brush or pencil as long as you live." In the secrecy of her isolation, however, she begins to write about what she is experiencing.

The bedroom she is confined to was formerly an upstairs nursery—the windows are barred and the bed nailed down, and it is covered with the hateful, sickly yellow wallpaper that seems to have a demonic life of its own. It was "One of those sprawling flamboyant patterns . . . when you follow the lame uncertain curves for a little distance they suddenly commit suicide—plunge off at outrageous angles, destroy themselves in unheard of contradictions. . . . The color is repellent, almost riveting, a smouldering unclean yellow. . . ." Although she complains to her husband and asks for a change of room, her husband scoffs and laughs at her, calling her "a blessed little goose."

Her views from the room are open to beautiful vistas of the bay and formal gardens. But soon the wallpaper begins to take on a fiendish life. "There is a recurrent spot where the pattern lolls like a broken neck and two bulbous eyes stare at you upside down. . . . There is one place where two breaths didn't match, and the eyes go all up and down the line, one a little higher than the other." There is also evidence that the children who were once consigned to this room hated it as well—the wallpaper is torn off in places, "the floor is scratched and gouged and splintered, the plaster itself is dug out here and there." Although she enjoys the views out the window, it is the wallpaper which is compelling.

When the light hits the wallpaper just so, she begins to "see a strange, provoking, formless sort of figure, that seems to skulk about behind that silly and conspicuous front design." She notices that "there are things in that paper that nobody knows but me, or ever will . . . it is like a woman stooping down and creeping about behind that pattern." One moonlit night she saw the figure shaking the pattern as if she wanted to get out.

The wallpaper increasingly takes on the appearance of her own madness when she begins to see clearly the woman behind the bars. By daylight the woman caught in the wallpaper is subdued, but at night she comes alive. The narrator becomes manic: she does not sleep at night so she can carefully observe the woman in the wallpaper. She begins to have visual and olfactory hallucinations—she begins to see creeping women everywhere and the smell of the wallpaper begins to permeate—"old foul, bad yellow things."

There is a sinister undercurrent at work. The woman's condition is compared to an abused child. The room is a nursery: the windows barred, the bed nailed down and "fairly gnawed," the wallpaper ripped off as high as a child could reach. The woman notices a funny mark on this wall, low down, near the mopboard— "A streak that runs round the room . . . as if it had been rubbed over and over." She wonders "how it was done and who did it, and what they did it for." This makes her dizzy.

Soon she becomes convinced that it is the wallpaper that keeps the woman confined, and she devises a plan to remove it. She starts to think that there may be more than one imprisoned woman in the wallpaper. In fact, she realizes, there are many, and she herself came from behind that paper. In the final scene she is creeping along the floorboard as her husband breaks into the room. She says to him, "I have got out at last. . . . And I've pulled off most of the paper, so you can't put me back!" In the chilling last sentence, she inquires of the reader: "Now why should that man have fainted? But he did, and right across my path by the wall, so that I had to creep over him every time!"

Gilman's description of a woman's descent into madness has encoded in it a powerful exposé of how an imaginative and creative woman finds herself captive, helpless over the conditions of her own life, her creative mind silenced. The constant infantilizing by her husband, the withholding of opportunities to work and engage in stimulating conversation, the assumption of emotional, financial, and medical control over her, all "for her own good," are efforts guaranteed to keep her off the pathway to her own sanity. She knows that if she were only able "to write a little it would relieve the press of ideas and rest me," but it is forbidden as if it were the writing that was making her sick.

We could say that Gilman's story is accurate for women one hundred years ago but certainly not applicable today. Yet as Mary's muzzled woman demonstrates, women still suffer from the culture's attempts to silence them, and oftentimes their treatment is not so far from what Gilman experienced. The prescription to stop writing as part of her cure is one aspect of an overall agenda to keep women muted, silenced, and muzzled, away from what could cure them, their own creative potential.

What happens to a woman living in the Belly of the Father, who would, against all advice, takes up the pen and begin to write? In the story Gilman tells us the writing does not save the woman from madness. Indeed, the unnamed woman's madness becomes her only means of revenge against those who would keep her from writing. Gilman, the author, however, did not go mad. She wrote "The Yellow Wallpaper" both as a warning tale for women and as her retaliation against the proscriptions that almost killed her. Gilman, the feminist, went on to have a full and active life. But others have been lost.

Virginia Woolf, no stranger to the fear and reality of madness that accompanies a woman writer, tells us her imaginary story of Shakespeare's sister, Judith, a genius equal in talent and drive to her brother, William. Woolf describes the impossibility of the task facing this imaginary woman. Aware of her own talent, but confronted with the inexorable demands of the culture on her womanhood, Judith Shakespeare resists marriage, steals away to the city to work in the theater, only to get impregnated by a man who has offered to help her. Pregnant and in despair, she kills herself. Woolf warns us lest we should be moved to judge her actions: ". . . who shall measure the heat and violence of the poet's heart when caught and tangled in a woman's body."[8]

Although she is thinking about Judith Shakespeare in the sixteenth century, the imputation of madness, craziness, still swirls around many women who would not be silenced. Woolf tells us how to spot these women hiding in the margins of our history books. "When, however one reads of a witch being ducked, of a woman possessed by devils, of a wise woman selling herbs, or even of a very remarkable man who had a mother, then I think we are on the track of a lost novelist, a suppressed poet."[9] Is it possible, I wonder, that the muzzled woman in Mary's dream is her own creative drive, incarcerated, held in hostage by an internalized negative father? Does contact with the muzzled woman, the woman unable to speak, bring with it the fear of creative possibility or the dread of madness?

It is a terrifying thing when a woman's mind begins to unravel. Even worse, however, are the conventional explanations put forth about what is happening to her or the treatments prescribed. Oftentimes, the most "enlightened" and rational interpretations of women's distress serve to keep them in confinement, while the "cures" dispensed could kill them. I wonder about Elizabeth Reis and what drove her to madness. Certainly our collective fantasies of happy agrarian life on the American frontier are easily countered by the known hardships imposed on people living under harsh conditions of climate, sickness, and isolation. What lethal combination of fear, sorrow, despair, what excesses of illness, religious piety, too much child-bearing, what amount of terror, rage and helplessness, led to her incarceration in an asylum and finally to such a violent act of self-destruction? These are questions that remain in my mind. What did she know and what knowledge did she take with her?

Isolation: Silencing Connection

Isolation is one of the major tools known and used by all captors. The isolation a woman can experience runs the gamut from actual incarceration in her own home to being jealously guarded and kept from associating with anyone outside her immediate family. In Gilman's story, the woman has been confined by her husband and physician to a bedroom in an isolated country house. In Mary's dream, the muzzled woman is held in isolation in the garage by her owner. Isolation can be effected by a rigid set of required behaviors that a woman comes to internalize.

Sometimes I ask a woman to make a map for me of what she feels is allowed and disallowed in her life. Most women know quite well how long their leash is, how far they can venture outside their homes without fear of reprisal. There are usually certain things outside the pale that a woman may know about, but could never imagine participating in herself. These things are often the very kinds of activities that would work to set her free. Even the thought of an overnight alone or with a woman friend is sometimes enough to make a woman feel subversive.

There are other ways that isolation occurs. The ban on speaking, breaking silence on all forms of abuse, does not have to be reinforced on a daily basis. Oftentimes a woman will come from a childhood in which she has had to bear secrets of shame, abuse, violence. She may have learned early on how to keep her mouth shut, to muzzle herself. The injunction about never "airing the family linen" in public is a rule that has sexual violation encoded within its metaphor. Being told never to speak in public about what occurs within the four walls of a family home for fear the neighbors will find out is a way of maintaining family privacy as well as enforcing isolation and keeping one from getting help. Often it is the women in the family—the mother, aunts, and grandmothers—who are most strict about this rule. The need to uphold the family's public image seems to fall within women's domain, and it is the women who are the enforcers.

Isolation, the inability to speak up, lack of access to resources, to information about getting help, are all part of the conspiracy of domination. These behaviors are reinforced most acutely when a woman's basic needs are dependent upon her husband. Particularly when a husband is her sole financial resource for food and shelter. "Family values" which would keep a woman out of the workplace, without resources of her own, without access to her own checkbook, without connections with other women, are colluding with and participating in a program that keep women in check and ultimately in captivity. As I was writing this chapter, many women referred me to *The Stepford Wives*, that chilling novel of women who were slowly but surely made into "perfect" wives.

Many women have understood their own madness and confinement in mental hospitals as a kind of political incarceration, a way to keep them silenced. Writing about political prisoners who have been tortured, Judith Lewis Herman makes links between that experience and childhood sexual and physical abuse. She includes, as well, women who are kept captive in their own homes, in their own marriages. She does not see these situations as separate but merely as different points on a continuum of coercion.[10]

A woman whose husband was a wealthy, highly respected business man came into counseling. Her appearance gripped me immediately. Although she was very expensively dressed, she had the body language and demeanor of a whipped dog. Her shoulders were caved in, she was very thin, she chain-smoked, and her face was haggard. Little by little, it came out that she was being kept hostage in her own home. Her husband, who had developed a powerful public persona as a generous philanthropist, was a maniacal tyrant at home. The control this man exercised over his family was total and complete, ranging from the most mundane of details to the most demeaning of demands. Unlike other hostages, she was allowed to go out of her home, but she had to be well-presented—thus the expensive clothes, the gold chains, and diamond rings that were her mandatory costume. However, she was not allowed to invite anybody into her home. Like many captives, she was kept in virtual isolation from other people. She said she had not been allowed to buy anything new for her home for twenty years. She described her household furniture as worn and tattered, couches with the stuffing coming out, drapes greying and torn, appliances inoperable or in a continual state of breakdown. She was allowed to buy towels or sheets only in a beige color. Her days were spent organized around preparing meals for her husband, who made erratic and unpredictable appearances at home demanding to be fed. She told of family car trips where neither she nor the children were allowed to take bathroom breaks or stop for food, and family vacations where they became virtual prisoners in wealthy resort settings.

As I listened to this woman's story week after week, I would also read in the newspapers how her husband was making large donations to various charities. It was understandable to me when she told me that she was sure if she told anyone about her situation, no one would believe her. She was right. Even people who were somewhat aware of her circumstances were not willing to help her because this man exercised so much power and influence in the community. Her state of psychological and economic dependence were immeasurably increased by the fact that she had several children. And over the years she and her children had developed survival strategies together—the children spent more and more time outside the home, and she sheltered and protected them as much as possible by taking the full brunt of his domination upon herself.

Many studies of battered women have shown that it is not necessary for a perpetrator to actually use violence as a means of control. Oftentimes threats are enough to keep the victim in a constant state of vigilance, fear, and compliance. Until recently, a husband's threats of violence towards his wife were commonplace, even a source of humor. One only has to remember Jackie Gleason holding his fist up to Audrey Meadows and saying, "Someday, Alice. Someday." And how we all laughed. Although this woman's husband never beat her or her children, he had, over the years occasionally engaged in violent outbursts. These eruptions were unpredictable, leaving her always afraid and always conciliatory.

It is hard for me to explain how or where this woman finally found the courage to come into counseling. She did it in secret at first, paying me cash, not using the family checkbook. I was aware that my office became the only place of safety for her and I was frequently in the position of "the only one who knew." The privacy of the therapeutic office, although an absolutely essential requirement for healing, oftentimes reinforces the sense of isolation from the larger community. Sometimes, however, it is the only place where a careful and intricate process of supporting a woman's move towards health and recovery can begin.

Over the course of several years, this woman was able to slowly but surely establish enough psychological strength to make some changes in her situation. Under terrible duress, she contacted a woman lawyer who gave her legal information about her status and her options. Eventually she was able, with restraining orders and help from the local police, to get her husband out of her house. During this time she was plagued by fears for her own and her children's lives. We did what we could to ensure her safety but she, as well as I, was aware of the potential for disaster—the husband's behavior was so erratic and unpredictable, his temper and emotional outbursts so violent. Neither of us had a great deal of confidence in the standard systems of protection. In a small community where a man wields so much influence and power, it is hard to find anybody willing or able to believe that he is capable of doing bad things much less to publicly go against him. Everyone wants to believe that any man with that much money and position must be right and the wife must be crazy or hysterical or exaggerating or ungrateful. It is even more impossible when one's job or one's charitable institutions are dependent upon his generosity.

With a great deal of support from a few very close friends, with the help of an unco-opted woman attorney, and with the strength she drew from the therapeutic relationship, she finally got a divorce and an adequate financial settlement as well. She went on to buy her own home and to provide a safe and emotionally stable environment for her children. She also began to go to small support groups, where she started to integrate herself and her experiences into a larger social context. Fortunately, this woman did not join the statistics of women who are killed by their fanatically controlling spouses. Her trauma and that of her children, however, will continue to take its toll. There is no quick or easy recovery and some of its effects will last a lifetime. Coming to terms with how she spent over twenty years of her life and the impact of that life on the children weigh heavily upon her. But her chances for having some joy, spontaneity, loving relationships, and personal freedom in her life are now greatly improved. Her life is in her own hands—for the first time.

A woman does not suddenly find herself in such a situation of captivity as an adult. Except in cases of actual hostage-taking, these things do not usually happen overnight. The long process of intimidation, the accretion of blows to her self-esteem, the incremental influences that shaped this woman's choices began in her early childhood—a childhood of captivity in her own home, a severe and demanding father who refused to allow her any form of independence, and a mother who absented herself through alcoholism, all conspired to make this woman vulnerable and susceptible to the abusive marriage she eventually made as an adult. Her own psychological internalization of father as tyrant and daughter as captive is what helped her re-create her family situation in her marriage. The collusion of the culture which protected the family's privacy and supported the father's/husband's rights over his family ensured that this woman would not escape. It is to her credit that she did.

Control: Silencing the Body

One way in which women may be held in captivity is through the psychological appropriation of their bodies. As Mary's muzzled woman dream shows, a woman's sense of body may not be her own. In general, women are not taught ownership of their bodies. As little girls we learn very early on that we can gain approval through the gaze of others. We are taught the importance of self-presentation—through our clothes, hair, "feminine" behaviors—for the pleasure of others. Much more importance is still laid on girls' appearance than on that of boys. This emphasis on appearance can frequently be directed towards the father's approval. Oftentimes it is the mother who will present the father with "his little princess." Although a father may be seemingly absent and unconcerned about his daughter's appearance, it is the father's more rigid standards for sex-typed behavior that are usually being met.[11]

One woman in her forties told me of an encapsulated memory of being dressed up in a frilly "feminine" outfit by her mother at age six. She was met with an overwhelmingly positive response by her father who, in his enthusiasm, swooped down to pick her up. She spontaneously repulsed him and turned away. To this day she cannot completely understand what it was that made her do that. She can say only that she wanted to be loved for more than just how she looked. Is it a strange irony that at age sixteen she would go on to become anorexic?

Adult scrutiny and control over a child's body can range from terribly invasive toilet rituals, like enemas, or restrictive eating practices, to highly rigid demands for proper behavior and dress, all in the name of physical health, politeness, or proper socialization. Physical abuse of this sort is one of the ways in which a child's psychological integrity begins to be compromised. Herman writes that: "in addition to inducing fear, the perpetrator seeks to destroy the victim's sense of autonomy. This is achieved by scrutiny and control of the victim's body and bodily functions."[12] Most women have experienced some sort of surveillance about their physical appearance by the time they are teen-agers.

Later, when she grows up, a woman will have already learned to divide her own vision. She learns to turn her gaze inward, scrutinizing herself with an unmerciful eye, while outwardly presenting herself for the judging gaze of others. Caught in this hall of mirrors, all of which are distorted, she must work continually at "keeping herself up." In an essay on seeing, John Berger tells us how this divided vision operates: "A woman must continually watch herself. She is almost continually accompanied by her own image of herself. . . . And so she comes to consider the *surveyor* and the *surveyed* within her as two constituent yet always distinct elements of her identity as a woman."[13]

Because we are led to believe that our bodies belong to others, we are extremely vulnerable to verbal comments on our appearance by others. We are continually being assaulted, no matter how subtly, by the "beauty myth." Because of our early training, many of us unconsciously collude with a culture that is ruthless in its depiction of what an acceptable woman should look like. We internalize these standards and become our own guards. When these tyrannizing standards are externalized, they can exist in our own homes, in our very love relationships, in the form of a husband who wants us to look a certain way. We accept this and do not recognize it as abusive. One woman told me of being hospitalized for anorexia while she was pregnant with her first child. The anorexia was self-induced due to her husband's disgust with her "getting too fat" during her pregnancy.

Women frequently tell of trying to meet their husband's or lover's standards of beauty. They do not claim ownership over their own hair, their weight, their clothes. Instead they will allow their partners to dictate how they should wear their hair, what their bodies should look like, what kinds of clothes they can wear. Oftentimes women will try to achieve a certain "look" because their husbands find it "sexy." One woman told me how her husband would buy clothes for her and then tell her what to wear when they went out together. He was dressing her up as if she were his doll. This woman expressed extreme disgust at herself for going along with his requests, but she had been doing it for so many years that she had no real sense of her own taste or what she, herself, really wanted to wear. She had been so used to living into her husband's fantasy of who she was that she had lost touch with her own sense of self. Sometimes this kind of controlling management will extend into the sexual relationship.

Some form of sexual coercion seems to be commonplace in many marriages. Women may find themselves being little more than prostitutes in their own homes. Ranging from marital rape to constant sexual innuendo, a woman may feel constantly pressured sexually. She may be asked to watch pornographic films, wear "sexy lingerie" that she herself would not be interested in, engage in sexual acts that repulse her, agree to sex more than she would like, all in order to keep her husband "satisfied." It is rare that a woman will question a man's sexual appetite. Women are trained to believe that men have a stronger and more insistent sex drive than they do and that men have little control over their sexual impulses. Women are taught that they must be the keeper and the container of men's sexual lives. Men must also, at some level, believe this as well. Women are blamed for arousing sexual interest and blamed for refusing it; women are called teasers and frigid. If a man wants sex three times a day, he is thought of as "highly sexed," maybe on the high end of a continuum of "normal," but not unusual. He is not thought of as exhibiting desperate and addictive behavior or as seeking self-medication for depression through orgasm.

If women have trouble comprehending some men's sexuality, they are frequently and deeply aware of men's emotional desperation. Herman writes that the women who return to battering relationships are "often persuaded to return, not by further threats but by apologies, expressions of love, promises of reform, and appeals to loyalty and compassion."[14] These, she says, appear to reverse for a moment the balance of power. The woman is led to believe "his fate is in her hands," she has the power to make everything all right again. Women, who have so little sense of personal power, are often easily convinced by these types of arguments, pleas, and persuasions. It is one of the disadvantages of women's socialization that we put relationships as such a priority—sometimes over our own well-being and that of our children. If women are led to believe that their self-esteem and worthiness comes primarily from maintaining close relationships, we will do so, sometimes at tremendous cost. Obviously there are no laws that regulate such subjugation.

Economics: The Silencing of Power

One cannot exaggerate the importance for women of some kind of financial viability. This applies not only to the majority of women who are the underpaid or undereducated poor, women least likely to be able to achieve a modicum of financial independence. It applies also to "well-kept" women—women who live off their husband's income. They do so at peril to their sense of dignity and self-esteem. This is one of the hardest facts for women to face. Women my age, in their fifties, still remember the "ideal family" model of the 1940s and 1950s, when moms stayed at home, wore aprons or housedresses, cooked Sunday dinners and cleaned their own houses, while men brought home the paycheck.

I remember a small incident that took place in my own family kitchen. It is a scene captured in my memory, as if caught in amber. My mother, who stayed at home to care for her large family, was asking my father for twenty-five cents to buy some nylon stockings so she could go out to her women's church group meeting. He refused. Whether he might not actually have had it (we certainly did not have much money) or whether it was an exercise in pure power, I don't recall. I do remember watching her helplessness and humiliation and vowed to myself at the age of eleven that I would never allow myself to be financially dependent. My awareness of what the power differential between my parents really meant was born at that moment. I sensed how trapped my mother was, and I, as her daughter, began to actively search for ways out.

Synchronistically, as I was writing this section, my mother reminded me of this very incident. She was remarking about how her current financial situation allowed her to make substantial gifts and loans to her children and grandchildren. She reminisced about how ironic it was that as a young woman she had no money to call her own, not even a few cents to buy a pair of nylons while now, as an eighty-year-old matriarch, she was playing banker to her extended family. As her oldest daughter who witnessed her early humiliation, I felt myself celebrate her good fortune while wondering where her anger went.

Depression: The Silencing of Rage

A woman sitting in the Belly of the Father experiences her rage as a kind of suppressed fury that comes over women who have been swallowed too long whether by being stuck in an insufferable marriage or being consumed by service to the patriarchy in a corporate job which demands that she work fifty to sixty hours a week. The rage of a swallowed woman is a particular kind of suffocating rage, like the smoldering fires in many women's dreams: the fire that is down in the basement and threatens to break through to the living room, the kitchen fires that are about to take over the whole house, the chimney fires that spontaneously burst through the masonry.

Rage in the Belly of the Father is primarily an energetic body event, a smoldering fire constantly fueled by guilt and shame. Life is perceived through a veil of smoky greyness, creativity choked off for lack of oxygen. It reminds me of women who smoke, whose faces are veiled in a wreath of cigarette fumes. This kind of rage produces a cold fire which does not warm. It is not incendiary, so it does not liberate nor will it illuminate. Until one is willing to use it, this kind of rage becomes the smothering rage that has turned in on oneself in the form of depression.

Depression is often thought of as rage turned inward. I imagine that any powerful passion when thwarted can turn to cold depression. I have frequently said that the only way to describe the feeling of being around my father at certain times was: "It felt like he put my light out." So convincing was the effect of his periodic cynicism, his pessimism, his propensity to find the one bad spot, that he could effectively kill my youthful joy, my enthusiasm, my spontaneity. It was during those times, when I still needed to feel his love and approval, that I would experience depression.

Daughters of Saturn are particularly vulnerable to depression. Their depression is like being caught in the dense, dark womb of the father, without access to nurturing warmth and light. This darkness is not fertile; nothing can grow in this gloom. In alchemy, this experience is called the *nigredo*. As the first stage of the alchemical process the *nigredo* is dominated by Saturn, the blackening, *putrefactio* and *mortificatio*—the colors are black and grey. Saturn is frequently thought of as temperamentally cold, weighty, heavy. All the feelings of paralysis and pessimism, the denseness and immovability of things, and the sense that one is bound by fateful limits belong to Saturn and his depressive influence.

Depression in women has been described at least since the Greek physician Galen noted it nearly 2,000 years ago. (Current studies consistently account women's depression as double that found in men.) Historically, men's melancholy was seen as a sign of their creative brilliance, and men's personal feelings of loss and grief easily became translated and accepted into the culture as art. But women have no claim to this grand tradition. It is clear that women's grief in patriarchal culture does not proclaim genius. Women do not count as the so-called great melancholics. Women's pain is dismissed with the banal and unprestigious term "depression."[15] What we learn from the long association of Saturn, melancholia, and male genius is that women's sorrow and its expression is not given the same cultural value and significance as men's grief.

This cultural "knowledge" filters down to us on a common, everyday level. Thus a man who is thought of as emotionally "sensitive" or artistic is admired, excused, and given a wide berth, while women expressing hurt are often derided and accused of "oversensitivity." Women, supposedly accustomed to loss and lack, are themselves overwhelmed when faced with men's grief. One only has to watch a film with Robert Bly and groups of men expressing grief to know that men's sorrow must be "deeper, more serious" than women's chronic complaining about their conditions. Faced with men's grief, women seem more than willing to forget their historical and political realities. I have frequently watched mixed-gender groups unravel along certain predictable lines. A woman will begin by sharing her pain and, rather then receive the woman's sorrow, some man will automatically intervene with his own list of grievances. Then women usually become very silent. Their silence almost always has an earlier referent, the awed silence felt toward the face of their own father's grief. A father's grief has the power to distract and disarm a woman.

A woman tells me her dream:

> Women are telling their stories, There is a rhythm to it—in and out, digesting and expelling, one woman speaking, another listening—a dynamic rhythm that was somehow holding everything together. My mother was telling a deep truth about her life. She was being "heard into speech" by a woman friend of hers, one of her old school friends from Norway. She told of how it was to leave Norway and come to Chicago, how lost she felt there, how she had lost everything. Listening to her now, I heard all this as if for the first time. That is: I really felt it for the first time. I began weeping. It was an amazing release, a kind of weeping I'd never done before.
>
> No sooner had I begun to give way to this sense of release, than my father's voice rang out "Lise!" "Lise!" calling from another room of the house. With the uncanny instinct he's always had for my moments of emotional distress, he was calling out in alarm, he was worried about me, wanted to know what was the matter. I tried to ignore him, go on with my weeping, but his call had already distracted me from my grief.

"It was my father," she says, "who distracted me from the grieving I really needed to be doing and the father version of grief is always so personal—like his depression." The daughter's necessary grieving for her mother's and other women's pain is swallowed by the father's insistently demanding and narcissistic melancholy. The myth of Saturn and his fearful and anxious devouring is the same story writ large—the melancholic father claims his patriarchal rights of primacy over the daughter's sympathies and occludes the desire for her mother. Creatively speaking, he devours all the daughter's available emotional resources, all her creative supplies.

Addictions: The Silencing of Passion

A woman captive in the Belly of the Father frequently finds herself addicted to something in order to anaesthetize her pain. An addiction to anything—a substance, food, buying things, another person—is a terrifying process to be in. The power invested in the addictive substance, to calm, excite, numb, stimulate, deaden, or otherwise alter, leads to an endless pursuit of the thing that produces, momentarily, the desired effect. After a while the struggle to maintain ego control is a battle that is continually lost. As any addict will tell you, the addictive process becomes more and more time consuming: more and more time is spent in pursuit, whether it be a shopping spree or a food binge; more and more time is spent in recovering, whether it be from the alcohol of the night before, or the loss of the latest lover. What starts out as a seemingly innocent activity—eating an ice cream cone, drinking a glass of wine, going on a date with a new acquaintance—can, in the life of an addicted person, end up with devastating consequences—a binge, a drunk, an empty one-night stand. Addictions work along a progressive continuum. The addictive substance is continually titrated for greater and greater effect.

Addictive behavior can sometimes become tangled up with a woman's relationship with her creativity. Oftentimes a woman who has difficulty surrendering to the creative voice inside will use some substance to break through her resistance. As Linda Schierse Leonard has so movingly shown, the glass of wine which once was taken to ignite the creative fires soon turns into the Demon Lover robbing a women of her true and vital passion. The bargain made with the addictive substance appears as a Moneylender who extorts higher and higher interest for the loan of a creative boost. The addictive process can be a shapeshifter, a Trickster, convincing a woman that she can control her behavior, then laughing in contempt as she falls into a terrifying addictive spin, and the one glass of wine she thought was enough ends in a blackout.[16]

Addictions take on a particular twist for women in our culture. I believe addictions are intimately tied to how women feel about themselves as women. The way an addiction is played out is necessarily gender-related. This is most obvious with so-called eating disorders which are, in my estimation, directly related to how women perceive themselves vis-à-vis the cultural prescriptions for femininity. But it is also true for compulsive consumerism, smoking, which is on the rise for women, and other forms of substance abuse. Probably the most common addictive behavior for women is what has been called co-dependency.

Relationship addiction for the Daughters of Saturn is almost an inevitable consequence of being swallowed by the father. What a woman learns as she sits in the Belly of the Father is that she has no rights within relationship. She becomes automatically attuned to the needs and wants of another at the expense of her own desires. Women are led to believe this is a virtue. Romance novels and romantic movies showing relationships predicated on a woman's capacity for sympathetic merger with her man are thought to be ideal. Women's drive to constitute a state of fusion within relationships leads them to deny their own individuality for the sake of union. To do otherwise is thought of as "selfish," or "self-centered"— words that are as devastating to women as are the epithets of "bitch" and "dyke." A woman who enters into addictive forms of relationship will have no energy left for developing a creative work. She will be continually preoccupied, her creative time swallowed up in "working on the relationship" or devoting herself to the needs of her partner. Or she may use her creativity to concoct a romantic image that she can feed off—a fantasy of marriage that sustains her while the reality remains something painfully different. Or she may spend her time feeding herself on romantic happily-ever-after plots, nurturing the romantic "hope" of someday reconstituting an old love relationship—giving the person an existence in her fantasy life which is frozen in the past—negating the possibility that the person has undoubtedly gone on with his or her separate life. Creative energies misused in this way can go so far as to become perverse.

Perversions: The Silencing of Desire

Addictions and perversions are related. Addictions happen when women give their power over to an external substance, thing, or person and that substance, thing, or person begins to control them. Perversions happen when women fetishise their partners, their own bodies, material goods, or anything else for the sake of fulfilling their hidden sexual desires. Women who are not granted vivid and powerful sexual lives tend to find ways to distort the culture's gender prescriptions for femininity and act them out in a sexual way. A woman trapped in the Belly of the Father will undoubtedly have a disturbed relationship with her own sexuality. She may even find herself engaging in sexually perverse behavior. As psychoanalyst, Louise Kaplan, has argued, perversions, in general, derive their emotional force from socially accepted and promoted gender stereotypes and are "as much pathologies of gender role identity as they are pathologies of sexuality."[17]

As Kaplan notes, female perversions are not obviously sexual. Rather, they are embedded in the socially accepted, stereotypical gender proscriptions for femininity which "serve as screens or disguises for a woman's forbidden and frightening masculine wishes."[18] If cultural constraints prevent fathers from enacting feminine attributes of softness and receptivity, their daughters and the women they become are deprived of expressions of power and active sexuality through the gender ideals of purity, cleanliness, modesty, and submissiveness.

To find the locus of female perversions, we must look, Kaplan says, "to our most revered social institutions—the family, the church, the fashion and cosmetic industries, the pornography industry, the department store and, not the least perverse among them, the medical profession."[19] Here the culture's denial and rejection of a healthy female sexual identity operates in collusion with the culturally encouraged pursuit of trophies from the male world. The true identifying mark of a female perversion is the fetishizing of the material world, or the lover's penis, or one's own body. In this way, women's erotomania is totally supported by the culture.

The Little Perversions of Everyday Life

Women who do not take up the pen, or in today's idiom, sit down at the word processor, or take up the paintbrush or the clay, women who do not move their bodies when their bodies are aching to dance, who do not scribble the poem down when it comes bubbling up in the middle of the night, are denying something at their peril. A woman who will not allow herself to create will undoubtedly and inevitably engage in a variety of perversions of that creativity, the little perversions of everyday life.

The seductions for women to engage in trivial (but deadly) distortions of the creative process are many. One only has to look at "women's" magazines to know where women are being told to spend their creative time, energy, and money. These "women's" magazines are like pornography: they drain off women's creative juices, are addictive, while their suggested activities with the promise of fulfillment are empty and sterile.

One woman told me how she threw her creative energies into cooking ever more elaborate meals for an unappreciative husband. The preparation of food is an art and can possibly be an art form. But only when women consciously choose it as their creative medium does it truly satisfy. Many an anorexic woman has involved herself in feeding others magnificently created meals which she herself would never dream of eating.

Another deflection of a woman's creative impulse happens when she creates herself as a work of art. The woman who will not attempt to become an artist can fool herself by attempting to turn her body into an artistic object. The incredible amount of attention and focus that goes into making oneself into a perfected and artistic object is truly deplorable. One woman who was too scared to begin painting made her self-presentation so desirable that frequently artistic men came up to her and asked if she would model for them.

Although women are acculturated to spend hours in front of the mirror, they are expected to look utterly "natural." The accusation of female vanity and narcissism is never too far away. Thus, would-be sculptors become "scalpel slaves" instead as they search out the latest surgical technology for perfecting their bodies.[20] From this perspective, one could even begin to place all bodily manipulations that women commit on themselves onto a continuum of perversity. The idea that women concede to each other "beauty hurts" becomes a complicated combination of sadistic revenge on one's one body as well as evidence for a well-known definition of perversion as "the erotic form of hatred."[21]

When women engage in these behaviors in the hopes of receiving some form of sexual gratification, they are participating in perverse scenarios. When a woman submits herself to cosmetic surgeries, she is embarked on a program of revenge against her own gender. This behavior becomes particularly destructive when she does this in order to please some man who wishes to fetishize her, i.e., make her into his own pornographic image. When she then presents him with a body that has undergone the requisite cosmetic changes, she offers herself up as a sexual object and any possibility for true emotional closeness or intimacy completely disappears.

Women who have been incarcerated in the prison of prescriptions for femininity will sometimes have dreams of mannequins. The stiff doll-like figure with a distorted woman's body becomes an image for the false self a woman has constructed. Sylvia Plath writes of the doll that a conventional marriage can make out of a woman.

> . . . in twenty-five years she'll be silver,
> in fifty, gold.
> A living doll, everywhere you look.
> It can sew, it can cook,
> It can talk, talk, talk.[22]

This "talk" is not speech. It more clearly resembles the mechanical repetition of gender prescriptions learned by rote.

In another poem, "Munich Mannequins," Plath writes: "Perfection is terrible, it cannot have children. / Cold as snow breath, it tamps the womb." The mannequins "naked and bald in their furs, / Orange lollies on silver sticks" are "glittering" but ultimately dead and white as snow: "Voicelessness. The snow has no voice."[23] In the Belly of the Father without a voice, or hearing voices, a woman is dead to herself.

∘III∘

The First Gate: The Awakening

Was I summoned?
Or did I rise
from my own emergency?

—*Kim Chernin*[1]

According to the myth, there are two ways in which the daughters of Saturn are disgorged from the Belly of the Father. In one variation of the Greek myth, the mother goddess, Rhea, tricks her husband, Saturn, into thinking that what he is swallowing is her latest child when, in fact, it is a stone wrapped in swaddling clothes. This causes him to vomit out his children.

It is common knowledge among some women that men are "stupid" when it comes to their own needs, that men can be duped into believing they are getting what they want. Women's reputation as dangerous, deceitful, cunning, comes from men's dim suspicion that they are being tricked. Men do not trust women for these reasons and rightfully so. What women harbor is contempt for the men who swallow their faked orgasms, duplicit devotion, and sham submission. Men's seemingly wilfull ignorance about this feeds women's hatred of them. But this kind of women's subterfuge is ultimately a strategy of the powerless. And so it is when Rhea gives Saturn the stone.

The Role of Metis

In another variation of the myth, Zeus hires Metis the Titan, an ancient wise woman who "knew more than all the gods or man," to concoct an emetic. Metis knows how to do this. Like a wily shamaness, she works with, not against, the orally aggressive, incorporative father. She knows he likes to eat so she feeds him. But what she feeds him—maybe a mushroom, a root, or an herb—is an emetic which works the cure and results in the release and liberation of the swallowed children.

Oftentimes women who have been captive in the Belly of the Father will meet up with some encouraging female figure, like Metis, who will work to inspire a woman's awakening. In writing about creative women, Carolyn Heilbrun notices that women's awakening follows a certain kind of pattern.

> It is fathers, as representatives of the patriarchy, who are the pivot on which, usually in memory, the new awareness turns. Mothers have no obvious role in this change, but some other female mentor or figure, often not even known personally, most often dead, operates in the new female plot to enhance the reaction from the father and encourage or inspire the awakening.[2]

Unfortunately, it is not usually the personal mother who is able to free the woman from her father. Mothers, for the most part, leave their daughters as yet unawakened. But sometimes the mother's sister, the unusual, interesting, or even crazy aunt, can act as a beckoning figure. Or sometimes the female mentor, the agent of change and awakening, will appear in a dream. Metis, who is well-known for her ability to shapeshift, can take many unusual forms.

One woman who had been living what looked on the surface to be a happy, normal life knew herself to be deeply discontented. She had followed the patented formula for success—married young, had two children, devoted her energies to her husband and family—but never found expression for what would have truly given her life meaning. In the beginning process of therapy, she dreamed:

> My husband and I are upstairs in our house. It is dark. There is a knock at the attic door. We are surprised by it, but I open the door. There stands a woman. She is seven feet tall. She is an alien—and she is pregnant! Almost ready to deliver!

This woman was surprised and bewildered by this alien woman's appearance in her dream life. Further work on the dream was revealing. When, in active imagination, the woman approached the alien, her first response was to her pregnant condition. Empathetically, she reached out to the alien and asked her what she needed to make herself more comfortable. The alien woman responded with the shocking reply that "Comfort is not a consideration!" The alien woman was giving the dreamer information that was, indeed, totally alien. As a representative of her own alienation from herself, the woman was being told that concerns about comfort were not only unnecessary but weren't even a category. In fact, thoughts about comfort were what had kept this woman from herself all these years. The inability to face the discomfort of disapproval, from family, friends, society in general, were keeping her life stuck in a deadly conventionality. While working with the image of the "alien," the woman realized that she had always had a deep desire to write. The "alien" continued to appear in varying disguises in her dreams and even once in her waking life. While she was sitting on a park bench, a neatly dressed woman, a tourist, came up and sat down beside her and asked "Are you a writer?"

Motivating Disasters

It usually takes an external event, what I call a motivating disaster, to move a woman out of life in the Belly of the Father—a divorce, a death, a severe illness, a hitting bottom of some kind, a breakdown of body or mind or both. With these experiences can come a kind of awakening, a recognition of her position. Although she may fall back asleep again and again, most women can document the event or moment when they first woke up.

My own awakening came at age thirty-seven when I was presented with the announcement of a divorce, an almost banal scenario from the annals of a contemporary woman's life. What led me to believe that this was going to be more than a divorce was the fact that I was overcome with full body tremors—for three days and nights! Although I had no idea what was occurring in my body, in retrospect I now understand that the creative energy I had been repressing for years was in the process of being unleashed. I had been holding on and holding back for years, afraid of my own creative potential, terrified of being overcome by something bigger than my little ego self. The divorce merely served to pull the cork, and any efforts to exert control over my life were now useless against the force of released energy. Luckily I had already established the practice of art-making into which I could canalize some of the intensity. But this upheaval demanded nothing less than a complete renovation of my life. The tremors were only the beginning of a years-long process of de-construction and re-construction of all the structures that had held my life together up until that point. Although I had been awakened to the reality of what I had been living in and shaken into the possibility of new life, my awakening was only the beginning.

As a woman begins to recognize where she has been living, she may undergo great amounts of disorientation. Behaviors and thoughts that once served her no longer work; things she once cherished and depended upon become ashes in her mouth. She will feel dislocated, estranged, and alienated. She will begin to react to her situation, critiquing it, which gives evidence that she is beginning to understand where she is living. And at this point, she will usually engage in lots of negotiations. Not completely wanting to change her residence, desiring to stay right where she is (with a few modifications), hoping she will not have to completely renovate her life, she starts to make bargains. She becomes legalistic and begins to broker deals.

Many women enter therapy with this attitude. They may want change but they do not want transformation. They may want to know what they can do to relieve their quiet desperation, but they do not want to leave a marriage that has been emotionally empty for years. They may want to begin their creative lives, but they do not want to give up the two glasses of wine they must have every night with their dinner. They may feel the urgency of something inside that wants to get born, but they do not want to give up their demanding social lives and subject themselves to the hours of serious labor and solitude that this work will demand of them. Women can go on like this for years. Eventually something happens. It is not always wonderful.

Ambivalence keeps a woman from engaging passionately with herself and her work. Doubt, hesitancy, feelings of uncertainty belong to all of us at various times. But many women will linger in ambivalence, languish in their aimless state, much longer than is necessary or helpful. Unable, for all the many reasons, to move directly toward what they want, they will vacillate, they will move into a piece of creative work and quickly move out again, letting long periods of wasted time go by. They will then scourge themselves from within, castigate themselves as lazy and stupid, unable or unwilling, perpetually wavering, always on the shore.

Submissiveness to one's situation, one's relationships, one's job, is also antithetical to creative work. Dutiful daughters, compliant wives, deferential employees, do not create, they resign themselves to their situations. They surrender, not to the creative fires within, but to the demands of the life of servitude the culture has created for them.

For women to begin to intentionally take up a creative process is usually terrifying. We are not that far away from those nineteenth-century literary foremothers "who feared their attempts at the pen were presumptuous, castrating, or even monstrous, (and found themselves) engaged in a variety of strategies to deal with their anxiety about authorship."[3] Jill Johnston rightfully observes that "women transform themselves, or set themselves on some path of achievement only after an awakening" and she recounts two in her life, both pertaining to her call as a writer. The first coincided "quite inconveniently" with marriage and motherhood, and caused conflicts of interest and responsibilities. "In the end, my awakening helped to cost me my new family." The second awakening "was of an interior nature." "I actually discovered" she says, "that things were going on inside me, that I had a whole life of thoughts, feelings, attitudes, rooted in a past that had been conducting itself autonomously, disconnected from my surface life." The second awakening centered on her long-dead father, whom she had never met, and who had never been married to her mother or even lived with her. Her second awakening and the new introspection it brought gave her she says, "for the first time the striking and novel idea that I had a story."[4]

Awakenings out of the Belly of the Father are not like the fairy tales where a kiss from the prince brings the sleeping daughter into life and love and happiness ever after. But sometimes an awakening does send a woman running back to her father. As Anne Sexton rewrites the fairy tale:

> He kissed Briar Rose
> And she woke up crying,
> Daddy! Daddy![4]

Once a woman has found herself outside of the Belly of the Father, she will have to learn ways to survive. Oftentimes a woman will find herself desperate for a man to save her from this eventuality. The false security found in wearing the "golden handcuffs" of a marriage of comfort and leisure, supported by a wealthy or even well-off husband or a well-paying, high-status job in an established institution which demands all of a woman's energy and attention, or belonging to a spiritual tradition that dictates what is acceptable behavior for women, will have to be seriously reevaluated and ultimately given up if a woman wants to live a life true to herself. Desires to "belong," to conform, be straight, be "normal" and conventional, must be seriously examined.

Unplugging from the patriarchal umbilicus scares most women, and for good reason. We are taught that this is the only place where we can get fed, only here will we be nourished, supported and sustained. We are taught to be dependent on these institutions of the fathers, that nothing can replace them. To go against this teaching, one must be willing to become a radical, a revolutionary or, in the case of the woman above, an alien.

In the late nineteenth century, when Charlotte Perkins Gilman found herself crawling into "remote closets and under beds in order to hide from the grinding pressure" of her depression, she had what she calls "a moment of clear vision."[6] In that moment of awakening, she saw what was making her ill. She wanted to be a writer and activist—she did not want to be a wife. Holding to the truth of her own vision, she divorced her husband and moved away. The madness she had experienced along with her awareness that the medical prescription for her "cure" had been potentially fatal led to her awakening. This realization was her radicalizing moment. Three years after her illness, she wrote "The Yellow Wallpaper." How important this moment of awakening was for her is indicated by the fact that she made it the measure of her life's work. After a full and accomplished life, years spent in activism and writing, she remarked in her autobiography that she had heard that her short story, "The Yellow Wallpaper," had influenced Dr. S. Weir Mitchell, the physician whose prescriptions almost killed her, and, since reading it, he had changed his treatment. "If that is a fact," she reflects, "I have not lived in vain. . . ."[7]

As anyone who has faced a disease knows, it is then that we begin to take our lives seriously, ask the hard questions, make the necessary changes. A woman who has confronted serious illness can often become a woman with a mission.[8] Adrienne Rich has said: ". . . in the very act of becoming more conscious of her situation in the world, a woman may feel herself coming deeper than ever into touch with her unconscious and with her body."[9] Sometimes it happens in reverse: a woman's awakening, her consciousness of her situation, will erupt through experiences of her body. Illness, in particular, can serve as a profound wake-up call.

A woman who is just waking up will undoubtedly be angry. Like the goddess Inanna, who returns from her stay in the underworld with demons swirling around her, she will have a wild look in her eye, and no patience for denial or sugar-coated solutions. She may be a woman just entering into recovery or getting ready to testify against a rapist; she may be in the process of getting a divorce from a battering husband, or breaking silence about her childhood abuse. She may be a woman whose sexuality has been awakened out of the stupor of a lifeless marriage or a woman whose mind has come alive to its own potential. She may have had a breast removed. Whatever has awakened her, she will not be easily lulled back to sleep.

A woman coming out of the Belly of the Father will have no patience left for other women who stay in denial, even and especially if it is her own mother. Facing abandonment by her husband, Ted Hughes, and the inevitable ensuing divorce, Sylvia Plath wrote to her mother from this place:

> Don't talk to me about the world needing cheerful stuff! What the person out of Belsen—physical or psychological—wants is nobody saying the birdies still go tweet-tweet, but the full knowledge that somebody else has been there and knows the worst, just what it is like.[10]

A woman's voice, when she is no longer in denial about where she has been, is a powerful agent for change. Truth-telling, breaking silence about any kind of terrorism, whether it occurs in a marriage or in a concentration camp, spells the beginning of the end of a woman's state of captivity. As Alice Walker has stated, "If you lie to yourself about your own pain, you will be killed by those who will claim you enjoyed it."[11] The hope for freedom through the simple act of speaking the truth is starkly expressed in Anna Ahkmatova's small prelude to her poem, "Requiem." The "Yezhov terror" is the name the Russians gave to the worst period of Stalin's purges. Yezhov was the name of the official whom Stalin entrusted with the operation.[12] Ahkmatova writes:

> In the fearful years of the Yezhov terror I spent seventeen months in prison queues in Leningrad. One day somebody "identified" me. Beside me, in the queue, there was a woman with blue lips. She had, of course, never heard of me; but she suddenly came out of that trance so common to us all and whispered in my ear (everybody spoke in whispers there): "Can you describe this?" And I said: "Yes, I can." And then something like the shadow of a smile crossed what had once been her face.
>
> 1 April 1957, Leningrad 13

Mary, the woman who dreamed about the woman with the muzzle, worked with her dream woman using active imagination over the course of several years. With infinite patience, gentleness, and attention, Mary was able to help the muzzled woman evolve. Once she had removed the muzzle, she made no other demands on her, letting her rest and heal.

> You need only sit here in new energy. The healing already has begun. You need only sit, be still, rest. It has ended. It was an aberration, cruel and over. We will go slowly, with your own flow. Sit and receive acceptance, goodness, kindness, humanity. I slowly dance around her, a dance of protection and energy.

Later, upon entering into another active imagination, Mary found the woman sitting in a molded orange plastic chair in a too brightly lit room with linoleum floors. She writes:

> It is like a holding place, institutional, like immigration. I go there to visit her. She is seated when I enter the room. We rarely speak, but we communicate without words. I open myself to perceiving what she needs to heal. Sometimes I just sit with her. Sometimes I hum. I wash her feet and give her lotion for her arms.

The woman seems to be in a transitional phase. There is a great delicacy in Mary's approach as she becomes attuned to the woman's needs. With this kind of attention, the woman's new-found strength becomes restored.

> Today the woman is sitting up straight in her chair. I ask how her arms are. She continues to need lotion to heal. I notice her hair that had been plaited in dirt and neglect is now tightly braided in long, thin braids. The braids move all along her body, past her shoulders to her waist. They are freshly done and clean. She seems very strong now. I hold her hand and she holds mine. I am disturbed by the strength and determination of her hand. I realize I am afraid that she is now healthier and stronger than I. I feel inadequate, uncomfortable—and afraid that now she will leave.

There is a significant shift in their relationship as Mary realizes the woman's strength may be used to leave her. This possibility arouses Mary's desire for this woman to stay, to be a part of her. The relationship moves deeper as the feelings of love and tenderness break down the simple division between victim and rescuer, and new channels of healing are opened. The woman who was once muzzled now becomes a source of comfort for Mary. Feelings of mutuality and reciprocity flow between them.

> I pray and listen. I hear words telling me to drink in comfort. I see the image of the Acoma woman with the gourd, dipping into the pool of

unconscious wisdom. I remember my own wisdom: to drink before I am thirsty. I think of drinking from the communion cup. I think of Aslan (the lion in Narnia), bathing the boy in cold water after he shed the dragon skin, and the wonderful sting of healing. I think of how much water I drink each day. I am resolved to accept that the state of peace I seek is one that requires consistent refueling—not because I am lacking, but because the process itself naturally requires a replenishing of energy. Drink before I am thirsty.

Mary says that now when she enters the room in her imagination, the woman reaches for her hand—just as she is about to wonder whether she should reach for hers, just before she wonders what to say, or if she should have come. She says, "She holds my hand firmly, a warm, strong gesture of warmth, welcome, connection."

A year later Mary revisits the woman.

When I imagine her now, she is living in an adobe house. I go to her by walking along a stone path, bordered by potted plants, sitting in bright sun. She always opens the door just before I would reach to knock, just before I would worry whether she will really want to see me. She is visibly glad to see me, smiling, greeting, hugging me, leading me into the house. We do not speak. She wears bright colors, beads, long Guatemalan skirts of multi-colored stripes. She takes me into a room with many windows, sunlight is streaming in. Sometimes there is tea waiting. Recently she has started to take me to sit on a couch. I lean against her and she just holds me, stroking my head, letting me just be with her.

Another year goes by and Mary goes once again to the woman. She is apprehensive this time because she has been so busy with the outer demands of her life. She worries: "It has been so long since I have tried this—or taken care of myself. I breathe deeply, try to move into the imagination, feel tense. I am afraid it won't work."

I find my way to her door, it opens as usual, she is there, looking the same, greeting me. I still am tense. She leads me to the couch. She sits there. I sit at her knee, on pillows. I lean my head on her lap. She strokes my brow. I say: "What can you tell me?" I repeat the question three times. At first there is no answer. I realize how tense I am—longstanding tension. She says, "I can tell you that I am still here. I am here because of you. I can tell you that this is your house." She starts to hum. I worry about what will happen next; will something happen next; can I sustain this? She moves down to the floor behind me, kneeling. I lean into her. She rocks me and continues to hum a simple chant. It is what

I need—time to recover, to reconnect—before I can expect to hear and learn more.

As Mary learns, the work of awakening is not always a sudden or immediate process. Oftentimes it is slow-paced, a gentle yet persistent unfolding. The evolution of her dream woman from a dirty, matted-haired, muzzled, victimized woman to a clean, nurturing source of comfort and wisdom has taken years.

Part Two

The Battlezone
of Culture

·IV·

"Unlearning to Not Speak"

> She grunts to a halt.
> She must learn again to speak
> starting with I
> starting with We
> starting as the infant does
> with her own true hunger
> and pleasure
> and rage.
>
> —*Marge Piercy*[1]

> Now, like a woman made frigid, I had to learn response, to trust this possibility for fruition that had not been before. Any interruption dazed and silenced me. . . . When again I had to leave the writing, I lost consciousness.
>
> —*Tillie Olsen*[2]

The Divided Life

When Saturn disgorges his children, the Sons of Saturn—Hades, Poseidon, and Zeus—triumphantly divide up the spoils: Hades resides in the underworld, Poseidon takes to the sea, and Zeus reigns over all on Mount Olympus. But the Daughters of Saturn—Hestia, Demeter, and Hera—are released out of the Belly of the Father and deposited onto patriarchal soil. Along with that "other" daughter, Aphrodite, the one born out of the foam of her father's castrated phallus, they are all made part of the new religious and social system led by their brother, Zeus. The Daughters of Saturn do not triumph or prosper in this male ascension to power; instead they suffer and struggle.

Like the mythic Daughters of Saturn, when a woman has awakened out of the Belly of the Father, she will find herself in a male-oriented system, a system that has already defined her. At first, she will use that system to react against in order to define herself. She will attempt to solve the problems that being a woman in a male-centered environment presents, and this will give her a measure of control, she will be testing and finding her powers. She will engage in strategies of rebellion and resistance. But she will inevitably find, as Adrienne Rich has so eloquently said, "Whatever my status or situation, my derived economic class or my sexual preference, I live under the power of the fathers, and I have access only to so much of privilege or influence as the patriarchy is willing to accede to me, and only for so long as I will pay the price for male approval."[3]

Most of us, who are at all awake, live here in this Battlezone most of the time. It is demanding and exhausting; it takes its toll on our bodies, minds, psyches, and souls. Virginia Woolf, writing in the late 1920s, gave voice to the dilemma women faced then, and the words never rang more true than they do for women today:

> Behind us lies the patriarchal system; the private house, with its nullity, its immorality, its hypocrisy, its servility. Before us lies the public world, the professional system, with its possessiveness, its jealousy, its pugnacity, its greed. The one shuts us up like slaves in a harem; the other forces us to circle, like caterpillars head to tail, round and round the mulberry tree, the sacred tree, of property. It is a choice of evils. Each is bad.[4]

Woolf is describing the two choices offered to women by the patriarchal system. It is within these two spheres—the home and the public world—that a woman must learn to channel her energies for work and love. The struggle to find work that is fulfilling and love relationships that support and nurture is an ongoing one for women. The choice is an especially critical one for women who wish to be creative in their lives. Nowhere is the influence and results of the melancholic father and the devouring culture of patriarchy more evident then when a woman seeks to find her creativity.

There are many ways women have learned to live as resistance fighters in the Battlezone of Culture. Once we have awakened we can become agitators, protest and dissent, object and critique. We are thought of as pathological, deviant. By unplugging from the father's umbilicus we have given up the hopes for fulfillment, happiness, satisfaction, if they are believed to come only from the institutions of patriarchy—traditional marriage; work as a wage-slave for an institution; participating in the "institution of motherhood," as Adrienne Rich has defined it; or giving our spirituality over to traditional religious forms. But we are still in a state of struggle when it comes to expressing ourselves in some creative way. We are still in the process of what Marge Piercy calls, "unlearning to not speak."[5]

One outcome of being a Daughter of Saturn is to suffer a divided life. If a woman is still trying to please the father, in his various forms, while simultaneously attempting to break into her creative life, she will feel terribly torn in two. Caught between two profoundly different realities, some women attempt to lead double lives, one as a dutiful daughter or compliant wife or employee, the other as a creative woman.

Even though a woman may think she has resolved her personal relationship with her father, his influence may have subtly and powerfully shifted on to her relationships with other men. Writer Jane Lazarre analyzes the dangers:

> I have to admit, with a great sense of loss, that up to now a strong connection to a man has undermined me, dissipated my energy, left me confused as to the validity of the most personal aspects of my vision of the world. That is something for which I can hold no one else responsible. The vulnerability is mine. It is not in an attempt to dissipate responsibility, then, but only in an attempt to understand origins and the ways in which the persistent force of those origins affect my life, that again and again, wanting to or not, I return to my father.[6]

If she is heterosexual, the creative woman experiences the subterranean pull of the personal father entering unbidden into her life frequently in the form of another man—most often the man with whom she is intimate. The woman then feels herself torn between two opposing forces—the desire for passionate connection (which for women seems to always include the possibility of loss of self) and the desire for her autonomous life as a creative woman.

> There is a connection for me between the ability to feel autonomous, to feel confidently creative, and a fear of certain kinds of love. The love, especially when it includes passionate sexuality, undermines my ability to be myself, pulls me away from open channels, reawakens in me a desire to succumb to the ferocious power of my father's needs.[7]

The desire for relationship and the desire to be fully oneself are frequently pitted against each other. Both desires imply a certain kind of abandonment: in one the woman abandons herself to a man, in the other, to "the open channels" of her self. The determination it takes for a creative woman to remain true to herself and her creative life in the face of another's wants and needs is almost impossible to sustain. In reflecting on Lily Briscoe, the woman artist, in Virginia Woolf's novel *To the Lighthouse*, Lazarre brings to our attention one of the few descriptions of a woman caught in the act of creation and how little it takes for that woman's attention to be subverted:

> The strength and impact of Woolf's description of a woman in the act of creation, in the moment of the separation of the autonomous self, lies in the recognition that the smallest details of behavior, the subtlest communication in the external world of love, may nevertheless be sufficient to draw a woman away from her work—from her self-definition.[8]

The effort to be autonomous is difficult because it runs counter to all that women have been taught. Lazarre recommends, "The use of my own name if I am married, the maintaining of my own desk—not sharing a single drawer of it." She notes that "these are unimportant details only to those whose sense of separateness is thoroughly secure."[9] To remove oneself, to separate from other's needs in order to create, is thought of as selfish at best and monstrous at worst. It is so much more acceptable and rewarding to be "good."

The novelist, Mary Gordon, wonders to herself, "Why was I so susceptible to the bad advice of men?" She asks, "Where did I acquire my genius for obedience?"[10] These questions take her immediately to thoughts of her father who "wanted her to be like him." Even though he died when she was seven, she knew that she was his child, not her mother's. "His mind was exalted, my mother's common" and thus she "learned the pleasures of being a good girl."[11] The ease of translation from father to other men came without a hitch. Only when she began to write did she have to question herself.

> It was easy for me to please my father; and this ease bred in me a desire to please men—a desire for the rewards of a good girl. They are by no means inconsiderable: safety and approval, the warm, incomparable atmosphere created when one pleases a man who has vowed, in his turn, to keep the wolf from the door?
> But who is the wolf?[12]

The wolf in question is the woman's hungry need to please a father who would, in turn, eagerly devour all of her efforts.

Ann, an accomplished sculptor, told me once what a great sacrifice it was for her to let go of her intense feelings of attachment to her son. She explained to me that these feeling were connected in her mind to her relationship with her father: "My father adored me!" she said. "And when I had a son, I felt those same feelings of adoration coming from him. Now, in order for us both to be able to grow, I find I have to let go of being adored like that." Adoration, it seems, does not fare well in human relationships, where it often threatens to revert to its opposite of detestation and hate. To be successful and enduring, human love demands more of us than a projection of the beloved on to others.

I am sure that my father adored me as well. Even when I began to individuate, separating myself from him through anger and rage, I still wanted to feel that delicious, idolizing love again. Because of the memory of that early love, it took me years to undo the habit of trying to please my father. An important part of my recovery included reclaiming my mother, valuing her and the life she chose. Initially it was hard to find any part of my mother's life and history that was artistically empowering for me. On the other hand, I could create nothing but unfortunate relationships with men until I found and located her and her history as a potentially enriching resource. Only by embarking on a process that led me through a reconnection with my personal mother, down into my mother-line and my grandmas, and all the way back to the most ancient goddesses, could I begin to find the wellspring of my own creative gift. All the tools given to me by my adoring father, my love for words, for language, for reading, for literature, story and poetry, even his belief in my creative potential were of no use to me, in fact were actually dangerous, until I found myself firmly grounded in my female center. Only then could I find my voice. Only then could I begin to create for myself.

The conflict that women artists wrestle with is founded on the culture's separation, when it comes to women, of love and power. The need to experience love and recognition while, at the same time, retaining an ambitious, autonomous artist-self, is something the culture gives easily to sons but not to daughters. Women learn early on to divide themselves and then must develop strategies to overcome that division if they are ever going to be able to create. The divided life poses particular problems that women sooner or later must confront.

Pathology as Resistance

Whenever we find ourselves mentally compartmentalized, emotionally disconnected, living in two worlds spiritually and creatively, we are susceptible and vulnerable to some kind of dis-ease. Pathology has as its root meaning the Greek, *pathologia*, meaning the study of passions. I believe that many of the so-called pathologies that we find ourselves confronting as women are a result of the silences entailed in living a divided life. Because of thwarted passion, we all suffer from some sort of battle fatigue. Women often wonder why their bodies ache, why they feel so tired. I think that living in this culture really takes it out of us. The demand on our energy—physical, emotional, creative, spiritual—comes at us from all quarters. If we aren't careful we get sick, in our bodies, our minds, our souls. Whether it comes as chronic fatigue syndrome, eating disorders, depressions, panics, rages, post-traumatic stress syndrome, or PMS, fibromyalgia, fibroid tumors, and other more lethal diseases affecting our femaleness like breast cancer, living in the Battlezone of Culture is dangerous for women. Our bodies, psyches, and souls are put on the line and register the impact and reflect the toll of our struggles. In this work I argue that for many women these so-called pathologies are not only the result of living a divided life but are also signs of our unconscious rebellion and resistance against a culture that would erase us. Only when we are able to bring our passion to consciousness can we move the resistance out of our bodies and into a conscious practice of resistance as a healthy and empowering process.[13]

This is not the first time in history that women have expressed their resistance in this way. In every era women have found themselves acting out against the restraint and imprisonment of their passion within cultural prescriptions for femininity. And in every era, including our own, women's resistance to the deadening of passion has been named as pathological.

Resistance as Pathology

If, as I noted before, melancholy has provided the historical and cultural trope for male genius, hysteria has been the sign of female weakness. Hysteria, or the disease called the "wandering womb," was a female malady noted at least as early as ancient Greece. In the seventeenth century, hysteria was thought to be the work of the devil and was implicated in the witch trials of that time. Women's fits and convulsions, erotically tinged emotional outbursts, strange and unaccountable paralyses, and chronic undiagnosable pains were all part of that great "phenomenon of struggle" called hysteria.

In the last two decades of the nineteenth century, when Freud began to work with women, hysteria had reached its peak of notoriety becoming, in certain medical circles, a kind of fashionable female pathology. Female hysterics mirrored the culture's perceptions of women; their hysteria was read as a perfect catalogue of female vices. Hysterics were excessive and uncontrollable, treacherous and deceitful. Imitating illness with its counterfeit symptoms, female hysteria "rendered public the hidden lusts, perverted religious passions and over-sensitivities of the weaker sex."[14]

During the late nineteenth century, the neurologist, Jean-Martin Charcot, in his immensely popular Tuesday lectures held at the Paris hospital, the Salpêtrière, provided live performances featuring the female hysteric and the male doctor. As Judith Lewis Herman remarks, "The patients he put on display were young women who had found refuge in the Salpêtrière from lives of unremitting violence, expoitations, and rape."[15] Although Charcot's scientific observations were an attempt to demonstrate that hysteria was primarily psychological in origin, not a case of simple female unmanageability, the emotional content and cause of hysteria was still overlooked. Although scientific investigation into hysteria gave its victims some credibility, the sexual nature of hysteria's etiology was ignored. Instead it became suffused into the erotically charged relationship between doctor and patient. The series of photographs taken by Charcot of these unfortunate women incarcerated in the women's asylum are unmistakably sexual, as lurid as any pornography of the day.

Charcot, the neurologist, was basically not interested in the inner life of these women but his young student, Sigmund Freud, was. What Freud began to find, through the process of hypnosis, was that these women's bodies were acting out in symbolic ways, both disguising as well as representing traumatic events that had been repressed from memory. As Freud and Breuer were to remark in their joint work on hysteria, "Hysterics suffer mainly from reminiscences."[16]

What Freud began to discover was that hysterical symptoms could be alleviated when the traumatic incidences were talked about. Thus Bertha Pappenheim (known as Anna O.), a brilliant woman with hysterical symptoms, called her "talks" with Breuer, "the talking cure"—an epithet still used today to describe psychoanalysis. Using the technique of hypnosis along with "the talking cure" Freud began to understand the source, or what he called the *caput Nili* (the head of the Nile) of these women's afflictions, namely, early sexual trauma.

As a self-proclaimed petit-bourgeois, Freud was initially repulsed by what he was finding, but, as a scientist, he could not deny the evidence. Freud understood that the hysteric was not just an intractable, self-assertive, unmanageable woman. He saw in her bodily symptoms a form of resistance, but he was not altogether clear what the women were resisting in this way. Although Freud was willing at first to accept women's stories of sexual trauma, he failed to understand, because he was a man of his time, the inherent impossibility of the woman's position. A woman's hysteria was not only a protest against her actual childhood trauma, but also against the unresolvable conflict of her gender. Since a woman was supposed to be pure, non-sexual and virtuous, an object to be esteemed and protected, the traumatized daughter became a silent pain-bearing woman, a self-denying servant of a man's hearth and home. Having no acceptable means available to express her trauma, her womanly body manifested symptoms not only as a remembrance of assault but as a "passive form of resistance against the system of social expectations organized round her sex." Her hysteria was "both the product and indictment of her culture." From this perspective these nineteenth-century women and their hysterical bodies acted out in a kind of "protofeminist protest."[17]

Psychology owes an enormous debt to these suffering women. Through his work with them, Freud learned a great deal about the psyche and its messenger, the body. Although Freud was right about women's resistance, he couldn't, in the end, believe that so many women had suffered childhood sexual trauma perpetrated by the men in their families. Because he was not able or willing to face the social (and personal) implications of what he was finding, he eventually repudiated his belief that these women and their bodies were telling him the truth and instead he formulated a concept that said they were engaged in wish-fulfilling fantasies. Freud could not confront the idea of a father's culpability, and so the burden of blame was placed on the sexuality of the daughters. The rest is history.

Freud, at one point, called one of his female patients "his teacher." These women are teaching us still. As we begin to listen to women more closely, we learn how women's bodies and psyches conspire to resistance against trauma. Women's extravagant bodily symptoms can now be read more clearly as a covert form of passionate protest against childhood abuse, as well as a resistance to a patriarchal system with its impossible demands. Individual trauma, when it becomes reinforced and secretly sanctioned by the culture, produces a particularly toxic effect, and a woman will experience that effect physically, psychologically, and spiritually. It is my belief that many psychiatric pathologies listed in such texts as the *DSM R IV* (*Diagnostic Standard Manual*) are, when it comes to women, actually forms of resistance to the culture. This is not to say that women who find themselves anorexic, agoraphobic, anxious, panicky, borderline, or depressed, or physically ill, are aware of using these pathological states as forms of conscious resistance; they obviously are not. But it does mean that in order for us, as women, to fully comprehend the nature of these "disorders," we must be able to take the perspective that sees psychological diagnoses, such as the *DSM R IV* represents, and physical diseases (especially autoimmune deficiencies), as descriptions of the traumatic effects of a toxic environment, both personal and collective, on women's body, mind, and soul. This is why I have called living in our culture a Battlezone.

Pathos and Pathology

The word "pathos" is related to "pathology" in the sense of passion and suffering. In his work on archetypal psychology, James Hillman points out that "the pathological is inherent in the mythical" and vice versa—that the gods and goddesses themselves are pathologized, exhibiting what he calls an "infirmitas of the archetype." "Thus each archetype has its pathologized themes, and each pathologized event has an archeytpal perspective."[18] Hillman, of course, does not contextualize Greek mythology as a patriarchal production; his work (along with many other Jungian-oriented psychologists) thereby tacitly privileges these myths as a higher form of cultural expression, not subject to cultural analysis. Although Hillman's work is sorely lacking in feminist perspective, he does offer a helpful way to look at how mythic images can inform our ideas and understanding of pathology. I wish to take Hillman's idea and reframe it from a feminist perspective. I find that the goddesses of classical Greek myth represent not a recommendation *for* women's behavior, but an analysis of Western women's resistance to being swallowed by a culture based largely on classical Greek ideals and of how that resistance is named by the culture as "pathological."

It is from this point of view that I wish to look at the mythic Daughters of Saturn—Hestia, Demeter, Hera—and that other daughter, Aphrodite. Their myths remain important to us today not because they tell women *how to live* but because they show *how women respond and resist* the weight of patriarchal systems in what I call the Battlezone of Culture.[19] In this way, contemporary women's experience in the Battlezone of Culture resonates with the mythologies of the Daughters of Saturn.

As Daughters of Saturn, these goddesses have undergone devourment in the Belly of the Father and diminishment in Zeus' patriarchal pantheon. In the Homeric edition of Greek mythology, where the goddesses become fully personified and storied, each goddess's reaction to the swallowing trauma is recorded. Their stories are full of pathos and pathology, of reaction and resistance, and are reflective of the collective response by women to living in the culture of paternal and patriarchal melancholy. As Christine Downing considers it, "Perhaps those years in Kronos's womb are analogous to the experience all of us have of growing up in a male-ordered world."[20]

◦ V ◦

The Mythic Daughters of Saturn and Their Mortal Sisters

Goddesses never die. They slip in and out of the world's cities, in and out of our dreams, century after century, answering to different names, dressed differently, perhaps even disguised, perhaps idle and unemployed, their official altars abandoned, their temples feared or simply forgotten.

—*Phyllis Chesler*[1]

The mythic tales of the Daughters of Saturn provide a window through which we can view the archetypal dimensions of the swallowed daughter. Each Daughter of Saturn responds in very different ways to her early ordeal with the father, as does that other daughter, Aphrodite. Each has her own particular psychological strategy, her passions as well as her pathologies, her resistances, and her means of transformation.

There are certain recurrent themes that characterize these goddesses. Their inheritance as devoured daughters sets them apart in certain symptomatic ways; they all have relational difficulties; they each struggle with various oral disorders; each has her particular need for psychic space; and all suffer from the lack of courageous mothering.

When the mythic Daughters of Saturn emerge from their shared experience in the dark womb of the father, Saturn, they go their separate ways. In some sense we could say that they have become more individuated and differentiated, but in other ways they are isolated, cut off from each other, their sisterhood denied, or at least not seen as a resource of support. In cult and myth, when Demeter's temple is open, Hera's is shut, making them somehow intrinsically opposed. Aphrodite has a little to do with Hera, but nothing to do with Demeter; and neither Demeter, Hera, nor Aphrodite interact with Hestia, confirming her isolation from her sisters. They have learned to live without benefit of maternal nurturing, warmth, and energy, and like sisters who don't speak to each other, once they are incorporated into the Greek pantheon, they don't acknowledge their early trauma and they try to go it alone. Such is life in the Battlezone of Culture.

The legendary struggles of the Greek goddesses provide archetypal themes which run throughout the stories of mortal women. In the following section, along with examples from contemporary women, I explore the lives and works of four writers—Emily Dickinson, H.D., Sylvia Plath, and Anais Nin. The poems, novels, letters, and journals document their struggles and strategies to live creative lives in the Battlezone of Culture.

1. HESTIA

Instead of marriage, Zeus the Father gave her a fair prize and
she took the choicest boon and sat in the middle of the house.
—Homeric Hymn to Aphrodite[2]

Nor yet are Aphrodite's works
for the venerable virgin, Hestia . . .
she swore a mighty oath . . .
that she would be a virgin all of her days . . .
—Homeric Hymns[3]

Renunciation is a piercing virtue.
—Emily Dickinson[4]

No is the wildest word we consign to language.
—Emily Dickinson[5]

Virginal Daughter of Hearth and Home

Hestia was counted as the oldest daughter of Saturn and Rhea. She was the first to be swallowed by her father and the last to be disgorged. Thus, we could say that Hestia spent the most time in her father's dark belly. It must have had its effect. In thinking about Hestia and how the Greeks described her, one is immediately struck by several things: She is very seldom imaged; she is almost completely unstoried. Unlike other Greek goddesses, no mythologies of drama and intrigue surround her. There is no doubt that she is old. Even Zeus acknowledges and honors her as an ancient goddess by declaring her to be "the first and the last" deity to

2. Vestal Virgin

whom libations were poured in any feast, yet she could very well be called "The Forgotten Goddess."[6] Classics scholar Sarah Pomeroy remarks about Hestia:

> There is little myth about Hestia, for she was the archetypal old maid, preferring the quiet of the hearth to the boisterous banquets and emotional entanglements of the other Olympians. Moreover, she is seldom depicted in the visual arts, for instead of having an anthropomorphic conception, Hestia is commonly envisioned as the living flame.[7]

As the goddess of the hearth and the hearth fire, Hestia is intimately linked with family, for the hearth was the center of Greek life. She presided over individual and familial well-being as well as the conviviality and hospitality of communal life. But there is another side to this goddess. As a swallowed Daughter of Saturn, now living under her brother Zeus' patriarchal regime, she appears silent, brooding, withdrawn. Although she is proclaimed as the most revered, this must refer to her more ancient goddess past. Now she has a proclivity for anonymity.

Hestia belongs to the general condition of anonymity that befalls women within a patriarchal culture. When a woman is praised for providing a voiceless and even faceless female ambience which is felt as warmth or creating the homebase where others may return for safe refuge, she comes into contact with Hestia.

Although devotion to Hestia can offer a woman a virtuous position within the family circle, there is no psychic room to harken to any other calls, either from the marketplace or the wilds. She is so basic that she frequently can be taken for granted, and although in myth she is always given the first offering at any festival and at the family meal, she can feel like any woman who is highly honored in theory but not truly appreciated in practice.

Women usually feel a great deal of ambivalence towards what Hestia represents. Her qualities as vestal virgin, in service to home and hearth, no personal story or image, no expressed sexuality, no lover, no child, runs too close to images of denigration: the faceless woman, a woman without a voice, without a life other than her place and function in the home. It is Hestia's attributes of unnamed, selfless service that give women pause.[8]

Agoraphobia: The Pathology of Hestia

Hestia can make her appearance in a women's life especially around issues of space and decisions that have to do with hearth and home versus activity in the outside world. In Hestian pathology, one is swallowed by the house. Feelings of entrapment and reclusivity, withdrawal from social life, fear of the marketplace— are all symptoms of a Hestian pathology. As a Daughter of Saturn, Hestia's pathos centers around her extreme introversion, her retreat into hearth and home, and celibacy. From this perspective, she is the patron saint of agoraphobes.

Traditionally, agoraphobia, the Greek-derived name meaning fear of the *agora* or marketplace, has been understood as primarily a women's disorder. Agoraphobia often develops secondarily to panic attacks—a woman will prefer to stay in her house and otherwise restrict her activities, thereby avoiding the experience of another panic attack. It is commonly understood that the occurrence of a first panic attack usually takes place in the late teens or twenties, when a young woman begins the process of separation from home. It is then that she is most severely confronted with society's expectations of her as a woman.

I imagine that agoraphobia is not only a woman's fear of entering into the marketplace, but a deeper fear that nothing will happen in her life. Women's losses—the absence of challenge, depression over loss of autonomy, loss of choices for their lives—are never usually factored into the traditional explanations for this kind of female malady. The absence of necessary stimulation, of encouragement to mastery and competency, is one of the biggest losses for many women.

It is commonly understood that a father's influence is important when it comes to a woman's ability to cope in the world. If she has had a father who was actively interested in her achievements and praised her accomplishments from childhood on—from her first steps to her first job—a woman will feel that life has something to offer her. If her father has ignored her or been too busy to notice her early attempts at independence and autonomy or actively sabotaged her efforts, a woman may later find herself unable to take the steps and support the risks necessary to find her place in the world. Women who have not been able to make a substantial bridge into the outer world often feel panicky when they leave the so-called safety of their homes. Yet inside the four walls of their domestic lives, they may suffer from the silent "trauma of eventlessness."

A woman in her mid-life came into counseling while she was making her final decision not to bear children. She and her husband worked through the intricacies of what this might mean for their relationship. Going through that process, and finally saying "no" to that form of creativity, plunged her into an even deeper decision: What was she to do with the rest of her life? As a woman in mid-life, she found that nothing held any juice, any spark for her. Her work life was basically uninteresting to her. The only thing she felt strongly about was maintaining the rituals of hearth and home—candlelight dinners, keeping house, and entertaining friends so that outwardly it would appear that her life was full and reasonably happy. But underneath the surface lay a very bleak and desolate landscape revealed to her in a dream.

> I am riding on an underground subway without a destination. As I sit there, I look up to see my own gaunt and empty face reflected back to me in the dark glass window opposite my seat. I am unable to move, almost catatonic, until a kind man comes and helps me get off this endless subway ride.

This dream image captured the "trauma of eventlessness," the quality of barreness she felt in her life. Swallowed in the belly of the underground subway, this woman was on a ride going nowhere. The dream gave her the opportunity to see herself—the gaunt and vacant face reflected in the window—so she could fully apprehend her condition. Her feelings of aimless futility were mirrored back to her in this quietly horrifying vision. Only when she saw herself this way could the agent of change and movement show up and help her off the track of meaninglessness.

While trying to understand how she had gotten on this ride with no future, she remembered her father's sudden death which happened when she was quite young. She felt that when he died a certain something in her had died along with him. He had been an energetic and ebullient man whose death had marked the end of her large family's sense of joy and zest for life. The family all honored this father, who was now believed to be in heaven, with a dull kind of routinized religiousity. The earthy and energetic man was replaced by an angelic and ethereal spirit, leaving the daughter no access to his worldly and embodied wisdom. Now there was no father to help bring her out into the world.

After a great deal of inner work, she began to realize that she did not have to make large and dramatic life changes to feel her connection with life. She found she could make her contribution to the larger world in ways that might seem too small or too local to others, but were right for her in that they fit her introspective personality. She learned that she could radiate out from the warmth and safety of her interior hearth by adding her energy to local community projects or responding to a neighbor's need. She did not have to leave the security of hearth and home in order to make a contribution to the wider world. She was able to transform what was once a fear of empty eventlessness into a centered place from which she could move out.

Many women walk the narrow path between wanting to make a home and needing to get out of it. It seems no surprise that the twinned condition of agoraphobia/claustrophobia is primarily a woman's disorder.

The same woman had also gone through great pains to create a special study for herself in her home, a place she prized for its feelings of security and sense of sanctuary, until she was presented with this dream.

> I am downstairs in my house being consumed by my household duties and other demands of life, so I retreat to the safety and protection of my study. I feel held, like in a cocoon, but soon I start to see that this small room has become a coffin—I see the nails coming through the walls as if I am on the inside of a coffin.

The woman in the dream is attempting to run away from the Hestian demands of household duties, so she retreats to the protective seclusion of her study. But now her precious study turns into a coffin. The comforting aspect of being enclosed and held in a protective, womblike space slips ever so easily over into images of claustrophobic, tomblike enclosure. Before her study can offer her the creative solitude she wants, she may have to return downstairs and encounter that pre-eminent female demon, the dark side of Hestia, what Virginia Woolf has called "the Angel in the House."

The Angel in the House

Virginia Woolf knew that the first tasks of a woman who would be creative are formidable. Her first assignment would be to confront the Angel in the House—that idealized, selfless woman whose life is justified by serving others. Trained to attend to other's needs, the Angel in the House is not a benign entity for women: she steals our time and our energy and eventually, over time, becomes a killer of creative women. "It was she," Woolf says, "who bothered me and wasted my time and so tormented me that at last I killed her. . . . I turned upon her and caught her at the throat. I did my best to kill her. I acted in self defense. Had I not killed her, she would have killed me. She would have plucked the heart out of my writing." How did Woolf learn to identify the Angel in the House? She studied her carefully, noting her mannerisms, her habits, her speech. She gives us such an accurately detailed description we can easily recognize her in our own lives:

> She was intensively sympathetic. She was immensely charming. She was utterly unselfish. She sacrificed herself daily. If there was a chicken, she took the leg; if there was a draught, she sat in it—in short she was so constituted that she never had a mind of her own or a wish of her own, but preferred always to sympathize with the minds and wishes of others. Above all, I need not say it, she was pure. . . . And when I came to write I encountered her with the very first words. The shadow of her wings fell on my page; I heard the rustling of her skirts in the room . . . she slipped behind me and whispered, "My dear, you are a young woman. You are writing about a book that has been written by a man. Be sympathetic; be tender; flatter; deceive; use all the wiles of our sex. Never let anyone guess you have a mind of your own." [9]

The need to carve out and protect one's creative time against the onslaught of relational demands is an ever-present challenge for women who would create. Taking time away from family duties or meeting others' needs goes against the grain of women's training to be caring people. Each woman has to find her own way of coming to terms with the ensuing guilt feelings. Knowing that she is abandoning an engrained set of cultural requirements to serve her own creative imperative leaves a woman vulnerable to accusations of selfishness, abandonment, coldness.

A Room of Her Own

Reflecting on the lot of nineteenth-century women writers, Woolf imagines the woman writer's struggle:

> In the first place, to have a room of her own, let alone a quiet room or a sound-proof room, was out of the question, unless her parents were exceptionally rich or very noble, even up to the beginning of the nineteenth century. Since her pin money, which depended on the good will of her father, was only enough to keep her clothed, she was debarred from such alleviations as came even to Keats or Tennyson or Carlyle, . . . (which) sheltered them from the claims and tyrannies of their families.[10]

As Woolf's essay shows, a creative woman's first struggle is not with her art, but with her attempt to establish the context of her life in such a way that she can "do" her art. It is noteworthy that even though many conditions have changed for women, the conditions for a woman artist are not so different as Woolf reflected upon. Being swallowed by the father—whether by demands and strictures of the personal father or constraints of patriarchal culture which sees women only as tenders of hearth and home, or a life in service to "the fathers," in the fathers' businesses and institutions—all this has a chilling effect on a woman's creativity. It is not unusual for a woman to feel forced to choose relational ties over her desire for creative work which demands a certain kind of Hestian solitude, introspection, freedom from relational demands of husband, lover, children, friends. It is not unusual for a woman to be driven by an unconscious need for her father's approval, the personal father's blessing, or the sanction of the cultural father's institutions, and thereby sacrifice her need for independent, self-authorized creativity.

It always amazes and pains me to learn of women who do not have "a room of their own." I am referring to both women in dire economic circumstances who do not have the luxury of separate space and women who live in spacious quarters but have not claimed one piece of it as their own. In patriarchal marriage the "whole house" is supposed to "belong" to the woman, as Anne Sexton wrote in her poem "Housewife":

> Some women marry houses.
> It's another kind of skin; it has a heart,
> a mouth, a liver and bowel movements.
> The walls are permanent and pink.
> See how she sits on her knees all day,
> faithfully washing herself down. . . .[11]

Although they may marry houses, many women live in utmost spiritual and creative poverty; they are in fact homeless.

Like other "Master" narratives that tell us how to live and think, standard architecture for the average middle-class home reinforces a women's sense of "homelessness" by creating a so-called "Master" bedroom, large and spacious, while other rooms are small and cramped by comparison. The kitchen is still thought of as a woman's domain and is usually built with her "concerns" in mind. A "den" is usually imagined as male territory, and the family room is what it says it is. Faced with these possibilities, a woman can fool herself into thinking she has the kind of necessary space by claiming a desk in the "Master" bedroom or by using the dining room table for her creative space. Although many women have made do with little or no private space and still have managed to create, they are working against powerful odds.

Hestia in her positive aspect is above all the goddess of place. I have watched changes happen in women as they begin to eke out a space of their own—a room they can retreat to for writing, painting, or just being—closets get transformed into small study "cells," attics get renovated, older children's bedrooms get confiscated after they go off to college. Women are always on the look out for a piece of real estate they can call their own. This imperative for "a room of one's own," as Virginia Woolf so rightly knew, is the one absolutely necessary first step for any woman attempting self-knowledge through her own creative process. This does not mean that a creative woman must live in isolation—or in some male mythology of the lonely, melancholic, starving artist. It does mean that a woman must stake her claim, become fiercely territorial, for the sake of her art. She must have a private place to work her creative magic, to think herself out of the cramped confines of patriarchal thought. One such woman was Emily Dickinson.

The Hestian World of Emily Dickinson

Very few images were ever made of Hestia by the Greeks. Of all the goddesses, she remains singularly unimaged and thus unimagined. So, too, there is only one extant photo of Emily Dickinson, a daguerreotype taken when she was sixteen. Her portrait is the only image we have to help us conjure her up. It radiates as much ambiguity and mystery as the Mona Lisa.

Dickinson was born in Amherst in 1830 and died there in 1886. From all outward appearances, her life was singularly uneventful: she spent much of her adult life as a dutiful daughter, housekeeping, gardening and caretaking for her family. But her inner life, as evidenced in her poems, bespoke a totally other existence. Her renunciations, her self-chosen decision to be housebound and celibate, her resolute refusal of conversion to traditional religious ideas, her adoption of a white "habit," her lifelong poetic interrogation of God make her poems of refusal and resistance stand apt and true for women today.

Dickinson lived her entire life in her father's house. By all accounts, Edward Dickinson was an austere, bleak, and ambitious man, both emotionally distant and demanding. Schooled at Yale, a lawyer by profession, he sought positions with political stature throughout his life, serving as state senator and in the U. S. House of Representatives. Although Amherst soon proved too small for the scope of his ambitions, he never chose to move his family to the seats of power in Boston or Washington, where he spent most of his time. Seldom at home, he maintained his family in Amherst, where he became their most prominent and influential citizen, a man "whom a whole village feared, in whose appearance there was that which terrified."[12]

3. Emily Dickinson

4. The Honorable Edward Dickinson

As biographer John Cody notes, Edward's worldly achievements were not gained by any charismatic brilliance nor any particular genius. He apparently achieved his fame and fortune through the dogged and determined means of industry, perseverance, painstaking and laborious effort, all fueled by his own over-determined drive for power and influence. His ambition was undoubtedly founded in part on his desire to overcome the personal and social humiliations caused by his own father's financial failures.

Throughout his lifetime, Edward Dickinson maintained a consistently disparaging and scornful attitude towards women who aspired toward any intellectual achievement or ambition outside of wifely duties. Although he believed that girls should be educated, he also felt it was mandatory that they ultimately renounce any potential ambitions other than domestic ones. He was known to attack "the Woman's Suffrage people."

While in the midst of his courtship with Dickinson's mother, Emily Norcross, he wrote a vituperative series of articles on "Female Education," under a pseudonym. These treatises demonstrate in full his hostilities toward educated women. Four years before Emily Dickinson was born, Edward would write to Emily Norcross about meeting a female "authoress" of whom he approved. Not content to leave it at that, he then issued his caveat:

> Tho' I should be sorry to see another Mme. de Stael—especially if any one wished to make a partner of her for life . . . different qualities are more desirable in a female who enters into domestic relations—and you have already had my opinions on that subject.[13]

Unlike many men whose ambition makes them powerful in the world but who seek solace and compensation in the sanctuary of hearth and home, Edward Dickinson's determination to dominate and control seems to have been unrelenting—his overbearing personality governed his worldly life as well as his family life. In general, he was regarded by Dickinson and her brother and sister, as "a stern and reproving deity."

Bearing the burden of paternal melancholy, Edward Dickinson was notably lacking in any of the more childlike expressions of delight, joy, intuition, humor, or play. Worse, for his daughter/poet, he repudiated any kind of fantasy life or the world of imagination. This attitude combined with the fact that he had no place in his world for poetry (Dickinson said "he reads lonely and rigorous books") must have had a devastating impact on her. Her father, who openly disapproved of "women literati," was utterly blind to the fact that his daughter was awake in the middle of the night working on her craft and calling as a poet. His inability to see that his daughter had capabilities beyond baking his favorite bread and pudding and playing the piano for him certainly must have caused Emily pain. Writing to her brother, Austin, she relates: "We don't have many jokes tho' now, it is pretty much all sobriety, and we do not have much poetry, father having made up his mind that it's pretty much all real life. Father's real life and mine sometimes come into collision, but as yet, escape unhurt."[14]

There is one incident told however that gives the smallest glimpse into what that "collision" might have looked like had it ever happened:

> One day, sitting down at the dinner table, he [Edward Dickinson] inquired whether a certain nicked plate must always be placed before him. Emily took the hint. She carried the plate to the garden and pulverized it on a stone, "just to remind" her, she said, not to give it to her father again.[15]

The rage expressed toward the offending plate was certainly displaced. It could not go toward her father, and it came dangerously close to being directed at herself—she eventually took it out on "God."

Although she undoubtedly at times must have loved her bleak and austere father, as biographer Cynthia Wolff has noted: "Sad to say, there is little evidence that Edward Dickinson returned this affection in any commensurate measure—or even that he took serious note of it. . . . He was not possessive. He did not scold her or turn his anger upon her or even reject her openly. He did, in the end, what was worse: he simply did not very much notice her."[16] Emily herself was aware of this, as she once wrote to her brother: "father is too busy to notice what we do."

A woman whose father is too busy, or always absent, may develop a tendency to idealize him, glorify his deeds, mythologize his life. If she does not have the situation where she can encounter her father in the numerous small, humanizing activities of day-to-day living, he can become a monolithic figure attaining heroic proportions. Usually such a father is a powermonger, a controller and hoarder of power who enjoys having "his women" under him.

Emily Dickinson's relationship to her father was undoubtedly complex. In a letter written shortly before her father died, she speaks about the vast remoteness emanating from her father who appears to her as an aged Saturn banished to the nethermost isle of Tartaros:

> My father seems to me often the oldest and the oddest sort of foreigner. Sometimes I say something and he stares in a curious sort of bewilderment though I speak a thought quite as old as his daughter. . . . Father says in fugitive moments when he forgets the barrister & lapses into the man, says that his life has been passed in a wilderness or on an island—of late he says on an island. And so it is, for in the morning I hear his voice and methinks it comes from afar & has a sea tone & there is a hum of hoarseness about (it) & a suggestion of remoteness as far as the isle of Juan Fernandez.[17]

It is hard to imagine a more unlikely father for such a gifted daughter. What was a daughter like Emily, who was secretly and seriously pursuing what she knew to be an object of scorn and humiliation, to do? What levels of deception and cam-ouflage did she have to maintain—this woman noted for her breathless, childish demeanor who was secretly working out poems of volcanic power and proportions? What would it have meant for her to be supported, albeit within the confines of the mores of the day, by a father who honored and acknowledged her aspirations?

The lack of such a father left Emily Dickinson, as it has left many creative women before and after her, exquisitely vulnerable to wanting the positive judg-ments and valuation of other men. For her, the father who she reports "is too busy to notice what we do" easily became the men who would not acknowledge her, and eventually the world which would not stop to see her, and the God who would not show his face. She did not consciously "blame" her father for his failure to see her, nor did she rage at him personally or fight with him; rather, she took her complaints, resentments, and sense of bitter injustice to a higher inner court. Much of her "wrestling" between the patriarch and the poet was written out in her poems about God.

When Edward Dickinson died, alone in a hotel room in Boston, Emily wrote to her mentor, Thomas Wentworth Higginson, that "his heart was pure and ter-rible." Her agoraphobia, which was fully manifested by then, prevented her from attending his funeral. Afterwards she drew the blinds shut for two years. She wrote to her cousins, "I dream about father every night, always a different dream, and forget what I am doing daytimes, wondering where he is."[18] She had lived forty-three years under his roof. Some say that after her father's death, her poetic drive drifted toward a permanent decline.[19]

"God save me from what they call households."

A father who is "too busy to notice" often creates an imbalance in the mother-daughter relationship, making it the only site for emotional expression and strug-gle. Emily Dickinson never allowed herself to express the anger she must have felt towards her father; it was the relationship with her mother that bore the brunt of it. Oftentimes, her mother was overcome with debilitating depressions which left Emily to fill her mother's role of housekeeper—a role that rankled and infuriated her and left her with a hatred of her mother, whom she equated with the house-hold duties imposed upon her. In a letter, Emily complains about taking on her mother's role of housewife and how that role ran counter to her needs as a poet.

> my hands but *two*—not four, or five as they ought to be—and *so many* wants—and me so *very* handy—and my time of so *little* account—and my writing so *very* needless . . .[20]

The italics give the emphasis to her biting and sarcastic, but finally helpless rage. The litany of feminine virtues, dictated by the culture of acceptable domestic femininity supported by the very person of her mother, left Dickinson almost hissing with fury. In the same letter, in a hateful, parodic way, she lets her mother's voice prattle on—

all the while letting her reader know exactly how the "good" maternal voices nibble away at one, by justifying and encouraging with all the cheerful, housewife bromides:

> mind the house—and the food—*sweep* if the spirits were low—nothing like exercise to strengthen—and invigorate—and help away such foolishness—work makes one strong, and cheerful. . . .[21]

All in all, Dickinson says "the path of duty looks very ugly indeed—and the place where I want to go more amiable—a great deal. . . . I don't wonder that good angels weep—and bad ones sing songs."[22] Singing for Dickinson always referred to the writing of poetry. By this time she had internalized the culture's prescription for a "good" woman and she knew herself, as a secret poet, to be "bad," or, as she sometimes put it, "wicked"—her badness a result of her willful non-submission to a husband, family, and especially to religion's demand for conversion.

Emily Dickinson undoubtedly perceived the power differential between her father and mother and between her father and herself and understood well that she was on the side of the powerless. She struggled vehemently against being identified solely by her mother's world. "My kitchen, I think I called it. God forbid it was or ever shall be my own—God save me from what they call households."[23] Throughout her life, she maintained a combination of resentment, scorn, arrogance, and frustration that she ever would be associated with this type of womanhood. What she craved was power—she had many intimations of the "immortality" of her poetry—and she was indignant and outraged that she would never find an adequate outlet to express her intellect, ambition, and creative passion.

Emily Dickinson is the documenter of the kind of female volcanic rage that exists in women who are held in anonymous domestic captivity. As she contemplates her surging craters—"Vesuvius at Home"—she knows that no one guesses at the molten fires, the potential for creation and destruction, surging within her. On the surface she looks safe and lovely. The primal forces of her fury create immense pressures from within and the effort to contain the fire are arduous.

> On my volcano grows the Grass
> A meditative spot —
> An acre for a Bird to choose
> Would be the General thought —
>
> How red the Fire rocks below —
> How insecure the sod
> Did I disclose
> Would populate with awe my solitude.[24]

For a creative woman, the struggle between feminine "goodness" and artistic "badness" does not seem to be time-bound. Many women today are as torn as

Dickinson was over a century and a half ago. Dickinson's life was one of constant negotiation between the demands of domesticity and her creative drive. It seems that she wrote most of her poetry at night.

It is most likely that Emily Dickinson did experience some kind of generalized anxiety disorder. Her mother had bouts of severe depression throughout her life, as did Dickinson. Many self-descriptions by Dickinson in her letters describe periods of depression and anxiety. I think it is important to acknowledge that Dickinson probably did suffer from a clinical entity called agoraphobia. Much of the poetry she wrote gives voice to a woman's ambivalence about her place in the home—where the need for safety and security bump into fears of being trapped and confined. Expressing the ensuing panic and the need to break free is a Dickinson specialty.

In a letter to Susan Gilbert, Emily Dickinson described in detail what is clearly recognizable as a panic attack situation. She tells of going to church and then hurrying home in a panicky state: "I walked—I ran—I turned precarious corners."[25] Her "breathless" condition noted by Higginson when he first met her was probably not so much a staged strategy of childish vulnerability as it was literally shortness of breath due to nervous hyperventilation, a common experience for people subject to anxiety attacks. In her twenties, trying to explain why she cannot respond to invitations, Emily writes to her friend that looking at "father and mother and Vinnie, and all my friends, and I say no—no, can't leave them, what if they die when I'm gone . . . ."[26] Today we would take a statement like that as evidence for pathologic dependence and separation anxiety. The agoraphobia was a condition that steadily increased throughout Dickinson's life until, as Cody describes it:

> . . . everything she needed had to be arranged for through others and brought to her. . . . She did not dine with her family in later life, but had her meals carried to her room. Finally she became incapable of the slightest transaction with persons outside the family. The clothes she wore had to be fitted to her sister because she could not face the seamstress. When she was ill, medical consultations were arranged by her worried family and executed by proxy because she would not see the physicians. . . . [m]usicians would be invited to sing and play in the parlor while she remained in solitude upstairs, overhearing.[27]

One can feel stifled and suffocated by the hermetic quality of her life, sealed up in a female space, pinched between the double claw of claustrophobia and agoraphobia. However, like many renunciates before her, she learned to use the almost vise-like constraints on her life and the enormous pressure of her passionate feelings to expand her consciousness. The poetry itself became her only passage out. Only through the discipline of her writing was she able to exercise some control over symptoms and circumstances that could easily overwhelm. Only through some terrific ability to withstand the tensions of such enclosure could she find the path which opened out into the spaciousness of her mind.

Dickinson's Room of Her Own

Emily Dickinson's niece Martha told how she once visited her aunt Emily in her room and how Emily made a gesture as if to turn an imaginary key to lock her bedroom door and said "Matty: here's freedom."[28] Dickinson's bedroom, a corner room, the best bedroom in the house, overlooking the main street on one side and her brother's house on the other, was the room in which she wrote most of her poetry.

Adrienne 0is one of the first women to understand Dickinson's agoraphobia as a strategy of resistance and survival. Convinced that Emily Dickinson consciously chose her sequestered life, Rich sees that "Given her vocation, she was neither eccentric nor quaint; she was determined to survive, to use her powers, to practice necessary economies."[29] She obviously lived in conditions that Rich says "could have spelled insanity to a woman genius."[30] With the help of Rich's insight, we can imagine that Dickinson's "pathology," her agoraphobia, became a necessary strategy of restriction. And then we have to question whether this strategy can be considered "abnormal" or "pathological" or whether it was, given the conditions of her life, the only possible choice. Choosing isolation for the sake of her calling makes her agoraphobia seem more a critique of the culture and family she lived in with its limited possibilities then a judgement on her fragile emotional make-up. From the perspective of her poetic vocation, her eventual withdrawal into her room can be seen as her way of resisting the press of culture and attaining those things necessary for creative work—solitude and uninterrupted time and space.

As Virginia Woolf was to state so clearly a half century after Dickinson's death: "five hundred [pounds] a year stands for the power to contemplate," and "a lock on the door means the power to think for oneself."[31] Dickinson did not receive her "five hundred a year" in the way Woolf imagined it; she paid for her upkeep by being the dutiful daughter, housekeeping, playing the piano, baking her father's bread and puddings, all of which intruded on her time to contemplate. Yet she was able to install a "lock on the door" and this certainly gave her the power to think for herself.

The Renunciations

One of Emily Dickinson's truly amazing accomplishments, given the context of her life, were her two major renunciations—religious conversion and marriage. Both events were conceived of by her as submissions to a masculine authority which entailed a breaking of will. She was willing to sacrifice any desires she may have had for sexual, social, and religious fulfillment if they could only be bought by conventional means, i.e., traditional marriage, conformity to an ideal of femininity, religious conversion. Dickinson knew her acts of refusal were radical and she knew the price she was paying when she wrote, "Renunciation is a piercing virtue." Although there was some sanction for her remaining unmarried, her refusal of conversion is astonishing for a woman of her time and her position. That she was able to withstand the sweeping forces of religious revivalism and not accept conversion took an almost unheard of amount of independent will. The final submission, that of death, she could not renounce, but she did sustain a lifelong interrogation of the Protestant God and his son whom she deemed sadistic, cold, and brutal.

When Emily Dickinson began to call herself "wicked," everyone she knew, both friends and her immediate family, including her father, was succumbing to religious conversion in what has been called "The Great Awakening." Dickinson's refusal to yield to the powerful tide of mass conversion ultimately led to her own personal awakening and the knowledge that she was a poet. Although her rejection of religious conversion caused her to think of herself as "wicked," it also sprung her free psychologically from the path of duty, the intellectual confines of her father's house, and the domestic confines of her mother's kitchen. It was to be the first of such renunciations.

According to the Greek myth, when faced with a choice of several suitors, Hestia swore an oath to Zeus that she would remain a virgin all of her days. Hestia's single recorded act in her mythology is to say "No" to the expected patriarchal script of marriage. Her decision for celibacy is clearly an act of renunciation and negation.

Emily Dickinson understood the Hestian imperative of refusal when she wrote, "No is the wildest word we consign to language." Like the goddess Hestia, Dickinson also chose a life of celibacy. Although the acceptable model of spinster, the unmarried woman who stayed at home, was available to her, her refusal of marriage was another monumental act of resistance. Again, the price of her refusal was costly but the alternative was terrifying to her.

It is clear that Emily Dickinson's fear of marriage was made up in part from watching her parent's troubled relationship and from observing the changes in her married female friends, including Susan Gilbert, her brother's wife. Dickinson's view of marriage and its deleterious effects upon women is encoded in the following poem:

> She rose to His Requirement — dropt
> The Playthings of Her Life
> To take the honorable Work
> Of Woman, and of Wife —
>
> If ought She missed in Her new Day,
> Of Amplitude and Awe —
> Or first Prospective — Or the Gold
> In using, wear away,
>
> It lay unmentioned — as the Sea

> Develop Pearl, and Weed,
> But only to Himself — be known
> The Fathoms they abide — [32]

In a letter known as the "man of noon" letter, Emily wrote to Susan Gilbert in early June 1852 about how she has seen women become transformed by the marriage relationship as they bow to "the man of noon":

> . . . you have seen flowers at morning, *satisfied* with the dew, and those same sweet flowers at noon with their heads bowed in anguish before the mighty sun; think you these thirsty blossoms will *now* need naught but—dew? No, they will cry for sunlight, and pine for the burning noon, tho' it scorches them, scathes them; they have go through with peace—they know the man of noon is *mightier* than the morning and their life is henceforth to him. . . .[33]

A major note in all Dickinson's perceptions of male/female relationships is master and slave. This was particularly true when she contemplated the husband and wife relationship. Dickinson consistently uses "the sun" to symbolize masculinity, which has the power to overcome as well as abandon femininity. The sun with its rising forcefulness (all sexual inuendo intended), its fierce scorching noon-time presence, and its inevitable fading absence—an inching away kind of abandonment—was, for Dickinson, the essence of male power, personified and experienced in her relationship with her father.

For Dickinson the price of her salvation was her agoraphobic withdrawal into her father's household along with a chosen exclusion from any directly passionate encounter with adult sexuality. Her choosing may not have been completely conscious; it was certainly complicated. It was a choice with many implications: she never crossed the threshold of sexual encounter. All of the other womanly rites of passage were also forsworn: marriage, childbirth, motherhood. She was well aware that she remained, in these respects, painfully uninitiated.

Rather than submit to what the culture offered, Emily Dickinson single-handedly undertook her own initiation. If the world was not going to offer its titles, or confer upon her the mantle of womanhood, she would initiate herself. Her self-investiture was something she could never have attained within the strictures of mid-nineteenth-century New England social system. Only through her poetic imagination could she achieve it.

The Initiations

Through the power of her poetry, Emily Dickinson is both baptized and wed—on her own terms. In these two self-initiations, she claims ownership of herself and her art and moves deeply into a full-fledged creative life, trading in the masquerade of childish innocence and naiveté for a woman poet's power. Although not recognized or acknowledged by the outer world, this double ceremony allowed her access to the reservoirs of her womanly power. Refusing the passivity of the religious ceremony, she names and chooses her self—and in this way she becomes a Queen.

> I'm ceded — I've stopped being Their's
> The name They dropped upon my face
> With water, in the country church
> Is finished using, now,
> And They can put it with my Dolls,
> My childhood, and the string of spools,
> I've finished threading — too —
>
> Baptized, before, without the choice,
> But this time, consciously, of Grace —
> Unto supremest name —
> Called to my Full — The Crescent dropped —
> Existence's whole Arc, filled up,
> With one small Diadem.
>
> My second Rank — too small the first —
> Crowned — Crowing — on my father's breast —
> A half unconscious Queen —
> Bui this time — Adequate — Erect,
> With Will to choose, or to reject,
> And I choose, just a Crown — [34]

Dickinson's poem of self-naming prepared her psychologically and spiritually for her second poetic initiation. In this one she appropriates for herself the "Title Divine," that of "Wife."

> Title divine — is mine!
> Wife — without the sign!
> Acute degree — conferred on me —
> Empress of Calvary!
> Royal — all but the Crown!
> Betrothed — without the swoon
> God sends us Women —
> When you — hold — Garnet to Garnet —
> Gold — to Gold —
> Born Bridalled — Shrouded —
> In a Day —
> Tri Victory

"My Husband" — women say —
Stroking the Melody —
Is *this* — the way?[35]

With supreme effort, Dickinson propelled herself out of a prolonged psychological adolescence which was threatening to become grotesque in a woman in her thirties. Without benefit of the socially sanctioned rite of passage into womanhood, marriage, which to her was fraught with terror—loss of self, loss of creative possibility—she managed her own wedding. As a result, with her newly created persona of "Bride," she entered into her mature creative life. Her voice no longer diminutive ("I am Nobody—Who are You?"), but authoritative, becoming "Wife without the sign" meaning wife without the loss of self she perceived was necessary for actual marriage.

Dickinson conjoined her naming ceremony in the phrase "Baptized a Bride"— indicating a sacramental intensification. In this sense she becomes her own woman "twice born," born again. Moving out, psychologically and spiritually, from under the patriarchal rule she creates her own sacraments of self-naming and self-choosing. As critic Paula Bennett notes, with these poetic initiations, Dickinson "became a self-defined, self-authorized and authenticated woman" in her own mind and imagination.[36]

The Trouble with God

It appears that Dickinson directly transferred her difficulties with her father onto her dealings with God the Father, since her lifelong interrogation of God was cast in terms of the daughter-father relationship.[37] Most of her poems about the Deity work to expose the Father's misuse of power in relation to her. As a disempowered daughter, she is constantly anxious, apprehensive and insecure: she does not trust God's good intentions; she is chary and secretive. On His part, the Father God is withholding: he is teasing and sadistic, he is narcissistic in his desire for all her attention, he is jealous, and he is unfair, unjust, and depriving. He becomes for Dickinson (like her personal father) both the source of power and the withholder. She approaches and reproaches God as "a daughter who has been treated poorly, unjustly abused, and humiliated, neglected and unseen, or when seen, threatened, maliciously teased or carelessly mistreated. Often she is reduced to a childlike state of dependence, smallness, impotence, and frustration."[38]

By adopting an "innocent" daughter voice in her poetry, Dickinson both gains the power to question this Father God and to express her complaints and distrust plainly in ways she never could with her own father. In her poetry addressed to God, Emily Dickinson is shockingly heretical. She would question God, blaspheme against him, accuse him of being *deus absconditus*. She is skeptical and critical, stand-offish, unconvinced. She calls God "a Swindler," and a "Mighty Merchant," "a Burglar, Banker, Father," and a "blonde Assassin." She frequently uses legal terminology, the language of her personal father's profession, when describing God—particularly His untrustworthiness. Dickinson's ultimate reaction is contempt for this Father who allows people to die but refuses to show His face and she mocks those in her family who pray daily to the "eclipse." She does not assume this stance without paying a tremendous price—guilt, doubt, fear, anxiety about death—all these generate in her an awesome energy that would deplete her if she did not write: "I work to drive the awe away, yet awe impels the work."[39]

For Dickinson to truly lay claim to her poetic powers meant that she had to encounter what Dickinson scholar Joanne Feit Diehl recognizes as her "murderous" impulses, "the desire to eliminate the forces (primarily male, primarily father/God) that would inhibit her through enforced feminine passivity or submission."[40] Encoded in Dickinson's poetry are her attempts at subverting that masculine power—they range from assuming an "innocent" childlike persona to presenting herself as self-sacrificial victim or more blatantly, by directly confronting and taking her power—as she did in her poetic self-initiations and in her poem where she declares: "Mine—here—in Vision and in Veto!"[41] As Diehl remarks ". . . murder repeatedly presents itself as a means to attain an individuating authority."[42] To rename and marry oneself may be possible "only if one murders the Father and feeds on his power."[43] Dickinson's "murderous tendencies" were not consciously directed at her personal father (as we shall see in Sylvia Plath's work), and the imagined murder was not without ambivalence. Since so much of her poetic effort was directed toward this withholding Father, she is indebted to him and she knows it: "Most—I love the Cause that slew Me."[44] As Diehl succinctly notes "In Dickinson's war with the Father (which is her war with the world), "All," as she knows, "is the price of All."[45]

Given the content, it is understandable that Emily Dickinson felt both fiercely protective and fearful about showing her poetic work to anyone. Although she went to her brother Austin, particularly when she was younger, seeking his intellectual companionship, he was not a fully receptive audience. One of the reasons Susan Gilbert, Austin's wife, was such an important figure in Dickinson's life was that Dickinson was able to give Gilbert her poems. But Dickinson's intellect was formidable and she met virtually no one who could meet and match her for intensity—although she continually tried to find them. She also had tremendous ambition and a driving creative daemon, something rather unheard or unspoken of for women in her time. Later in her life she developed some clear intuitions about the "immortality" of her work, and on this she really gambled all. Although there was really no one who rose to her requirements, there were several men who were able, more or less, to "receive" her. Thomas Wentworth Higginson was sought after in hopes of publishing, and Samuel Bowles was likewise courted for this reason. But none of these men could comprehend her scope nor take the measure of her circumference, and in retrospect she seems to have been wise to have been so wary and careful with her treasure trove. In the end she relinquished hopes of publishing in her lifetime. Although this obviously wounded her and caused her to become even more isolated, she eventually moved to a place where she could tell Higginson that the idea of publishing was as far removed for her as "fin to firmament." Of her 1775 poems, only seven were published in her lifetime and these were edited by others. All the rest she stitched together in packets and secretly laid away in a chest in her bedroom.

Emily Dickinson undertook poetic material unheard of for a woman poet of her day. By dint of her enormous genius, she used the lack of blessing from her distant and unreachable father, her society's inability to grant her legitimacy, and her supreme distrust of the Father God's promises as material for her art. As surgeon and seer into her own soul, she anatomized her womanly pain in relation to such lack of approval and sanction. With her own colossal destiny in mind, unbeknownst to any but herself, she fashioned with unstinting care and passion poems documenting the widest range and depth of the female soul. Reading her poems today, we can see that they still pose the most serious and provocative existential questions, exploring the deepest categories of psychological experience, the most profound religious argumentation, the most penetrating understanding of the creative process as well as the most critical questions of gender. Although the poet announces the Hestian heat of her calling as an "unanointed Blaze," a poetic fire without the blessing of her culture, she does lay claim to the creative process as her own "White Election" and she has left us with her legacy.

2. DEMETER AND PERSEPHONE

I begin to sing of lovely-haired Demeter, the goddess august,
of her and her slender-ankled daughter whom Zeus, far-seeing
and loud thundering, gave to Hades to abduct.
                    —*Homeric Hymn to Demeter*[1]

We knew, of course, that there had been a preliminary stage of
attachment to the mother, but we did not know that it could be
so rich in content and so long-lasting, and could leave behind so
many opportunities for fixations and dispositions.
                    —*Freud*[2]

The mysteries remain
I keep the same
cycle of seed time
and of sun and rain;
Demeter in the grass
I multiply . . .
                    —*H.D.*[3]

5. Demeter and Kore

Mothers and Daughters in the Battlezone

Demeter is an earth mother goddess. Her realm is the above world of agriculture, the seasons, grain, all growing things. Although she has many stories the mythology of Demeter is primarily focused on her relationship with her daughter, Persephone. In fact, so close are they that Demeter and Persephone are frequently thought of as a double figure. In essence the story of Demeter and Persephone is a profound story of mother-daughter love as it occurs in patriarchal culture. It is Demeter's response to the loss of her daughter through abduction and rape by a male underworld god that determines Demeter's mythology. The following is the myth as told in the "Homeric Hymn to Demeter."

One day the young maiden Persephone was playing with her friends in a field of flowers, away from her mother. As she gathered roses, crocuses and beautiful violets, iris, and hyacinth, she happened upon a narcissus placed there by Zeus "for a girl with a flower's beauty." Upon seeing this beautiful flower with its "hundred stems of sweet-smelling blossoms" she was dazzled and reached out with both hands at once whereupon the earth gaped open and Hades, "the many-named son of Kronos," sprang out upon her. "Against her will he seized her" and carried her away as she wailed. Persephone's cry was heard by her mother, Demeter, and "A sharp pain gripped her heart, she tore/ the headband round her divine hair with her own hands./ From both of her shoulders she cast down her dark veil and rushed like a bird over the nourishing land and the sea, searching."

For nine days Demeter wandered the earth with bright torches in her hands, and in her sorrow she never ate or bathed. Hearing that her daughter was abducted by Hades with Zeus' permission, "a pain more awful and savage reached Demeter's soul" and she withdrew herself from lofty Olympus and wandered the earth in her grief as an old woman, unseen and unrecognized by mortals.[4]

The First Bond

Once she has been disgorged from Saturn's belly, Demeter is absorbed into the Zeus religion. She becomes pregnant through a rape-marriage by her brother, Zeus, and like her sister, Hera, her relations with him are forced and do not last. Her primary attachment, her deepest soul connection, her sacred *coniunctio*, is with Persephone, her daughter. Their union is an old and familiar one, taking Demeter and Persephone back to their ancient heritage as Neolithic goddesses, when lineage was traced down through the mother-line and the story of female becoming was understood as a continuous mother-daughter unfolding.

In the Greek version of Demeter-Persephone, although deep memories of matrilinearity are ever present, the mother-daughter story takes place within the context of a patriarchal culture. In Greek myth, the story is no longer one of mother-daughter continuity; instead, the plot centers on the forced separation between mother and daughter perpetrated by a male abduction. In this myth the vicissitudes of the mother-daughter relationship as it occurs in patriarchal culture are encoded. In this story the great archetypal mother-daughter motifs are vividly portrayed: the early blissful merger of the first bond broken into by a rape from the masculine Underworld; a profound period of separation characterized by deep grief and yearning; a euphoric reunion which, in the mythology, results in a re-flowering of the world.

As the Greeks tell it, Demeter acts primarily as a mother—the points at which her story turns are all maternal in nature. But she is not only a positive earth mother but also a depressive goddess, and it is her depression that is significant. To really understand the depths of Demeter's suffering, it is necessary to go back to her own early development.

As a Daughter of Saturn, she spent time in the Belly of the Father. She lived in that cold, coagulation of matter without benefit of the nurturing warmth and protection of her own mother. In a sense, this is the background to the Demeter-Persephone myth that is seldom recognized. With this in mind, it makes Demeter's maternal desire for everlasting connection with Persephone over-determined. Like that of many women today, her practice of mothering is colored by her own maternal deprivation. As often happens with women who have felt mother-loss, they imbue their daughters with an additional emotional significance and their attachment to them gains a certain ferocious intensity. This is what creates the binding, almost incestuous quality of some mother-daughter relationships.

When Demeter loses her beloved daughter due to an over-powering male force, a rupture in the mother-daughter bond occurs, one that echoes Demeter's loss of her own mother when she was swallowed by Saturn. As I read it, the classical Greek version of the Demeter-Persephone myth is a tale of the struggle of mothers and daughters to retain their connections in what I call the Battlezone of Culture. As Adrienne Rich has said, "This cathexis between mother and daughter—essential, distorted, misused—is the great unwritten story."[5]

Since patriarchal culture ensures that women will be separated from each other, many women experience what can only be called a Demeter-Persephone re-enactment of the mythic cycles of attachment, separation and loss, grieving, and longing for reunion and renewal. In fact, it is made into a sign of our normality. Freud's psychology tells us how it happens: The girl at the threshold of maturity is expected to leave her mother behind and turn instead to men for love, emotional support, and nurturance. Although Freud acknowledged that this was indeed a difficult thing for a girl to do and that the process in effect leaves a woman exhausted, he did not understand fully why it happened.

In a paper entitled "Some Psychical Consequences of the Anatomical Distinction Between the Sexes" (1925),[6] Freud outlined in detail the process of psychosexual development for girls. This paper was delivered at the International Psychoanalytic Congress, strangely enough, by his daughter, Anna Freud. I say "strangely enough" because in this paper Freud develops some of his deepest understandings about mothers and daughters and some of his most outrageous and devastating ideas about female sexuality. In this paper he basically comes to the conclusion that women are "failed men."

In the beginning, Freud says, both boys and girls are involved with the same original love object, the mother—the pre-oedipal mother, the original source of love, security and pleasure. But as they start down the long and treacherous road of development, boys and girls follow divergent paths. For girls, the path begins with their castration complex, which is initiated when, Freud says, "They notice the penis of a brother or playmate, strikingly visible and of large proportions, at once recognize it as the superior counterpart of their own small and inconspicuous organ, and from that time forward fall a victim to envy for the penis." This "discovery" happens, Freud notes, "in a flash." "She has seen it and knows that she is without it, and wants to have it." This sudden realization sets into motion a girl's "masculine complex." She has seen the superior organ and she wants it. Her penis-envy leaves her with two choices—she can go on wanting it, wanting to be a man, or she can disavow her "castration" and go on thinking she does have it and go on to behave like a man: "After a woman has become aware of the wound to her narcissism, she develops, like a scar, a sense of inferiority." She develops contempt for her own sex while acknowledging the superiority of the phallus, and this leads to a "loosening of the girl's relation with her mother as a love-object"—a necessary separation that ensures the girl's mature heterosexual development.

Freud goes on to describe another aspect to this perilous journey. After the great penis revelation, a girl discovers, through the process of comparison, "the inferiority of the clitoris." Freud always assumes that masturbation for young girls is an active, "masculine" activity and that "the elimination of clitoridal sexuality is a necessary precondition for the development of femininity." He equates clitoral pleasure with the phallic phase when a little girl actively loves her mother. However, for a girl to truly reach her feminine identity, she must learn to repudiate her active, clitoral, "masculine sexuality," which thus far has been directed towards her mother, and move toward a more mature, passive, receptive vaginal sexuality. She is helped along in this process by her "narcissistic sense of humiliation"—the hopelessness of ever gaining a penis. It is at this point that Freud sees that "the girl's libido slips into a new position," offering her the possibility of having the "penis-child." This she hopes to attain by enlisting her father as love-object. Her mother then becomes an obstacle to this desire and is met with strong feelings of jealousy. Thus a girl enters into her version of the Oedipus complex where her development becomes rather vague and diffuse and eventually seems to fade out. In his paper entitled "Female Sexuality" (1931), Freud sums it up:

> In girls, the motive for the demolition of the Oedipus complex is lacking. Castration has already had its effect, which was to force the child into the situation of the Oedipus complex. Thus the Oedipus complex

escapes the fate which it meets with in boys: it may be slowly abandoned or dealt with by repression, or its effects may persist far into women's normal mental life. . . . [f]or women the level of what is ethically normal is different from what it is in men. Their super-ego is never so inexorable, so impersonal, so independent of its emotional origins as we require it to be in men.[7]

Thus women tend to have, according to Freud, less sense of justice, less moral fiber; their judgments are more easily influenced by their emotions. Their journey to adult acceptance of their womanliness, Freud wearily concluded, has left women "exhausted" and with "no paths open to further development."

Toward the end of his life, Freud began to acknowledge, if not understand, the deep influence and attachment that a girl has for her first love object, her mother. In one of his favorite analogies to the field of archaeology, Freud makes a remarkable comparison: "Our insight into this early pre-Oedipus phase in girls comes to us as a surprise, like the discovery, in another field, of the Minoan-Mycenean civilization behind the civilization of Greece."[8] He goes on to say: "Everything in the sphere of this first attachment to the mother seemed to me so difficult to grasp in analysis—grey with age and shadowy and almost impossible to revivify—that it was as if it has succumbed to an especially inexorable repression."[9] In an unwittingly prescient observation, Freud had a glimmer of two profoundly connected realities; first, that in fact, there was, as we now know, a highly developed social, political, and religious civilization (one that even pre-dates the Minoan-Mycenean culture) which was organized around the worship of the goddess.[10] Secondly, like the goddess-oriented Minoan-Mycenean culture which lay buried under the masculinist culture of Greece, so too, does a woman's deepest memory of connection with her mother lie repressed in memory, replaced with all the structures and strictures of patriarchal culture built on top.

The question of what happens in our culture to a woman whose first love bond is with her mother is still largely unanswered. Does she in fact change her deepest allegiance from mother to father and then later to another man as Freud would have us believe? How does this switch of love object happen? There is no doubt that a woman may look to her father to lead her into the pleasures and experiences of the wider world. In the myth Zeus planted the narcissus as a lure to move the daughter away from the vigilant eye of her mother. But must the process necessarily be such a wrenching, severing one? Psychoanalyst D. W. Winnicott imagined the introduction of the "father" into the mother-daughter pair as a joint project initiated by them as a way to make a space in which separation from the mother can then occur. But can the father, or later the husband, possibly be a substitute for the lost first love? Won't a girl's vulnerability and openness, like that of Persephone, be exploited and confiscated? Won't she, as a woman, be secretly disappointed that her husband cannot satisfy her longing for the past unitary experience? Won't she remain in a lifelong state of ambivalence because she has been forced to choose between her father and her mother, and cannot? Given the choices, a woman may find that she has no path open to her except the well-worn one of silent submission to cultural scripts, or she may set out on her way back to reconnection with the maternal circuit and the company of women, or she may feel herself to be living on the fault-line, a perpetually isolated misfit, as Phyllis Chesler writes of in her work on women and madness:

> Persephone does not wish to be raped, nor do women today. Neither do they wish to recapitulate their mother's identity. But the modern Persephone still has no other place to go but into marriage and mother-hood. Her father (men in general) still conforms to a rape-incest model of sexuality. And her mother has not taught her to be a warrior, i.e., to take difficult roads to unknown and unique destinations—gladly.[11]

The separation of Demeter and Persephone as told in the "Homeric Hymn to Demeter" is an unwilling one; it does not emerge naturally out of their relation-ship: it is, like all rape, against their wills. As we can see in the Hymn, the shock of losing, the search for the lost one, the resultant depression, grief, and mourning all belong to the great psychic break in the mother-daughter bond as it occurs within the context of a male-determined society.

Separation, as the primal issue between mother and daughter, runs through-out women's stories. In the annals of traditional psychology, masculine develop-ment demands a separation from the mother as the only means of sailing out on the great adventure towards autonomy and individuation. This vision of develop-ment has left women standing on the shore. Unable to completely disengage from their mothers, women have been seen, in traditional psychoanalytic think-ing, as less developed, weak, foundering on the rocks of relationship, unable to set sail towards their own destiny. It has taken us, as women, a long time to understand our turn away from the mother as well. Many women still pray that they "will never be like my mother" and are horrified when they realize the deep level of their similarities. This horror seems to arise out of a recognition of the mother's conformity to patriarchal scripts. Seeing what her mother has paid for surviving in a male-dominated culture, a woman will understandably want to dis-tance herself.

Only recently have women begun to understand that their inability to com-pletely disengage from their mothers is not due to some inherent weakness in women's make-up, but is an unnatural requirement placed on them by masculine culture.[12] Demeter and Persephone were wrenched away from each other by the growing emphasis on the Law of the Father. We are just beginning to realize, as Kim Chernin has so clearly said, "When the daughter at the crossroads rejects her mother and chooses her father instead, it is because she cannot find within the mother-world a way to grow into the full promise of her original female

being."[13]This is not an innate problem between mother and daughter but a manifestation of our struggle under the Law of the Father. We are just starting to
understand the ways we, as women, can move out of the enclosed maternal circuit without denying the importance of our mothers and losing our connections
to each other.

Demeter and the Mother's Search for the Daughter

In the Greek myth, we see how the goddess Demeter goes "mad" over the loss of
her daughter to Hades. She falls into a deep depression, and we do not question
her emotional pain. Demeter's response to her loss is extreme: she wanders the
earth for nine days without bathing or eating, she sits speechless and brooding on
the "Laughless Rock"; she lies pining with longing on the navel of the earth
attempting to make re-connection. Today we are suspect of such extravagant
reactions to daughter-loss. As a monument in commemoration of her experience,
Demeter ordered temples to be built and established the Eleusinian Mysteries.
(One wonders what a woman's memorial would look like today.) Many women
would be astounded to think that their mothers would raise such a ruckus over
the loss and rape of her daughter. Yet as Adrienne Rich remarks: "Each daughter,
even in the millennia before Christ, must have longed for a mother whose love for
her and whose powers were so great as to undo rape and bring her back from
death. And every mother must have longed for the power of Demeter, the efficacy
of her anger, the reconciliation with her lost self."[14]

Persephone and the Daughter's Search for the Mother

As the daughter in the myth, Persephone suffers as well. She is torn away from
her mother against her will. She sits alone and unhappy in the Underworld longing for home. Like all women who have lost connection with their mother bond,
she, too, is depressed. As Adrienne Rich reminds us, this relationship is "the great
unwritten story."[15] Although it may be "unwritten," it is not unknown. Many
women have attempted to enter into the meaning of this primal connection.

Oftentimes, women, particularly women who have been father's daughters,
will feel themselves to be what Rich has called "wildly unmothered." This
unmothered condition sets up a longing and yearning for a special kind of touch
and holding. Many women, of course, seek it in men, looking to their husbands
or mates for that which only another woman can offer. This can be a source of
deep and secret dissatisfaction. Men can give women many things, but they can
never give the kind of touch, warmth, nurturance that connection with another
woman's body can provide. In order to love oneself fully, physical cherishing from
another woman must occur as a registered knowing in our body cells. If we do not
get this from our personal mother, we may seek it in dreams, find it through our
daughters or sisters, or receive it from another woman. However it happens, hap-

pen it must. Until a woman knows this experience, she will never be able to feel herself united body and soul.

We barely understand how the separation of Demeter and Persephone can be a gateway to a woman's deeper understanding of herself as a creative woman. As Kerenyi has noted, in her aspect as Goddess of the Mysteries of Eleusis the goddess Demeter, "herself in grief and mourning entered upon the path of initiation and turned toward the core of the Mysteries. . ."[16] It is this turning inward that deepens and enriches the mythology of Demeter and Persephone, as well as the life of any woman who consciously participates or is unwittingly thrust into their mysteries.

Deciphering Demeter with the Poet, H.D.

In his later years, Freud finally confessed his ultimate bewilderment about female development. In what feels like resignation or even defeat, he said, "If you want to know more about femininity, enquire of your own experience of life, or turn to the poets, or wait until science can give you deeper and more coherent information."[17] Taking Freud's directive, I have turned to the poets, in this case to the poet whom Freud himself analyzed, Hilda Doolittle, or H.D. as she has come to be known.

H.D. was born in Bethlehem, Pennsylvania in 1886. She died in 1961, at the age of seventy-five after a long, hard, and fruitful life, most of it spent as an expatriate in Europe. Her life spanned both World Wars, and all the contingent upheavals of those years affected her psychologically, artistically, and spiritually. Her most important relationships reflect the richness and the depth of her life. Engaged to Ezra Pound who recognized the poet in her, analyzed by Sigmund Freud who helped her understand the driving forces in her life, supported by her lifelong companion and lover, Winifred Ellerman (Bryher), H.D. lived a life that was uniquely her own, frequently outside of social sanction, a life fashioned by her own hand. It is H.D.'s changing relationship to her often-conflicted experiences of being a woman, a mother, and an artist that is at the core of her work, and it is through her struggle with these issues that I wish to look at her life.[18]

The Struggles

The traumatic and determinative events of H.D.'s life fall within a short span of several critical years. H.D. experienced pregnancy three times. In 1916, during World War I, a year before the publication of her first book of poems, H.D.'s first child was stillborn. The loss of this child was compounded by her growing loss of confidence in her capacities as a woman, and helped to engender her sense of being a misfit as a woman poet. As is often the case, the combined loss of child and confidence greatly contributed to the breakdown of her marriage. Her second child, Perdita ("the lost one"), born out of wedlock in 1919, survived despite H.D.'s own near death from double pneumonia. This pregnancy, accompanied as it was by severe illness, was also emotionally complicated by the concurrent deaths

6. H.D. and Frances Perdita

7. Professor Charles Leander Doolittle

of her beloved brother and her father. H.D. survived the traumatic birth and the second set of losses with the help and support of Bryher. These were the critical events that gave shape to H.D.'s life, the meaning of which she would work to decipher through her poetry.

The first pregnancy had thrown H.D. into confusion; her female identity and her poetic identity, she felt, were at odds, dissonant. She translated the guilt, pain, and grief over the stillborn child into an inability to create at all. The subsequent birth in 1919 of Perdita, a healthy, beautiful daughter, gave her life resonance, regenerated her sense of herself as a woman, and renewed her courage to become a serious creator of poems. The last pregnancy came in 1928, a year after her mother died. She was forty-two. This pregnancy was aborted in Berlin. Writing to Brhyer and Kenneth Macpherson (Bryher's "screen husband"),[19] H.D. assures them both that terminating the pregnancy was "ALL FOR THE GOOD." Although Macpherson was undoubtedly the father of the child, H.D. writes to them that "the whole experience brought me near to you both, brought us into some exquisite psychic rapport and certainly brought me to my senses. . . . Your tenderness and sweetness will always now be a part of my life and I don't want playing about with any 'and ors' and things, old or new fashioned it may be."[20] A relief and an apparently guiltless experience, the abortion cleared the way for a further deepening of her creative life. For H.D., the three experiences of pregnancy would always be set up in her mind in comparison and juxtaposition to her work—the stillbirth, a metaphor for blocked creativity; the birth of Perdita, (H.D.'s Persephone) a sign of creative renewal; the abortion, a conscious decision between the two, an empowered choice. These events formed the nexus of what she termed her "personal hieroglyph," the meanings of which she would spend a lifetime decoding.

H.D. was proficient in Greek and used the familiar topics of classical Greece for her own poetic purposes. Not surprisingly, she was drawn to the Eleusinian Mysteries—Demeter and Persephone's ritual cycle of rebirth; the mother and daughter *heuresis*; the "finding again." She worked this mythic round of birth, death, and regeneration throughout her life and on many different levels.

One of H.D.'s earliest creative struggles was wresting her poetry out of the realm of her intellect and bringing the wisdom of her woman's body to bear on her poetic imagination. In an early essay written shortly after Perdita's birth, she worked to understand the interconnection between body and spirit. Using a Demeter-like agricultural metaphor, she imagined the body as the ground upon which the seed of the spirit is cast. Although in this early work H.D. used masculine gender, I have taken the liberty to change it, as I imagine she, too, might have understood it.

This is the mystery of Demeter, the Earth Mother. The body of the Eleusinian initiate had become one with the earth, as her soul had become one with the seeds enclosed in the earth.

No woman by thought can make the grain sprout or the acorn break its shell. No woman by intellectual striving can make her spirit expand.

But every woman can till the field, can clear the weeds from about the stems of flowers. Every woman can water her own little plot, can strive to quiet down the overwrought tension of her body.[21]

Drawing together the cluster of associations from agriculture, the mother-daughter goddesses, and her creative process, H.D. embarked on her lifelong quest to shape a woman-based theory of creativity. But even by her mid-forties she still had not found a way to write that truly gratified her, "I have never been completely satisfied with any of my books, published or unpublished." Using her usual maternal metaphor, she says, "My books are not so much still-born as born from the detached intellect." Even in her poetry, she says, "There is a feeling that it is only a *part* of myself there."[22] H.D's dissatisfaction with her work continued up until her analysis with Freud.

H.D. and "The Professor"

In 1933 H.D. was accepted into analysis with Freud in Vienna. He was then seventy-seven years old; she, forty-seven. The Freud that H.D. met is not the misogynist of some of his writings. He is an old man who will die within five years; he is a Jew about to flee the Nazi holocaust; he is frail, sometimes tender-hearted, as well as irascible. The analysis lasted three and one-half months. In 1934, she concluded the analysis with another five-week series of sessions.[23]

About her motivations to begin analysis, H.D. writes, "I wanted to dig down and dig out, root out my personal weeds, strengthen my purpose, reaffirm my beliefs, canalize my energies."[24] She goes on to claim, "You might say that I had—yes, I had something that I specifically owned. I *owned* myself." Feeling herself and all of Europe at that time in the early 1930s drifting toward some unknown disaster, she compares her soul-self to a "narrow birch-bark canoe." In a beautiful metaphor, she describes her other reason for seeking out Freud:

With the current gathering force, I could at least pull in to the shallows before it was too late, take stock of my very modest possessions of mind and body, and ask the old Hermit who lived on the edge of this vast domain to talk to me, to tell me, if he would, how best to steer my course.[25]

H.D. had already experienced several mental and physical breakdowns, the most serious of which was during World War I when she had the stillbirth. She knew that war was again imminent, and she wanted to be able to withstand it this time.

H.D. began her analysis with Freud on March 1, "a Holy Day," as she notes: Ash Wednesday. She goes on to say, "This is March, astrologically the House of Sorrow. It is traditionally the House of the Crucifixion." Historically, the month of March had brought death and loss for H.D. It was the month her father died, as well as her mother. But she remembers, "the end of March sometimes coincides with the spiritual vernal equinox, the resurrection."[26] And indeed, March was the birth month of Perdita "who arrived in the vernal equinox, and at the high time of the sun, at noon." "Surely," H.D. reflects, "the high tide of her stars brought fortune to me."[27] Going back to touch the memory of her good fortune, gave her the courage to remember the loss of her first child. Writing in her journal after the first session with Freud, she recalls that traumatic time of loss.

> I cried too hard . . . I do not know what I remembered: the hurt of the cold, nun-like nurses at the time of my first London confinement, spring 1915; the shock of the Lusitania going down just before the child was still-born; fear of drowning; young men on park benches in blue hospital uniform; my father's anti-war sentiments and his violent volte-face in 1918; my broken marriage; a short period with friends in Cornwall in 1918; my father's telescope, my grandfather's microscope. If I let go (I, this one drop, this one ego under the microscope-telescope of Sigmund Freud) I fear to be dissolved utterly.[28]

It is to her credit that she did let go and subject her ego to the penetrating lenses of the fathers and their science. But she did not let go, as we shall see, of the woman wisdom in her bones.

As one would expect in undergoing analysis with Freud, H.D. returned in her mind to her childhood. Her mother, Helen Wolle Doolittle, was a talented women with a strong Moravian heritage. But there were problems. H.D. told Freud how as a child she had admired her mother's painting and boasted about it to visitors, but, she added, "My mother was morbidly self-effacing."[29] And, although her mother had a beautiful singing voice, H.D. recognized that "she had some sort of block or repression about singing,"[30] which her mother attributed to having been mocked for it by her father when she was young.

Despite Helen Wolle's lack of confidence, H.D. strongly identified with her beautiful and artistic mother. But even as a child, H.D. struggled with her own feminine identity. She often felt a misfit as the only surviving daughter in a family with five boys. At first her awkwardness was felt as a physical thing. As a young school-girl she felt her height was inappropriately unfeminine: "I am a misfit. I am . . . too advanced in some ways, backward in others. I am either at the head of the school procession or at the tail, because I am so tall."[31] Her feelings about being the ugly duckling were exacerbated because her beloved mother noticeably favored her older brother, leaving H.D. to deepen her feelings of unworthiness.

It is not unusual for a daughter to feel crushed when her mother prefers her brothers. When a mother has not found ways to express her own ambitions, she will frequently attempt to live that part of her personality out unconsciously through her sons. A woman who has not been given access to a life outside the home will look upon her daughter with affection, perhaps, but not with the glowing devotion she directs toward her sons, who are the more likely candidates to carry the mother's unlived life out into the world. When a mother's favoritism for her son combines with the culture's preference for males and masculine values, a gifted daughter can feel doubly unrecognized and betrayed.

Like the mothers of Emily Dickinson, Sylvia Plath, and Anais Nin, H.D.'s mother was defined by and defined herself through her relationship with her brilliant and distant husband. How this kind of mother affects a daughter who wishes to be something other than a servant to male "genius" is painfully clear. The daughter learns that if she is to salvage the possibility for a creative life, she must reject and deny her self-effacing, "feminine" mother as a model for her life in favor of an identification with an idealized version of her father. By refusing to take the mother's "normal" feminine path, a woman finds herself outside the easy comforts of conventionality.

The painful longing set up in a woman who has not had an affirming mother is evident in H.D.'s struggle. Writing about her mother, she remembers: "But one can never get near enough, or if one gets near, it is because one has measles or scarlet fever. If one could stay near her always, there would be no break in consciousness"[32] This desire for fusion, in Freud's view, represented a regressive desire for the mother. For H.D. it meant reconnecting with her deepest self, a Demeter-Persephone reunion.

H.D.'s father, Charles Doolittle, was forty-three when H.D. was born. A professor of mathematics and astronomy, a scientist with honorary degrees, and an author of books on astronomy, he was a distant man who "mapped the stars at night and napped until noon." She describes her astronomer father: "Father, aloof, distant, the provider, the protector—but a little un-get-at-able, a little too far away and giant-like in proportion, a little chilly withal."[33]

Freud asked H.D, "Was your father a little cold, a little stiff?" She explained that "he was what is known as 'typically New England,' though he was one remove from New England, his father having moved to the west."[34]

Although her father was distant, he was not averse to encouraging his only daughter to pursue nontraditional interests. In fact, he actively supported her to become what was then called "the new woman." Soon, however, she proved to be a disappointment to him because, like many verbally gifted daughters, she had failed mathematics dismally, an event which effectively canceled out her father's ambitious hopes for her to become a scientist. Subsequently, H.D. dropped out of Bryn Mawr after her first year. Her father, she said, had "wanted to make a mathematician of me, a research worker or scientist like (he even said so) Madame

Curie." In retrospect, she goes on to note ironically; "He did make a research worker of me but in another dimension."[35]

Early in her analysis with Freud, H.D. related an important story from her childhood, a story that encapsulated her dilemma as her father's daughter. In her father's study, on one of the topmost bookshelves there was a stuffed snow owl. "It was an extremely large owl. It was very white. It lived under a bell-jar, it had large unblinking gold or amber eyes." Little Hilda had asked her father, "May I have that white owl?" Her father, she remembered, consented to his young daughter's wish and gave her the owl. But, of course, with one condition, which Freud immediately recognized: "Ah—yes—he gave the owl to you, on the condition that it stayed where it was."[36]

As this early childhood story aptly demonstrates, having a father who says to his daughter that she can have anything she sets her mind to is not a guaranteed recipe for the daughter's later success. Certainly it is better than having a father like that of Dickinson, who had no expectations for his daughter at all except that she bake his bread and puddings, or like that of Nin, a narcissist who only recognized her for her beauty. But even an encouraging father cannot prepare his daughter for what her life will be like as a creative woman in a male-centered culture. He may expect, like my father did, that his daughter would achieve and accomplish, but he cannot guess the price. It is especially costly when a daughter's success is bought at the expense of her female identity, when she chooses the path of her father's ambition over her love for her mother.

H.D. felt split by the parental discord in her own psyche. For her the division appeared as a gender split, the same one embodied by her parents—the artist mother versus the scientist father, the emotional woman versus the rational man, the woman lover versus the male mate. Her inability to choose between these two, to fully commit to one path over the other, left H.D. exhausted. Her struggle was not merely a personal one. It had deeper dimensions as well: to chose her mother meant denying her creative gifts and identifying with being a victim, to choose her father meant worldly success while exercising too much power over others. The struggle is one that is familiar to many women. Determined to resolve the conflict within herself, H.D. relinquished the victim stance, reclaimed her mother's artistic powers as her own heritage, and found her relationship to her father's science in Freud's science of the unconscious. Her analysis with Freud helped her to bring long internal divisions to resolution: "I am on the fringes or in the penumbra of the light of my father's science and my mother's art—the psychology or philosophy of Sigmund Freud."[37]

H.D. identified Freud with her scientist father and grandfather, calling him "Papa" or "Our Professor" in her letters to Bryher. But she was aware that Freud was not the same as her father or her brother: "They called my father the Professor and my half-brother the young Professor. Our Professor was right, they do not resemble this Viennese Herr Professor Sigmund Freud. He is nearer to the grandfather and that religion, 'an atmosphere'. . . ."[38] As a father-figure, Freud helped H.D. to bridge into a realm that she already had access to, the realm of the unconscious. H.D. felt, too, that Freud's particularly appealing mix of masculine and feminine interests, that of scientist and mystic, were related to hers. Because of that combination, she understood how Freud's science went back before the science of her father: "My father studied or observed the variable orbit of the track of the earth round the sun, variation of latitude, he called it. He spent thirty years on this problem, adding a graph on a map started by Ptolemy in Egypt. The Professor continues a graph started by the ancestors of Ptolemy."[39] With Freud's help in decoding her dreams and visions, H.D. found her own spiritual and philosophical underpinnings. Most importantly, she recognized that Freud's science had much deeper implications for her then her father's: "My father went out of doors; the stars commanded him. Human souls command Sigmund Freud."[40]

H.D. called Freud her "midwife to the soul."[41] And it is clear that he was instrumental in helping H.D. find her own solution to the "mother-father" thing that had torn her so apart. Their work together enabled her to draw out "the hieroglyphs of the unconscious."[42] Eventually she learned to understand what Adrienne Rich has, years later, so beautifully stated: "I knew I was not an incorporeal intellect. My mind and body might be divided, as if between father and mother; but *I had both*."[43] In her own unconscious, decoded with Freud's help, H.D. found their place of union, and the wellsprings of her own creative inspiration.

"I had two loves separate"

From her writings, it is clear that H.D. was not merely a suppliant at Freud's altar: she was an active participant in what can only be called a creative collaboration. Freud was, by this time (and by his own account) an "old man." H.D. was a woman in her mid-life. They frequently disagreed about things, particularly Freud's interpretations of femininity. As H.D. remarks, "About the greater transcendental issues, we never argued. But there was an argument implicit in our very bones."[44] In her poem "The Master," she would recall "I was angry with the old man / with his talk of the man-strength, / I was angry with his mystery, his mysteries, / I argued till day-break."[45]

One of her arguments with Freud was about the meaning and importance of her love for women in regard to her creative life. Throughout her life H.D. loved both men and women. Although she lived with Bryher for almost three full decades in a lasting relationship which endured through Bryher's two "screen" marriages with Robert McAlmon and Kenneth Macpherson, as well as her own affairs, she felt basically unresolved about her love relationships.

H.D. never used the word "lesbian" to describe her relationships with women, nor did she allude directly to her physical relations with them. She was compelled instead by the psychological aspects of her love. She was not male-centered in her love for women as many acknowledged lesbian women of that time were (including Brhyer, who claimed she felt like a boy trapped in a woman's body). H.D.'s consciousness was definitely female-centered. Her lesbianism, as she wrote it out in her poems and novels, was not a mere replication of heterosexual love between two women, but more a deep remembrance of early mother-daughter or twinned-sister love. But H.D. also loved men. Indeed, her love for men, although sometimes equally intense as her love for women, was also often abject. With men she fell into what Rachel Blau du Plessis calls a "romantic thralldom,"[46] a condition which almost always proved disastrous for her life and her work.

In the analysis, Freud assumed H.D. to be bisexual. Writing to Bryher, H.D. comments: "The Professor said I had not made the conventional transference from mother to father, as is usual with a girl at adolescence. He said he thought my father was a cold man."[47] Freud, she says, thought she was a "perfect bi." To his credit, Freud understood that bisexuality was the natural state of human beings but that socialization eventually forces one to repress the homosexual longings. In the case of acknowledged lesbians, he believed the heterosexual desires were submerged. Although Freud's judgments were not completely value-free, his opinions did manage to release H.D. of some of her feelings of estrangment and probably some of her homophobia as well.

It is hard for us, especially today, to determine what label to use for our varied love relationships, or to want to use labels at all. Certainly to be able to "name" our loving is empowering, but to "label" can be restrictive and reductive. Although she has been severely challenged, I still find Adrienne Rich's definition of "lesbian" most useful especially because she is talking about the connection between "lesbian" and women-centered creativity:

> it is the lesbian in every woman who is compelled by female energy, who gravitates toward strong women, who seeks a literature that will express that energy and strength. It is the lesbian in us who drives us to feel imaginatively, render in language, grasp, the full connection between woman and woman. It is the lesbian in us who is creative, for the dutiful daughter of the fathers in us is only a hack.[48]

Using Rich's sense of the word, one could say that H.D. was truly and deeply lesbian; that although she also loved men, she gained energy and strength from women; and that her life and quest were profoundly woman-identified and woman-centered. Obviously, our vocabulary is still limited and does not permit us yet to speak, in a more differentiated language, of where the complexities and multiplicities of our sexuality can take us in our creative lives. Until we find that language, most sexually labeling language feels limiting.

A testimony to Freud's and H.D.'s collaborative relationship around the issue of her love for women can be found in her poem "The Master," where she says, in simple unadorned language what happened:

> I had two loves separate;
> God who loves all mountains,
> alone knew why
> and understood
> and told the old man
> to explain
> the impossible
>
> which he did.[49]

The Poet's Search for the Mother

The critical aspect of her analysis was H.D.'s recovery of an emotional connection to her mother which Freud helped to facilitate, even though he told her "I do *not* like to be the mother in the transference—it always surprises and shocks me a little. I feel so very masculine."[50] By deconstructing the image of an internalized, authoritarian father who blocked her creativity, she was able to reassess her relationship with her mother's legacy and powers. On a personal level, it meant that she could dig deeply into her mother's Moravian heritage to find what she would later call *The Gift*[51]—maternal love as the source of creative and spiritual life.

In her earlier writings, before the analysis, H.D.'s desire to reinstate female love and female speech at the center of her writing had been framed as an attempt to unseat the figure of her scientist father with his "mathematical-biological definition":

> Words may be my heritage and with words I will prove conic sections a falsity and the very stars that wheel and frame concentric pattern as mere very-stars, gems put there, a gift, a diadem, a crown, a chair, a cart or a mere lady. A lady will be set back in the sky.[52]

The reassertion of the Lady is a theme that runs throughout H.D.'s early work. In part it is her desire to confront her father's scientific "truths" with her more intuitive knowing, but it is also representative of her own internalization of this conflict:

> Papa is so fantastic. There were, he had assured us no gods. There was a firey pain at the back of my head and I had been taught that pure reason was the only goodness. Goodness, Goddess. There were others, I was certain. There was the Cytherean.[53]

The reference to "the Cytherean" here is to H.D.'s certainty about Aphrodite. In patriarchal Greek myth Aphrodite and Demeter have little to do with each other. This "fact" becomes translated into everyday life when we are taught that mothers have no sexual desire. But for H.D., Aphroditic knowing lies outside the realm of paternal authority; she knows "the Cytherean" from her own experience. But the collision between her father's knowledge and her own knowing creates "a firey pain" at the back of her head. It is the process of breaking through to her own womanly wisdom that creates the pain. It means cracking through the paternal prerogative which names "reason as the only goodness" and reaching through the father's authority to find the goddess. It means going past the father's mind back to the mother's body. As Adrienne Rich would later remember it: "the early pleasure and reassurance I found in my mother's body was, I believe, an imprinting never to be wholly erased, even in those years when, as my father's daughter, I suffered the obscure bodily self-hatred peculiar to women who view themselves through the eyes of men."[54]

Mother-Daughter Reunion

In the Demeter-Persephone myth, there is a great rejoicing at the "finding again," the *heurisis*, when mother and daughter are reunited. Writing about her early love with Bryher, she disclaims the power of words, her own precious medium as a poet, to describe pre-verbal love between women.

> it was beyond words;
> there were no words
> even in our glorious speech
> that could hint the joy we had then;
> how can we to-day in a crude tongue,
> in a strange land hope to say
> one word that can hint at the joy we had
>
> when the rocks broke like sand under our heels
> and they fled?[55]

Because she knew "in her bones" that her love for women was crucial to her creative life, she was able to steer clear of Freud's more debilitating theories of femininity. Wisely, Freud made H.D.'s relationship with her mother the focus of her analysis. Through his prompting, she came to see how her relationship with her mother was in need of repair. But she took this direction much further than Freud ever imagined possible. Reconnecting with the rich heritage that came down through her mother line, from her beloved grandmother through her artistic mother, H.D. gathered the strength to tap into the more universal, collective mother-goddess as a wellspring of poetic inspiration and spiritual wisdom. In forging her links back to her mother, H.D. experienced, like Persephone with Demeter, a spiritual reunion and a re-flowering of her creative gift. She writes: "Obviously, this is my inheritance. I derive my imaginative faculties through my musician-artist mother."[56]

H.D.'s analysis with Freud took place six years after her mother had died. During her analysis, H.D. recorded a dream in which she had been trying to get back to her London flat. The way upstairs was barred by a man and a "rough boy" who threatened and terrified her. (In her notes she associates these males with "news of fresh Nazi atrocities"). She calls out, "Mother" and then finds herself back out on the pavement where she is looking up at the window of her flat. "A figure is standing there, holding a lighted candle. It is my mother." She was "overpowered with happiness and all trace of terror vanished."[57] As critic Susan Stanford Friedman comments: "In dream, Helen Wolle could 'return' to her daughter as a Demeter-figure whose loyal strength would guard her beloved Persephone trapped in the man-created Hades of a world approaching the second holocaust of the century."[58]

Finding the Goddess

In a letter to Bryher during her analysis, H.D. recalls another dream:

> We got to the country. I looked up. There was a giant moon, bigger than the sun. It was rainbow coloured and like a pool of rainbow in the sky. Enormous. As I looked, there was a dim figure of a woman in the moon. She was clothed with "samite, mystic, wonderful," if you know what I mean, draped in flowing rainbow coloured robes, seated like a madonna in a curved frame. Yet she was not Madonna in that sense, she was Greek, she was Artemis, yet she was pregnant. A perfect renaissance idea . . . VIRGIN but pregnant.[59]

H.D.'s "VIRGIN but pregnant" is the paradox that Jungian analyst, Marion Woodman, explores in *The Pregnant Virgin*.[60] For Woodman the pregnant virgin is "that aspect of the feminine . . . that has the courage to Be and the flexibility to be always Becoming. Rooted in the instincts, the virgin has a loving relationship to the Great Earth Mother. But she is not herself the Great Mother."[61] As H.D.'s dream shows, the mortal woman has been given a vision of the goddess, she is not the goddess herself. However, because she has seen the goddess she can come into some creative relationship with her. Unlike Plath's mortuary vision in her last poem, where "the woman is perfected," H.D.'s vision of wholeness or completeness is not perfectly dead or sterile, she is the very image of living fertility.

In her examination, Woodman says that women who are in touch with the pregnant virgin archetype "have been through the joy and the agony of the daily sorting of the seeds of their own feeling-values in order to find out who they authentically are, and they continue to do so. They are strong enough and pliable enough to surrender to the penetration of the Spirit and to bring the fruit of that union into consciousness."[62] Certainly that is what H.D. was doing as she let go and subjected her ego to the daily analytic sessions with Freud.

H.D. equated the pregnant virgin of her dream with her own poetic process, which was originally inspired and continued to be affirmed and supported by her love for women. She was also born under the sign of Virgo, the Virgin. Although it always remained something to be negotiated at the social level, for H.D. the power of erotic love between women was, at the deep creative level, unproblematic. The pregnant virgin also gave her imagination an image outside the very real dangers posed by actual pregnancy and male relationships, both of which had been so dangerous and devastating to her.

The process of psychoanalysis allowed H.D. to find for herself how the power and wonder of women's sexuality was, in itself, not deficient as she feared it might be, or lacking "satisfaction" as Freud would have it, but simply, like the integrated completeness of the pregnant virgin, "perfect."

> O God, what is it,
> this flower
> that in itself had power over the whole earth?
> for she needs no man,
> herself
> is that dart and pulse of the male.
> hands, feet, thighs, herself perfect.[63]

H.D. had learned through her analysis with Freud that her original love bond was with the mother and that her poetry arose from that same erotic source, not from the conventional notion of the child made from the charged relationship between man and woman. She made this more primary bond the basis of her theory of creativity, one that would counter the phallocentrism of her male contemporaries.[64] Claiming her spiritual godhead in the form of a woman was healing for H.D. psychologically, creatively, and spiritually, as it has been for many women. Naming and claiming her legacy from the goddess—"you are near beauty the sun, / you are that Lord become woman"[65]—helped to unleash her poetic voice. As her muse, the goddess became, as Susan Stanford Friedman notes, "the female divine spirit embodying the power of regenerative Love in the midst of a fragmented, death-centered modern world. Her manifestations in myth, dream, and religious experience transform the misogyny of patriarchal tradition and validate H.D. as woman, as poet."[66]

It is ironic in the deepest sense of the word that it was Freud, that promoter of phallocentrism, who helped her discover this. As Friedman says, "H.D.'s work began immersed in patriarchal imagery: Freud's psychoanalysis and esoteric mysticism. She used these images to restore the bond with her mother, to resurrect the Goddess, to revise woman as a cultural symbol, and thus establish a valid dimension of women's quest."[67]

Prophecy

Deconstructing the scientific and religious superstructure of the Fathers, H.D. reconstructed her own creative life on the basis of the deeper spiritual authority of the Mother. Taking a metaphor from classical archaeology, she made a personal excavation that reveals the foundation stones on which everything depends:

> Under every shrine to Zeus, to Jupiter, to Zeus-pater or Theus-pater or God-the-father . . . there is an earlier altar. There is, beneath the carved superstructure of every temple to God-the father, the dark cave or grotto or inner hall or cellar to Mary, Mere, Mut, mutter, pray for us.[68]

In *Trilogy*, written during the war as she lived through the Blitz in London, H.D. wrote out her vision of the goddess. She is not the Madonna, "The Child is not with her," instead: "she carries a book but it is not / the tome of the ancient wisdom, / the pages, I imagine, are the blank pages /of the unwritten volume of the new. . . ." Her goddess of wisdom "is not shut up in a cave / like a Sibyl;" in the way that Greek patriarchal culture consigned its visionary women. Nor is she "imprisoned in leaden bars / in a coloured window" in the way that Christianity held Mary's powers captive. Instead, H.D.'s goddess of "the unwritten volume" is a goddess of deep and ever-evolving metamorphic power: "she is Psyche, the butterfly / out of the cocoon."[69]

The pregnant virgin contains, as Woodman points out, the idea of the chrysalis as the mode of creation. It is an image that H.D. uses throughout her poetry as the *sine qua non* for psychic and spiritual transformation. She is the butterfly emerging, Psyche, the female soul, born out of the dark chamber of the chrysalis.

H.D.'s analysis with Freud paradoxically enabled her to break free from the paralyzing grip that patriarchal tradition and authoritarian men had on her creativity. It allowed her to break open into her own deep womanly knowing revising patriarchal traditions in order to spin a new mythos which reclaimed the power of the goddess: as she wrote, "And it was he himself, he who set me free to prophesy."[70] Reflecting on H.D.'s struggle, Friedman notes, "Her lifelong revolt against traditional norms and expectations set her apart from the literary mainstream but her resistance led her ultimately to no less than a woman-centered mythmaking and radical re-vision of the patriarchal foundations of western culture."[71]

3. HERA

Of golden-throned Hera I sing, born of Rhea,
queen of the gods, unexcelled in beauty,
sister and glorious wife of loud-thundering Zeus,
All the gods on lofty Olympos reverence her
and honor her together with Zeus who delights in thunder.
                              —*The Homeric Hymn to Hera*[1]

The husband is almost always so to speak only a substitute, never the right man; it is another man—in typical cases the father—who has first claim to a woman's love, the husband at most takes second place.
                              —*Freud*[2]

They thought death was worth it, but I
Have a self to recover, a queen.
Is she dead, is she sleeping?
Where has she been,
With her lion-red body, her wings of glass?
                              —*Sylvia Plath*[3]

Becoming a Wife in the Battlezone

The remnants of Hera's earliest mythology show that she once was a central figure in the worship of the Great Goddess of Old Europe. But Hera and her worship became severely compromised with the arrival of the conquering peoples of the north. Memories of Hera's prehistoric heritage carried over into Greek mythology when she was made, through a marriage to the proto-Indo-European sky and weather god, Zeus, into the greatest female deity of Olympus, the Queen of Heaven. This so-called "marriage" was a patent attempt to co-opt the powers that Hera once held—Great Goddess powers for renewal and regeneration. As Kerenyi comments, "The "marriage" of Zeus and Hera is usually thought of in simplistic terms as the union of the boisterous father god of the immigrants on Mycenean territory with the mighty female deity of the countryside."[4] What is

8. *The Holy Marriage of Zeus and Hera*

more accurate is the notion that this marriage represents the forced union of two very different religious systems and social structures, a merger predicated on the domination of the goddess-worshipping cultures. It is said that Zeus and Hera's courtship lasted three hundred years, which probably indicates the time it took to establish the Zeus religion over the indigenous worship of the goddess, Hera.

The Reluctant Goddess of Marriage

When we meet Zeus and Hera as the divine couple in classical Greek mythology, a profound shift in social and religious order has already taken place. Along with the new patriarchal religion came the institution of marriage, over which Hera now presided. Remarking on the social structure that Zeus and Hera represent, classicist Jane Ellen Harrison (1850–1928) says: "Undoubtedly they represent that form of society with which we are ourselves most familiar, the patriarchal family. Zeus is the father and head: though Hera and he are in constant unseemly conflict, there is no doubt about his ultimate supremacy."[5] Writing in the early part of this century, without benefit of all the recent archaeology on the Neolithic era of Greece, Harrison instinctively knew that it was Hera who was "of the old matriarchal type; it is she, Pelasgian Hera, not Zeus, who is really dominant; in fact, Zeus is practically non-existent."[6] In a more personally empathetic comment, Harrison notes: "Hera has been forcibly married, but she is never really wife."[7] By all accounts, this marriage was not an easy alliance.

If Hera is the "goddess of marriage," it is certainly not the kind of marriage imposed upon her by the Greeks. The forced character of the union between Zeus and Hera is one that remains in the collective memory of women. It does not fade with time, but rather, like all women's oppression, becomes another installment in our memory bank, funding our knowledge, as is hinted in this small exchange: "Women," says Praxinoe to Gorgo, in the famous Syracusan Idyll of Theocritus, "Women know everything." "Yes, and how Zeus married Hera."[8] Needless to say the marriage was full of conflict and it is this tormented relationship that is recorded in classical Greek myth.

There are two aspects to the classical Hera mythology that are particularly poignant—her infertility and Zeus's unfaithfulness. The union between Zeus and Hera was fraught on the one hand with Hera's inability to produce offspring within her marriage and on the other by Zeus's infidelities, which produced most of the Greek heros. If Hera was bound to a form of fidelity dictated by patriarchal marriage, Zeus was not. Famous for his sexual athleticism and his rape/matings with other gods, goddesses, and mortal women, Zeus had, one could say, a compulsion. This caused Hera no end of suffering, and she wreaked terrible revenge on those she could implicate in Zeus's affairs. Although she herself does not seek out other lovers, one of her supreme acts of revenge is to use her ancient power of parthenogenesis to produce offspring without his participation. But these male offspring, Hephaistos and Typhaon, are misbegotten and rejected by Hera; and her daughters, Eileithyia and Hebe, mere doubles of their mother, are only pitiful reminders of her own more powerful past. In this mythology, it is clear that Hera's relationship to her own creative efforts is troubled because she uses her creative powers as weapons of revenge. Ultimately she is left frustrated and disgusted by what she produces.

Like the other ancient great goddesses who were subsumed into the pantheon by the political and religious takeover of Zeus-worshippers, Hera's original powers are co-opted and modified until she has no real function except to be Zeus's wife. Hera is wholly unsuccessful within the confines of patriarchal marriage—she becomes terribly diminished and distorted until finally she devolves into the shrewish, jealous, destructive, vindictive wife portrayed in Homer's telling.

Ever since Zeus married Hera, the marriage plot has been a problematical one for women. Because we are still attempting to come to terms with the effects and inequities of the patriarchal marriage system, I see Hera's story encoding a number of struggles that are relevant to women. In particular her mythology reveals a woman's perilous quest to maintain her power and identity while attempting the difficult task of attaining a marriage of equals in a patriarchal culture. This is one of the most fundamental of all creative challenges facing women today.

If a woman is heterosexual, her search for a marriage partner does not begin when she is an adult. It is well known that a woman's earliest experiences of her father set the tone for her later love relationships with men. When a daughter has had a swallowing father there are lasting effects. The devouring tendency will most likely reappear in her intimate relationships as a confusion between psychological merger and love. In her search for intimacy, a woman may seek to duplicate her childhood position and attempt a return to the Belly of the Father. Phyllis Chesler writes: "Psychologically, women do not have initiation rites to help them break their incestuous ties. While most women do not commit incest with their biological fathers, patriarchal marriage, prostitution, and mass 'romantic' love are psychologically predicated on sexual union between Daughter and Father figures." She goes on to wonder, "What would female sexuality be like if women did not violate the incest taboo, did not willingly marry Father figures, or were not unwittingly raped by them?"[9] It is important to clarify that Chesler is *not* talking here about women who have actually been incested by their fathers as children, rather, she is talking about the culture which would have us replicate incest in our marriages.

A Daughter of Saturn may find that her choice of partner turns out to be someone who comes close to her father in his possessiveness, depression, his pattern of distancing, his emotional withdrawal. A woman's efforts to achieve a fatherly esteem and recognition from this sort of man will leave her continually begging. She may learn to pose as a perpetual daughter with men, a *puella aeterna*, an eternal girl, playful, teasing, saucy, and secretly anxious, or she may insist on being identified with him, with his specialness, his romantic genius, his gloomy and intellectual outlook. If her father has been physically absent from her life, or actually dead, a daughter may find herself engaged in a desperate search for him in other men.

A daughter's deepest longing is to *know* and be *known* by her father, not in a physical way but in an emotionally honest way. When this is not fulfilled, she may later translate her longing into her adult life as a "love" quest. But it soon becomes something else. By abandoning herself to a dominating partner, she clearly risks losing her sense of self. By fragmenting herself, projecting her strength onto a man, she creates *his* power, allows *him* to possess a coherent self, a self in which she can finally take refuge. By sacrificing her own sense of self, she appears to gain access, however circumscribed, to a more powerful one. Although it is greatly feared, most women have experienced this process. It is almost *the* paradigmatic definition of a marriage relationship—for women. We have been taught that this is how to love. Many women who enter into marriages based on this kind of pattern sooner or later find themselves deeply dissatisfied.

Revolutionary Marriage

In her exploration of women's life narratives, Carolyn Heilbrun searches for the kind of marriage that would support a woman's creative life. She comments that "The marriage of a woman and man of talent must constantly be reinvented: its failure has already been predicted by conventional society, and its success is usually disbelieved or denied."[10] She defines this kind of marriage as a revolutionary marriage: "one in which both partners have work at the center of their lives and must find a delicate balance that can support both together and each individually. This means of course that the man, or the exceptional woman in an all-woman relationship, must be equally, probably more, nurturing and supportive than the usual "husband."[11] "Equality in work and money seems to be one of the most important factors in the make-up of a revolutionary marriage. Heilbrun does not take up the hard question of children in a marriage. Raising children is what tips the balance in many potentially equal marriages.

While many women seek the kind of partner who is, as Adrienne Rich describes it, "merely a fellow-creature / with natural resources equal to our own,"[12] few have found them. The poet Sylvia Plath was one such woman. Seeking a revolutionary marriage, a marriage of equals, she encountered instead the marital hells of Hera.

Sylvia Plath and the Marital Hells of Hera

Three years after Sylvia Plath was born on October 27, 1932, her father became ill. For the next five years, in a sustained pique of Prussian stubbornness, Otto Plath willfully misdiagnosed and then ignored his increasingly serious symptoms— weight loss, exhaustion, and fits of rage—thinking he had lung cancer when in

9. Sylvia Plath and Ted Hughes

10. Otto Plath at the blackboard

reality he had diabetes. Refusing to see a doctor until it was too late, he died, at age fifty-five, of complications due to the undiagnosed and neglected diabetes.[13]

Sylvia Plath's life and work reveals in many ways her response to this early trauma of father-loss. Plath's suicide attempts, her search for the missing father in the man she married, her desire for a "marriage of equals" and the marital hells she encountered in it, her final poetry of liberation, and her death are all anchored in this traumatic event.

"The Old Myth of Origins"

Her father was, by Plath's later recollection, a withdrawn and intimidating personality—"an old man." In her journal, written in her twenties while she was living in Boston, she attempted to come to terms with the event of his death by sorting out and assigning guilt and blame:

> Me. I never knew the love of a father, the love of a steady blood-related man after the age of eight . . . the only man who'd love me steady through life: she came in one morning with tears . . . in her eyes and told me he was gone for good. I hate her for that. [omission] He was an ogre, but I miss him. He was old, but she married an old man to be my father. It was her fault.[14]

When Otto Plath married Aurelia, he was forty-three and she was twenty-two. The marriage was predicated on paternal hierarchy; he was the quintessential Prussian *pater familias*, organizing the family around his work, while Aurelia became his secretary-typist—a primary role to her secondary occupation as housewife and mother. When Sylvia was little, Aurelia was busy helping Otto prepare two large scientific works. Both Aurelia and Otto practiced the Germanic veneration of hard work. They sacrificed many personal pleasures—no small self-indulgences, no social life—for the sake of Otto's work. Sylvia's early years with her ill, tired and angry father were carefully mediated by Aurelia, a process that helped to forge the dangerously fused alliance between mother and daughter, which Aurelia would later refer to as their "psychic osmosis."[15] When Aurelia announced to her children that Otto Plath had died, eight-year-old Sylvia responded with the childish but chilling declaration, "I will never speak to God again."

With his death Sylvia must have felt some piece of herself go with him. Much of her writing life feels like an attempt to get him back, or at least to get that piece of herself back, as well as, in the end, getting back at him for so profoundly abandoning her. All of her life Sylvia believed at some level that her father had committed a kind of suicide. And as Adrienne Rich has rightly noted, "it was Plath's father who set the example of self-destructiveness."[16] Her whole psychic life seems to have been organized around the void her father left. His absence worked like an energy vortex, a saturnian black hole exerting a relentless pull on her psyche. She sought her father out in her poetry and tried to re-create him other men. When she met Ted Hughes, her husband-to-be, Plath wrote to her mother, "He is better than any teacher, even fills somehow that huge, sad hole I felt in having no father."[17]

When Sylvia was thirteen, Aurelia took Sylvia into Boston to see a production of Shakespeare's *The Tempest*. There for the first time she heard Ariel's Song about the death of a father.

> Full Fathom Five thy father lies;
> Of his bones are coral made;
> Those are pearls that were his eyes:
> Nothing of him that doth fade
> But doth suffer a sea-change
> Into something rich and strange.
> Sea nymphs hourly ring his knell.

Thirteen years later, when she was twenty-six, Plath wrote a poem entitled "Full Fathom Five," plumbing the deep sea image in search of her own father, that "old myth of origins."[18] In this poem the father's seduction is felt as a call from the deeps; the subterranean pull of the unfathomed sea is dangerous—the poet's relation to her sunken father is an immutable iceberg of which she can perceive only the tip and barely imagine the treacherous, underlying mass. An archaic Poseidon, the sea-father surfaces seldom. As she walks along the shore, she realizes that there is no substitute for him, "You defy other godhood." And in a strange, ominous, and incestuous desire to identify with and join him, she declares: "Your shelled bed I remember / Father, this thick air is murderous / I would breathe water."

It appears from all reports that Aurelia never took her children on a trip to the cemetery where their father was buried. It was up to Sylvia as an adult woman to undertake this journey to her father's grave site in Winthrop's Town Cemetery. There she found his tombstone located in a place ironically called Azalea Path. There were no azaleas, only plastic flowers on another grave, as Plath would state in her poem entitled "Electra on the Azalea Path."[19] Identifying herself as Electra in this poem, she speaks to her father, admitting to him that she will "borrow the stilts of an old tragedy" to understand her relationship to him. In the Greek tragedy, Electra is the bereft daughter plotting revenge against her mother, Clytemnestra, who has killed her beloved father, Agamemnon. In her search for the man who contains her "old myth of origins," Plath is also building on "the stilts" of psychoanalysis which names the Oedipal daughter, Electra. The poem is another of her many attempts to disentangle herself from the disquieting effects of her unrequited love and loss of her father. After the visit to his grave she wrote in her journal: "Felt cheated. . . . My temptation to dig him up. To prove he existed and was dead."[20]

In her poem she acknowledges the difficulties his death caused her, including her own suicide attempt at twenty: "The day you died I went into the dirt. . . . It was good for twenty years, that wintering— / As if you never existed . . ." Her trip to the cemetery is marked as "The day I woke," and in her lament she cries: "I brought my love to bear, and then you died. / My mother said; you died like any man. / How shall I age into that state of mind?" The sensation that all life stopped for her somehow at the moment of his death is something that she cannot get beyond, cannot grow into. The end of the poem insidiously and incestuously mingles their fates: "I am the ghost of an infamous suicide, / My own blue razor rusting in my throat." And in a strange mixture of anger, guilt, and grief she asks: "O pardon the one who knocks for pardon at / Your gate, father—your hound-bitch, daughter, friend. / It was my love that did us both to death." In this poem Plath understands that her father's death is related to her severe depression, breakdown, and first suicide attempt at age twenty.

Plath seemed to use her writing as a compensation for loss, certainly not a new idea, but one that had special significance for her. At first, she worked to restore her father's presence by conjuring him as "a buried male muse"[21] who would help her write. Eventually she would have to poetically assassinate him in order to find her own voice. She also transferred her wild ambivalence, her desperate need for love, and terrible fear of loss, onto her husband, Ted Hughes. When Hughes did in fact leave Plath, the old wounds of father-loss were re-opened and she swung from euphoria and a creative frenzy to despair and completed suicide.

The Search for the Marriage of Equals

Sylvia Plath, like many women who have suffered the early loss of a father, had a tendency to overinflate men and their powers. In this, she was certainly helped by the culture of the 1940s and 1950s, a culture that supported the notion of creative power as singularly male-centered. In particular, as an aspiring poet, she was faced with the formidable literary canon of male writers. With male creativity as her paradigm, she could easily imagine "God as the Supreme Stylizer"[22] and the male intellectual as a fictionalized and poeticized "Colossus."[23]

Plath was already the recipient of many honors and had many encouraging and supportive mentors when she graduated summa cum laude from Smith College. But no one had prepared her for what she could expect after college. When Adlai Stevenson gave his commencement address to her graduating class, he performed the task of assigning her a well-worn place in patriarchal culture. Marriage and family, he argued, will not take you away from the "great issues of the day," rather you will be brought "back to their very center." Moving these gifted young women out of any thoughts or aspirations they might have entertained about public life, Stevenson placed them firmly and squarely back where they belong, into private, family life:

> The assignment for you, as wives and mothers, you can do in the living room with a baby in your lap or in the kitchen with a can opener in

your hand. If you're clever, maybe you can even practice your saving arts on that unsuspecting man while he's watching television. I think there is much you can do about our crisis in the humble role of house-wife. I could wish you no better vocation than that.[24]

These words out of the mouth of the most prominent liberal of the day are enough to really give us pause. Can we hear the echoes of Emily Dickinson's father who wrote vituperative essays on women's education? Are we, ourselves, so far away from this day in June 1955? The betrayal and frustration of these edu-cated women who were taught to write poetry and then expected to use their skills reading recipes and writing grocery and laundry lists was profound. Later Betty Friedan, in *The Feminine Mystique*, would identify women's reactions to this wholesale sell-out of their talent as "the problem that had no name."

Throughout her college years, Plath developed and struggled with her enor-mous literary ambitions. Her desire to write, to be seen and acknowledged as an important writer, was of the utmost importance to her. But side by side ran her need to make, as Adlai Stevenson had suggested, "a creative marriage." When she received a Fulbright scholarship to study literature in Cambridge, she was ecstatic. Yet the need to keep an eye out for the right man was ever present. She was obsessed with finding a husband who would provide her with a family and home. But she was also concerned with "making a self, in great pain, often, as for a birth."[25] Both projects were intertwined for her.

Plath's obsession with marriage came not only as a cultural imposition. There seemed to be an inherent need in her personality for marriage. The roots of that need were tangled—part cultural, part resolution to her troublesome sexuality, part affirmation of herself as a woman, part need for male love and constancy. But Plath's marriage meant more than the usual solutions to these perennial problems. Above all else, she married a poet.

From the beginning, there was a turbulent undercurrent of erotic violence in Plath's description of her relationship with Ted Hughes. Meeting Hughes for the first time at a party for poets, she described him as "that big dark, hunky boy, the only one there huge enough for me. . . ." and in the midst of a stamping, shouting match, she says, "he kissed me bang smash on the mouth and ripped my hair band off . . . and my favorite silver earring: hah, I shall keep, he barked. And when he kissed my neck I bit him long and hard on the cheek, and when we came out of the room, blood was running down his face."[26] She was attracted to this man who could meet and match her force, although she was also aware that he was "a breaker of things and people." Plath herself had a grandiose sense of her own power, a power caught in a woman's body. Struggling with the contradictions inherent in being powerful and female, she had written in her high school diary : "I think I would like to call myself 'The girl who wanted to be God.' Yet if I were not in this body, where would I be—perhaps I am destined to be classified and quali-fied. But, oh, I cry out against it. I am I—I am powerful—but to what extent?"[27]

As "The girl who wanted to be God" she needed her mate to be of equally mighty and mythic proportions—"the strongest man in the world . . . with a voice like the thunder of god."[28] His violence could feel to her "like a blast of Jove's lightning." But she herself, as a goddess of equal intensity, could withstand the force.

After her marriage the power differential radically shifted. She found herself to be not a goddess at all but a mere mortal. Identifying more with Eve, she began calling herself "this Adam's woman":

> I can appreciate the legend of Eve coming from Adam's rib as I never did before; The damn story's true! That's where I belong. Away from Ted, I feel as if I were living with one eyelash of myself only. . . .[29]

And so Plath, like many women before her and since, embarked upon that strange process of diminishment which happens upon marriage: "Her virtue exists in direct proportion to how much of her self is whittled away, and how much of what is left she is willing to not keep to herself."[30] The girl who wanted to be God becomes, in the process of marriage, a woman whose highest goal is to be without a self. Plath not only began denying her power as a woman, she projected her own poetic genius onto her husband. That she chose to marry a poet put her, as a poet-wife, into a severely conflicted position—both servant to the male poet and his competitor. She frequently served Ted's poetry as her mother had served her father's scientific writing. It was Sylvia who sent out carefully typed drafts of Ted's poems to magazines and journals in America. It was Sylvia who, when Ted's first volume of poetry came out, said in a letter home to her mother:

> I am more happy than if it was my book published! I have worked so closely on these poems of Ted's and typed them so many countless times through revision after revision that I feel ecstatic about it all. I am so glad that Ted was first.[31]

One can feel in these sentences the dangerous moment of blurred boundaries where a woman can fool herself into thinking that the success her husband has attained, by virtue of her labors, is somehow hers. In writing this to her mother, Sylvia was mirroring back what she must have watched as a small girl—how her mother had served as father's secretary and scribe, researching, writing, typing, and editing his great scientific works. That Aurelia undertook this task as her duty, that her daughter, Sylvia, picked up where her mother left off, is not surprising. The need that women have for being married to powerful men is so great that they themselves will gladly serve as distorted reflectors. As Virginia Woolf wrote in 1928, "Women have served all these centuries as looking-glasses possessing the magic and delicious power of reflecting the figure of man at twice its natural size."[32]

Sylvia must have felt and yet denied her mother's enormous resentment at receiving only secondary acknowledgment from her husband for her secretarial efforts and the sacrifices they entailed. (Aurelia Plath refers to her first year of marriage as "the year of THE BOOK" and the second "the year of the CHAPTER."[33]) But Sylvia was not her mother. Although her great supply of ambition was being used to fuel Ted, she did not take herself out of the race. And yet there were frequent occasions, especially social, where Ted was the acknowledged poet and Sylvia was merely the wife—a situation that deeply rankled her. Only momentarily, and this mostly at the beginning of their marriage, could she imagine them living together as gods, as Zeus and Hera, a match of equals.

Threats of violence appear frequently in the Zeus and Hera mythology. Hera's jealous rages at Zeus's infidelities only increase her feelings of helplessness. She often wreaked vengeance on the mortal women whom he had seduced, but calling her to account for her acts of revenge, Zeus reminds Hera of his ultimate power. Calling her incorrigible, he asks Hera:

> Have you forgotten the time when I strung you aloft with a couple of anvils hanging from your feet and your hands lashed together with a golden chain you could not break? There you dangled, up in the air and in among the clouds; and the gods on high Olympus, though they rallied round you in their indignation found it impossible to set you free.[34]

Sylvia Plath and Ted Hughes seemed to have also been caught in this kind of marital hell. While they were living in Boston, the quarrels between them grew intense as Sylvia nursed a growing sense of jealousy. Her suspicions that Hughes was seducing other women became more and more a source of rage and fury for her. After she came upon Ted with a Smith student, Sylvia and Ted fought physically. She ended up with a sprained thumb, he with fingernail marks on his face. She wrote later: "I got hit, and saw stars for the first time—blinding red and white stars exploding in the black void of snarls and bitings."[35] As in their first meeting, her violence and his had met again.

Later, towards the end of their marriage, Sylvia answered a phone call from Assia Gutmann Wevill, a mutual friend and the woman whom Ted had been secretly seeing and with whom he would eventually live and have a child.[36] Recognizing what the phone call was, Plath ripped the phone wires from the wall. Days later in a fit of rage, she built a fire in the backyard and, with her mother looking on, burned her latest manuscript page by page. The manuscript was about marriage and was intended, Plath said, to be a birthday present to Hughes. Like Hera, whose revenge at times turned against her own creative efforts, Plath destroyed her own work.

Her fury, however, was not only self-directed. On another occasion, Sylvia burned some of Ted's belongings—waste paper, poems, and letters—and proceeded to dance around the fire. This was not the first time she had unleashed her rage by destroying Ted's materials. Earlier in their marriage, Hughes had returned late from a luncheon with a woman who was interviewing him for a job. Plath, smelling treachery, tore up Hughes' notebooks, working manuscripts, drafts, and his beloved *Complete Shakespeare*.[37] Several days later she miscarried. Like Hera, like any woman brought to her knees by jealousy and a man's unfaithfulness, Plath's destructive energies were ultimately turned in on herself—the burned manuscript, the miscarriage, all preludes to the final act of self-destruction.

The depth of Plath's search for and desire for recognition from a powerful other certainly has its origins in the "great sad hole" created by her missing father. This paternal vacuum developed in her, like many women, as a later attraction and susceptibility to domination scenarios.

The stark rage in Plath's late poems can also be seen as attempts to move herself through what psychiatrist John Bowlby calls "pathologic mourning," a condition which demands expressions of anger and aggression in order for healing to take place.[38] There is, in the wisdom of the psyche, a deep understanding of how destruction and survival, death and regeneration, are inherently creative powers. The deeper impulse of Hera's manifestation is the birth, death, and regeneration cycle that belongs to the Great Goddess. This theme of cyclical renewal is one that also runs throughout Plath's poetry. One could say she was fairly obsessed with the idea. It was a process of natural interest to her as a woman born under Scorpio, the astrological sign of death and rebirth, the phoenix rising out of the ashes.

Hera as Moon Goddess

Plath's later poems move deeply into Hera's matriarchal consciousness when she takes the moon as her muse. It was not an untroubled relationship. As the Moon Goddess moves through her lunar phases of birth, death, and regeneration, so too, did Plath track her course.

Plath had a fear and dislike of "barrenness." Early in her marriage, fearing she might not be able to conceive because of erratic ovulation, Plath writes

> I have worked, bled, knocked my head on walls to break through to where I am now . . . I want a house full of our children, little animals, flowers, vegetables, fruits. I want to be an Earth Mother in the deepest richest sense. I have turned from being an intellectual, a career woman: all that is ash to me.[39]

Plath did go on to have two children. Her pregnancies and births were easy, at-home events, attended by a midwife. Moving fully into her fertility goddess persona, Plath, like Hera who was frequently referred to as bovine, called herself "cowy" or "cowlike." She says in an effusive letter to her mother "I think having babies is really the happiest experience of my life. I would just like to go on and on."[40]

The experience of birthing is a woman's special prerogative, it belongs to her as a woman and as such is rightfully hers to claim—as literal motherhood and as metaphor for the creative process. Plath was concerned with both these. Along with her enormous literary ambitions, Plath had protean energy for creating and celebrating her life. As earth mother, Eve, "this Adam's woman," she was devoted to her babies, gardening, cooking, sewing. She even took up beekeeping. Despite the fact that Plath had chronic sinusitus and desperate depressions, one cannot help but feel her inherent vitality. She was tall, athletic, and full of energy—she speaks of ten mile walks on the English moors. And, unlike Dickinson, who cultivated a hunger-aesthetic, Plath loved to eat and cook. Her journals and letters are full of descriptions of delicious food, prepared and eaten. She was also a gardener. As a teen-ager she worked summers on a farm in New England. Later, in Devon, she gathered armfuls of daffodils in spring to sell and give to friends. She had a large vegetable garden and many fruit trees. But all of her love of and response to natural growth and fruition did not easily translate over into her work.

"My true deep voice."

Many women have a desire to write but feel they cannot find their voice. Finding one's voice, written or spoken, is central to establishing a woman's sense of self and is at the core of some of our most mutinous and subversive relations with men. A compliant, dutiful daughter and wife does not speak or write her own mind. Instead, she serves the ones who own the language. Finding one's voice, for a woman, can oftentimes mean engaging in seditious activities like stealing (Alicia Ostriker calls it "stealing the language"). Women who would write have to come to terms with their relationship with male language and traditional and acceptable forms of using that language. Some comply; many resist. Some like Sylvia Plath are caught in the tension. Plath, educated in the 1940s and 1950s, was fed on the traditional literary canon of male authors, and she married a man on his way to becoming a highly recognized poet. It was against this literary legacy and poet-husband that she measured her own writing ambitions and felt herself wanting.

Feeling like a fraud is a common experience for many women—especially if she has, like Plath, excelled in some external way at the expense of her inner development. If a woman has been raised to think that her self-worth depends on what she can produce, praise and recognition from outside authorities do not give the desired result of higher self-esteem; instead, they set up fearful obsessions about being "found out." How Plath ties her lack of internal clarity and direction to her father is demonstrated in *The Bell Jar*, where Esther Greenwood, when asked by her boss what she would like to be, replies, "I don't really know." Shocked by her own reply, she says, "It sounded true, and I recognized it, the way you recognize some nondescript person that's been hanging around your door for ages and then suddenly comes up and introduces himself as your real father and looks exactly like you, so you know he really is your father, and the person you thought all your life was your father is a sham."[41]

Plath struggled throughout her marriage from what is commonly called a "writer's block." Openly confronting her father loss, her subsequent capacity to overinflate men and their power, and her own feelings of failure, she wrote in her journal: "Dreamed last night I was beginning my novel . . . : a girl's search for her dead father—for an outside authority which must be developed, instead, from the inside."[42] This novel never did get written, but the energy of the dream fed into her poetic process informing her poetry of struggle with "the jealous gods": the male muses who ruled over poetic creation, the male poetic authorities who could so easily exclude her, the successful poet-husband who so easily left her, the father who had so early abandoned her.

As she began an open rebellion against the internalized male poetic authority that kept her own voice suffocated, Plath implored, "What inner decision, what inner murder or prison break must I commit if I want to speak from my true deep voice?"[46] She understood that the only way to find her own "true deep voice," a voice that was hers, a woman's voice, is through murder or escape. The "prison break" in her life was unwittingly facilitated by Hughes desertion. After Hughes left, her difficulties in writing disappeared "as if domesticity had choked me."[44] As for many women before her and since, betrayal by a man became the means for her liberation. The glass caul that Plath referred to as "the glass-dam fancy-facade of numb dumb wordage"[45] was shattered when Hughes deserted her. It was then that Plath began, with great determination, to take up her own identity as a poet. She now mocked and satirized the connubial bliss she once celebrated. Realizing she had been sold out by the image of the toy doll wife, she wants her life back with a vengeance. If ending the marriage was her "prison-break," killing off her father was the "inner murder" which released her from a deeper captivity.

Killing the Father

When Plath asks what murder she must commit, she is on her way to writing one of her most powerful poems, "Daddy."[46] In this poem she went up against all tradition. She imagined herself committing patricide.

It is most interesting that there are hardly any myths, stories, or fairy tales of daughters killing the father. As writer Jane Lazarre asks, "Why had this murder not taken place in literary history?"[47] Myths, which have no moral aim, can conjure many fantastical acts, bizarre behaviors outside the law of social order: sons like Oedipus, may sleep with their mothers and kill their fathers. They may, like Orestes, kill their mothers. Daughters can also conspire in matricide, as did Orestes' sister, Elektra. They may even express desire for their fathers or have sex with them, but they do not kill them off. We have to wonder why this is so. Women are not faint-hearted. They kill abusive husbands, lovers; they even sometimes, like Medea, kill their children. All of this, though horrifying, has been told before. But no woman in myth, story, or fairy tale does, can, or will, kill her father, even though many myths show the father killing the daughter. As has been shown, patricide is a primordial deed in the Greek myth of genesis, as it is in Freud's vision of history in "Civilization and Its Discontents," where it stands as the mark of male maturity, a sign of relinquishment of all claims to childish needs for paternal protection. In these versions, patricide is a masculine gesture which women are not allowed in fact or fantasy. In the few obscure tales where daughters do murder fathers, it is usually because she is caught between father and lover, and she is inevitably punished by the lover's later abandonment. To what depths must we go to reach the source of this taboo? How can a woman expect to overthrow the patriarchal social structure if she is not at least *willing* to contemplate patricide in her imagination? Why does this particular act cause so much cultural anxiety? Since women are not immune from feelings of rage, revenge, violence, or even competition, why don't they enact, in myth, literature, or even actual life, what is such a commonly accepted homicide for men? What are the ways women have found to psychologically and imaginatively separate themselves from their fathers? Do we do it like Emily Dickinson did with her "murderous tendencies," without ever having to face up to what we are doing? Or are women's ways of killing off the father different and therefore not readily apparent or visible?

Sylvia Plath broke the taboo against "killing the father" in her powerful poem of liberation. When she read her poem "Daddy" on the BBC, she introduced it by saying: "Here is a poem spoken by a girl with an Electra complex. Her father died while she thought he was God."[48] Addressed to her dead father, Otto, she resurrects him only to assassinate him. But this poem moves quickly beyond the personal father and reaches deeply into the archetypal father:

> You do not do, you do not do
> Any more, black shoe
> In which I have lived like a foot
> For thirty years, poor and white,
> Barely daring to breathe or Achoo.
>
> Daddy, I have had to kill you.
> You died before I had time—
> Marble-heavy, a bag full of God,
> Ghastly statue with one gray toe
> Big as a Frisco seal.

Identifying herself as a Jew, Plath sees her father as Hitler. In taking the Holocaust as her allegory, she focuses on the sado-masochistic relationship, the dominance-submission theme that runs throughout her experience of male-female and father-daughter relationship. The woman/Jew/daughter is victimized by the man/Nazi/father. The relationship is saturated with sadomasochism: "Every woman adores a Fascist, / The boot in the face, the brute / Brute heart of a brute like you."

Hitler easily slips into becoming the devil and the poet comes face to face with evil.

You stand at the blackboard, daddy,
In the picture I have of you,
A cleft in you chin instead of your foot
But no less a devil for that, no not
Any less the black man who

Bit my pretty red heart in two.
I was ten when they buried you.
At twenty I tried to die
And get back, back, back to you.
I thought even the bones would do.

Linking the death of her father and her own suicide attempt at twenty, she senses that her marriage to Ted Hughes was made to a man who could carry her father's stamp. The poem, written as her marriage was breaking up, four months before she died, ties together and then demolishes the images of husband, daddy, Hitler, the devil.

I made a model of you,
A man in black with a Meinkampf look
And a love of the rack and the screw.
And I said I do, I do.
So daddy, I'm finally through.
The black telephone's off at the root,
The voices just can't worm through

If I've killed one man, I've killed two—
The vampire who said he was you
And drank my blood for a year,
Seven years, if you want to know.
Daddy, you can lie back now.

There's a stake in your fat black heart
And the villagers never liked you.
They are dancing and stamping on you.
They always *knew* it was you
Daddy, Daddy, you bastard, I'm through.

Many interpreters cannot understand Plath's rage—she was not Jewish, her father was not a Nazi, nor is there any "evidence" that he mistreated her—so how could she have manufactured a poem that is such a sustained work of unadulterated fury, revenge, and, above all, murder? In light of the fact that this "murder" did not, in the end, liberate her or exorcise the demonic influences that fed her madness, the poem is chilling. However, it still stands as one of her best works articulating for many women the need and desire to somehow at last be quit of the demonic father and his power. In any case, it is one of the few works that have directly and purposefully broken the taboo of daughters committing patricide.

Although rooted in it, clearly the poem "Daddy" is more than a working out of Plath's personal father relationship. One feminist critic believes the poem should be "read as an allegory about the way in which the father-daughter relationship dominates the female psyche in our culture. Father and daughter are exaggerated figures of authority and obedience—exaggerated . . . in order to explode the tragic glory of father worship in the Electra myth."[49] Plath's strategy is to kill the father in order to get herself back.

The poems Plath wrote from September 26, 1962 to February 5, 1963 are the ones for which she is best known, the ones that come from her "true deep voice." Four months before she died, she wrote: "I am a writer . . . I am a genius of a writer; I have it in me. I am writing the best poems of my life; they will make my name."[50]

In these last poems, she murders and escapes, she drives a stake into the heart of her father complex, she eats men like air, she looses the lioness, and she flies away in "the upflight of the murderess into a heaven that loves her."[51] Her true self takes many forms. Disguised as "a queen bee, bear, superman, train, an acetylene virgin, a horse, a risen corpse, an arrow, or a baby,"[52] Plath labors to give birth to herself. No longer a passive male-defined Eve ("this Adam's woman"), she begins her process of poetic incarnation. In these later works, Plath reclaims her female body and its processes as metaphors for her poetic labors: "Plath manipulates her body as a psychic and physical space; imaginatively transforms it into fantastic shapes; submits it to fire; freezes it into statuary; and translates it into figures of speed and flight."[53] Through imagery of fire and air, she fuses her woman's body with her poetic process, forming "a female body of imagination" that gives rise to her most transformative poetry.

Plath also takes on God, not as a child but as a woman. "O God, I am not like you, / In your vacuous black, / Stars stuck all over, bright stupid confetti. / Eternity bores me, / I never wanted it."[54] Like Dickinson who referred to God as an "eclipse," Plath calls God the "great Stasis" and asks, "What is so great in that!"

Like Dickinson, Plath also undertook several variations of the regeneration theme by appropriating the Christian myth of Jesus raising Lazarus from the dead. In her poem "Lady Lazarus,"[55] she addresses her capacity to die—"Dying / is an art, like everything else. I do it exceptionally well."—and, to raise herself from the dead—"I have done it again. / One year in every ten / I manage it—" Lady Lazarus assumes the position of Christ—not Christ as savior, but Christ as masochist, since these dyings and revivings are performances done at the behest of "Herr Doktor," "Herr Enemy." Putting herself in an abjectly masochistic relationship with the male deity who raises her from the dead in these theatricals, she mocks him as "Herr God," "Herr Lucifer." Naming his resurrections of her as a carnival show for "the peanut crunching crowd," she directly confronts, challenges, and warns the male patriarch with her own version of resurrection. "Beware, Beware." Usurping Jesus' miraculous power for her own, she performs a female act of resurrection that is, if nothing else, aggressive. A female phoenix rising: "Out of the ash / I rise with my red hair / And I eat men like air."

"Lady Lazarus" has been read as "an allegory about the woman artist's struggle for autonomy. The female creature of a male artist-god is asserting independent creative powers."[56] This is an accurate assessment, one that reconciles with Plath's own intention. But Plath's description of the poem also includes a very down-to-earth practicality. In the BBC reading of the poem, she describes "Lady Lazarus" as "a woman who has the great and terrible gift of being reborn. The only trouble is, she has to die first. She is the Phoenix, the libertarian spirit, what you will. She is also just a good, plain, very resourceful woman."[57]

In addition to "Lady Lazarus," many other poems from Plath's last four months are infused with the metaphor of death and rebirth, making this a poetry filled with the desperately hard labor of de-structuring and re-creating herself anew: Lady Lazarus, the acetylene virgin, the queen bee, and the lioness are distinctly sexually aggressive females intent on their own trajectory. Working with the alchemy of fire and air, Plath uses her female passion to fuel her art.

She confronts the tyranny of standards for female normalcy which her mother modeled and she herself strove for with a vengeance—relational attachments, pleasing others, self-sacrifice. She understands them now as building blocks of the prison, the wax house, the mausoleum. In her beehive poems, Plath appropriates her father's craft of beekeeping for the metaphor needed to vent herself. As the returning, raging, vengeful daughter, she emerges from the hive as queen bee.

> ... I
> Have a self to recover, a queen,
> Is she dead, is she sleeping?
> Where has she been,
> With her lion-red body, her wings of glass?
>
> Now she is flying
> More terrible than she ever was, red
> Scar in the sky, red comet
> Over the engine that killed her—
> The mausoleum, the wax house.[58]

Escape was the only route out of a life of "Measuring the flour, cutting off the surplus, / Adhering to rules, to rules, to rules."[59] No longer "the little toy wife" she springs forth as the lioness. Her rage becomes "creative violence."[60] Like Dickinson, who once dared the reader to "see a soul in white heat," Plath, in the furnace of her own creative fires, becomes a self-seeding, self-fertilizing, self-pleasuring virgin—needing no man, she performs her poetic parthenogenesis.

> Does not my heat astound you. And my light.
> All by myself I am a huge camellia
> Glowing and coming and going, flush on flush.

> I think I am going up,
> I think I may rise—
> The beads of hot metal fly, and I, love, I
> Am a pure acetylene
> Virgin
> Attended by roses
>
> * * * * *
>
> (My selves dissolving, old whore petticoats)—
> To Paradise.[64]

Plath's trajectory towards transformation is desperate and extreme, its annihilating intensity determined by the forces of past suppressions of self.

Her deep, intuitive drive for rebirth feels to me like a remembering of ancient female wisdom. Like that most famous of goddess symbols, the regenerative snake, she is frantic to shed her skin: "And I, stepping from this skin / Of old bandages, boredoms, old faces"[62] In Plath's poetic mythology, Hera's Great Goddess Moon cycle of birth, death, and regeneration, the natural rhythm so severed by the culture of enforced femininity, seems to be the unconscious driving force.

Perfection

Sylvia Plath died by her own hand on February 11, 1963, during the coldest, bitterest winter in recent London history. When Plath turned the gas oven on in her apartment, she was just thirty years old, a mother of two small children. She was in the process of getting a divorce from the poet Ted Hughes, and she had been writing the most powerful poetry of her entire life. This poetry was inversely proportional to the letters she had written home to her mother during all of her adult life. If the letters home had been drenched in sweetness, her last poetry was bitter and violent; if the letters to her mother had been consistently and determinedly bright and optimistic, her poetry was filled with ghastly, haunting imagery. If the daughter was a bubbly, effusive, all-American girl, the poet was a wild, orgiastic, sexual creature. The disparity between these two personas has provided many Plath critics with the evidence to prove that Plath suffered from a kind of "split personality" which led to her destruction. There is no doubt that Plath's strategy of a double self was one born out of psychological desperation.

Plath's struggle between the "two selves" is written out in the poem "In Plaster,"[63] where the clean, perfect, white plaster "nice self" who is so "superior" gives way to "Old Yellow," the ugly, hairy and yellow one who lives inside the impeccable white plaster shell. It is "the yellow one" who has the last word, and in a chilling final stanza announces: "I'm collecting my strength; one day I shall manage without her, / And she'll perish with emptiness then, and begin to miss me."

Many feminist critics of Plath understand her life and work in terms of the impossible dialectic waged between these two split selves, one warring with the other.

In some ways, Plath knew that the perfection demanded of her—by her mother, her man, her culture, herself—would kill her. By contrast, the imperfect woman filled with rage, the "ugly and hairy" hag who is petty, jealous, vindictive, vicious, and cruel is also the emotionally honest poet. When Plath finally appears in her poetry as her true self, in her "Ariel" persona, she is a high priestess, moon goddess, a female Lazarus arising from the dead, a queen bee, a sexually passionate, self-pleasuring woman who creates parthenogenically. Birthing herself in rage and pain, she rises out of the ash with her red hair, eating men like air. But her very last poem swings irrevocably back to the other perfect, white persona. In this poem, she offers the perfected woman up to those who liked her best when she was good: "The woman is perfected / Her dead / Body wears the smile of accomplishment."[64] In short, Plath says, a perfect woman is a dead woman.

It is said that no other goddess was punished by Zeus as Hera was, and it could equally be said that no other woman poet has been so slandered as Plath has been after her death. Called an "Oedipal victim," a "violated little girl," accused as a manipulator, a pornographer, and a "bitch goddess," a "priestess cultivating her hysteria," "a woman who despises herself as a woman," a "pseudo-male," and "the Marilyn Monroe of the literati," Plath has obviously hit a nerve in our collective psyches.[65]

The goddess Hera retained into classical Greek times two important vestiges of her earlier powers over which she still reigned supreme: only she could bestow the gift of prophecy on any human or beast she pleased, and only she could punish with madness. Sylvia Plath was the recipient of both.

4. APHRODITE

"And it is I who empowered these moist espousals,
I, the great Aphrodite. . . .
—*Aeschylus, The Danaides*[1]

I cannot think of any need in childhood as strong as the need for a father's protection.
—*Sigmund Freud*[2]

I believe if I have genius it is a genius for loving.
—*Anais Nin*[3]

I am a writer. I would rather have been a courtesan.
—*Anais Nin*[4]

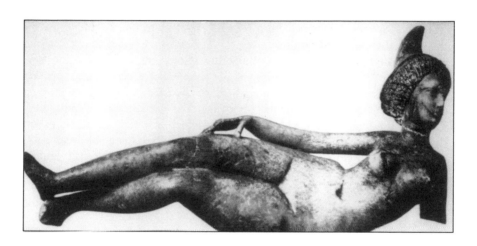

11. *Reclining Woman*

Sexual Desire in the Battlezone

In the Greek myth of genesis, after Saturn castrates Ouranos, he tosses his father's severed genitals over his left shoulder. The detached phallus lands in the lap of the great ocean mother, inseminating her. Out of the foaming froth arises the goddess Aphrodite. Born out of her father's castration, the goddess of love emerges from the salty sea waters in full-bodied bloom. She is not a true daughter of Saturn, she has not been swallowed by the father, nor has she spent time in the Belly of the Father. Rather she has been tossed aside. Landing in the stormy seas where the waves carried her for a long time, she develops on her own, outside the central drama of devouring.

When Aphrodite emerges from the sea, she sets foot on holy Cythera. "There she came forth, lovely, much revered, and the grass grew up beneath her delicate feet." From Cythera she went, again by way of the sea, to the island of Cyprus which was encircled by waves. From Cyprus she came to Greece. Her entry into the classical Greek pantheon from "out there" gives some indication of her "otherness," a condition that remains with her throughout time.

As the goddess of love, Aphrodite is not simply, nor even first and foremost, an expression of the instinctual mating instinct; she is not about reproductive fertility, like her half-sister, Demeter, whom she does not appreciate. Aphrodite is the great sensualist. She is not wild. She is refined, she tempers erotic passion through the cultivation of the arts of lovemaking. Beauty is her aphrodisiac.

On Mount Olympus she is greatly revered, yet always regarded with ambivalence. With the exception of her sworn-to-virginity sisters—Athena, Artemis, and Hestia—she exercises her powers over everyone. Even great Zeus is not safe from her powers of persuasion and the potential madness of her effect. In Greek myth, Aphrodite herself is not always in charge of what happens when her powers are loosed, and sometimes even she suffers from her own medicine. Attempts to control her fail miserably, and although Zeus marries her off to the crippled artisan, Hephaestus, her energy remains fluid and unbounded, definitely not containable in marriage. Apprehension and distrust of her untamable powers are countered by the yearning desire for her blessing. This double-edged response to Aphrodite travels from ancient Olympus down to the present time.

Today the deep human impulse to connect with Aphrodite is both desired and demeaned and devalued. Men look to *Playboy* magazine to get the gift of her quickening and then look to the ordinary women in their lives to satisfy their sexual fantasy. Women look to *Cosmopolitan* for their instruction on the art of love and find their powers trivialized.

Oftentimes a woman who is beginning to wake up will find herself in conflict about her sexuality. If she has overstayed in the Belly of the Father she will find herself still operating within the "daughter complex," where her sexuality remains caught within the confines of conventional heterosexual arrangements, particularly an immature marriage. She may marry an older man, a man like her father. But if she is in the process of awakening she will realize, like Jane Lazarre, that a womanly sexuality does not mix with fatherly prescriptions for his daughter. Writing about her father's response to her sexuality, Lazarre becomes aware of his need to have her be an Athena daughter, one whose sexuality was contained and far from chthonic:

> He wanted me to follow him into the labyrinths, my willfulness hope-fully chiseled into a responsible courage, armed with convictions in the face of inevitable adversity, but he wanted me to follow him fully dressed, and more: well-groomed in a *dignified* manner, a manner which could be trusted to contain the disturbing sexuality with its blood, its discharges, its sensuous odors, its complicated and unpre-dictable *desire*, that ebbed and flowed underneath.[5]

As Lazarre's insight reveals, a father's love and encouragement of his daughter may run counter to her own knowledge of sensuality. With this kind of fatherly "loving," the erotic desires of a woman may be easily lost. She may find herself married to a man similar to her father, a man who, although he may sincerely want her as a partner, denies the range of her womanly sexuality. A woman in this situation may find herself happily married yet erotically silenced.[6]

It often comes as a terrible surprise to a woman that she is so split in two. She may not even be aware of this until she is swept up, willy nilly, into an affair with a man who can meet and match her sexually. Oftentimes this is the only way she can find to break the patriarchal rule of being a "good" girl: by being "bad" she can have her sexuality and possibly her own autonomy. One woman in this position dreamt of being offered a beautiful cake and told that she could have just the frosting if she wanted. She realized in the dream that she wanted the cake, too, and then was told that she could have the frosting anytime, even with sandwiches. This dream gave her an interesting twist on having her cake and eating it, too. But the stakes of having a sexually satisfying affair while maintaining a successful marriage are often high and the balancing act strenuous, despite the immediate boon to one's renewed sense of self.

On the other hand, a woman may find herself falling deeply in love with another woman, pulled into the love that has no name. As Susan Griffin writes in her essay, "The Uncharted Body," this love happens against all odds: "Ringed by an alliance of institutional and cultural prohibitions, silence, or rather, the muting of speech, it is a miracle every time the desire of one woman for another is pro-nounced."[7] Reclaiming one's sexuality, re-establishing ownership over one's own body, learning to love and trust the wisdom of one's body can be a long, lonely, and painful process for a Daughter of Saturn. It is a hard fact of our culture that a woman has to work tirelessly to keep herself undivided.

Many women feel the deep impulse of Aphrodite in their lives, but they do not know her name or to whom they are in service. Women who intuit that their sexual energy is a power for healing, women who are moved to create a sexual ambience in which soul talk between a man and a woman can occur, women who are driven by their desires to touch, awaken, and inspire other women through their sexuality are often confused by the power that lies within them, the power that has not been rightly named. Oftentimes a woman with this kind of energy will live a double life, she may be by all accounts an ordinary-looking, conventional, even proper woman. But emanating from her very essence, in her gestures, her clothes, in how she holds her body, there is a palpable message, an aura of knowledgeable sensuality. A woman like this is likely to imbue every activity with a kind of golden sheen, making everyone feel special in her presence. If she is at all conscious of her abilities and if they have been gained outside the injurious force of early childhood sexual abuse, the woman will be seen as marvelous, fascinating, magical in her ability to transform an ordinary event into a special moment. If, on the other hand, her motivation arises out of revenge for past sexual injury, she may use her powers in a manipulative, coercive, and defensive way.

It is an extremely sensitive and delicate issue for women. Most women have been hurt in some way by the highly sexualized culture in which we live, whether experienced acutely through actual sexual transgression or subtly through the constant bombardment of sexual innuendo and pressure to be sexually attractive and available. It takes a great deal of consciousness for a woman to salvage a relationship to her sexuality that feels truly her own, in bondage to no one. Most women are not taught that the sexual fire that lives inside their bodies is a source of healing and transformation both for themselves and for the people they wish to share it with. We are taught that sex is powerful, dangerous, good if in the right context, but we are not taught that it is sacred.

The effort to reclaim and use our erotic energy as a resource for change is a radical and revolutionary act. Any woman who learns how to awaken the sacred fire in her body must move through layers of confusion, depression, anger, and fear. Confronting the forces, both personal and collective, that have kept us away from this ultimate source of female knowledge and power is never easy.[8] As Audre Lorde imagines it, the erotic exists in that highly charged space between the self and "the chaos of our strongest feelings."[9] Once we have experienced the fullness of this deep feeling, all else will be measured in relation to its magnitude.

The connection between sexual energy and creativity is profound. It is almost impossible for a woman to have one without the other. This does not mean that a woman has to be genitally active to be creative, but it does mean that she has to be in contact with her own erotic life if she wishes to feel her own creative juices. When a woman learns to touch and claim her connection with erotic energy, this gives her the power to transform all aspects of her life, including and especially her creative work. As Lorde says, "Within the celebration of the erotic in all our endeavors, my work becomes a conscious decision—a longed-for bed which I enter gratefully and from which I rise up empowered."[10]

Anais Nin: A Genius for Loving

The effort it takes for a woman to aspire to a clear place of reverence and joy for her sexuality and her creativity is nowhere expressed more completely than in the life and work of Anais Nin. Her biography, fiction, and diaries tell of a long career dedicated to exercising her sexual powers to the fullest extent possible, all the while exploring the darkest corners of her own desires. She combined her drive for self-expression and creative fulfillment through sexual experience with a deep devotion towards documentation of her progress towards that end. She has left us with a monumental record of a woman's sexual and artistic development— an intricately detailed 150-volume diary which spans a period of over fifty years.

Anais Nin's childhood struggles with a narcissistic, physically and sexually abusing, and abandoning father left a permanent mark upon her life. Her efforts to undo, retaliate against, and repair the damage through a multitude of sexual relationships are also what drove her creative process.

Nin's story is filled with the perils of being a priestess of Aphrodite in a pro-fane world. Her rage, revenge, and grief at having her riches devalued are familiar to many women, while the extremes she went to for restitution are unusual, breathtaking, and outrageous. Through her story, we can begin to understand what a tremendous undertaking it is for a woman to restore the damage of abuse and consciously claim the power of her sexuality. For Nin that quest informed what became her most important creative work.

The Return of the Repressed

If we think about her at all, Anais Nin exists in most of our minds as a diarist, a woman who charted what Freud called "the dark continent" of women's sexual desire. She is mostly known for her passionate affair with the novelist Henry Miller, the quintessential pornographer of *Tropic of Cancer*. Her diaries have been in print, in a censored version, for over twenty years, and even in that sanitized form they have inspired many women who recognized in Nin the ultimate "woman" artist.

Nin's diaries, which she began in 1914, provide the most extensive psychologi-cal documentation of the development of a woman artist that we have. They are not purely accurate recordings and reportage, however, since Nin did not main-tain the usual distinction between art and reality—the diaries underwent frequent and lifelong revisions, editings, even self-censorings. Unlike her lover, Henry Miller, Nin was not a "realist." She was a premier illusionist. She made her life into art and created art out of her life. Driven by an aphroditic aesthetic that demanded beauty above all else, she worked and re-worked her diaries until they became legendary, mythic. Despite the fantastic proportions, they reveal a vivid interiority, appointed with the most intricate tracings of a woman's psyche. The diary process served different purposes throughout Nin's life. At first, it was meant to be a document to her missing father; then it became a place where she

12. Anais Nin

13. Joaquin Nin

allowed her real feelings to be explored and expressed; at certain times in her life the diary was the only centering device amidst a welter of fragmented subpersonalities. Finally it became her literary claim to fame.

Nin seemed to know all along that the ever-increasing document was her most important work. Throughout her life, she carefully protected the diaries from loss, salvaging them from war-torn Europe, carrying them with her when she moved back to New York City from Paris, installing them in a bank safety-deposit box. The diaries were her personal and creative treasure cache, which she herself plundered for most of her fictional writing—her serious short stories, as well as her mercenary-inspired pieces of "erotica."

While the diaries have been published and available to readers in expurgated form since the 1970s, the unexpurgated work arrived only recently as *Henry and June* and *Incest*. The early expurgated diaries veiled the deeper driving force behind the work, the damage, the abuse, the abandonment by her father. The recent publication of the unexpurgated versions of her adult diaries allows for a fuller appreciation of the cruder material Nin was trying to refine, the lead she was turning into gold through her aphroditic alchemy of sexuality and the creative process.

The Struggles

Anais Nin (1903–1977) was born in Paris. Her father, Joaquin Nin y Castellanos, was a well-known Cuban-born composer and concert pianist whose career took him on extensive tours throughout Europe. When Anais was ten years old, her father, a self-acknowledged Don Juan, completely abandoned his wife and three children to live with a younger woman. Following this desertion, Nin's pragmatic and resourceful mother packed her family up and moved them to New York City. It was during this transatlantic passing that eleven-year-old Anais began to write her first diary. Composed primarily of letters filled with longing for her absent father, she began this precocious piece of work by pasting in a nude photograph of herself. The photograph was one out of "countless pictures" that her father had taken of her as a young girl.

This childish gesture would set the tone for all her later desires to be seen by men. As an adult, she would report about these photographic scenes with her father, "He wanted to see me naked. All admiration came by way of the camera."[11] Her father's abusive voyeurism in photographing his young daughter in this way, his use of her small body as sexual object, puts him in the category of sexual perpetrator. In her earliest diary, she tries to remember the violent quarrels between her parents and recalls begging her father not to leave, his hypochondriasis, his quirky vegetarianism. She also remembers his brutal acts: killing a cat in anger, beating her and her brothers, spanking her on her bare bottom. His emotional and physical abuse of her mixed and fused in her psyche with his abandonment. Her adolescent longing for him and his love would result in what later amounted to a relentless pursuit of male admiration.

After her father's desertion when she was ten, Nin saw her father once briefly in her early twenties and not again until their fateful meeting when she was thirty. His influence, however, was always there, prompting, pushing, in her blood. When she met him again as an adult, she made an instant identification with the dark side of his sexual narcissism and she called him her "Double," her "dearly beloved Shadow."[12] The wrongful sexual attention in combination with his emotional and physical abandonment set up a powerfully destructive explosive in her psyche, one that took her a lifetime to defuse.

As I have noted before, a father's response to his daughter's developing sexuality is an important factor in her feelings about herself and her future sexual choices. If he is respectful and unafraid, the daughter will learn to find and expect that from her own lovers. If he is dismissive, unavailable and distant, a girl will feel tentative and weakened. Nancy Chodorow describes the effects of a distant father on a girl's subsequent heterosexual relationships:

> The young girl (and the woman she becomes) is willing to deny her father's limitations (and those of her lover or husband) as long as she feels loved. She is more able to do this because his distance means that she does not really know him. The relationship, then, because of the father's distance and importance to her, occurs largely as fantasy and idealization.[13]

This is exactly the effect that her father's abandonment had on Nin. Although she would later "remember" his violence and his abuse, what is most memorable is his emotional distance, and how that created in her an unmitigated idealization as well as a driving desire to get him back in some way:

> I never saw my father living and talking intellectually, brilliantly—never heard the vigourous blasphemies and obscenities Mother complained of later; but it was enough to catch a glimpse of Father's face as he passed me on his way out of the house or into the parlor, that awakened, alert, vital face; it was enough to have tasted the flavor of the wall-covering books, to have heard from afar the reverberations of animated talks and music—enough to create an atmosphere which, from then on, I have wistfully sought to recapture.[14]

Her father's abuse and abandonment also set up an aura of fragility around Nin as a woman, a quality that she would learn to cultivate because she knew men found it irresistible. But hidden behind the many veils of vulnerability would be a woman seriously engaged in exercising her powers of seduction and retribution.

For most of her adult life, Nin's choice of partners turned out to be men who came close to her father in their depression, their pattern of distancing, their emotional withdrawal. Her efforts to achieve a fatherly esteem, approval, and

recognition from these men left her continually begging. As in the early photographs, she learned to pose as a perpetual daughter with them, a *puella aeturna*,
an eternal girl, playful, teasing, seductive, and secretly anxious. She concealed her
identification with her father—his specialness, his romantic genius, his gloomy
and intellectual outlook, his promiscuity—confessing it only to her diary.

Although Nin's father photographed his daughter nude, he also called her
"ugly" and frequently judged her looks as if she were already a womanly sexual
object. A father's proclamation about or mismeasurement of his young daughter's
erotic appeal puts a heavy weight on her. The more actively disparaging or cruel
the father is toward his daughter in this regard, the more devastated she will feel,
her self-worth and self-esteem lost in the paternal calculation. If the father's attitudes are left unrepaired by the mother's affirmation, a daughter may later find
herself on a rebellious rampage to find and win the recognition and attention for
her body and her sexuality she desires.

As a society, we do not have much understanding or compassion for the promiscu-
ous behavior of women. Nor do we provide ways for girls and young women to break
out of that kind of destructive pattern for seeking paternal love; rather we support
them in it. As Phyllis Chesler writes: "Psychologically, women do not have initiation
rites to help them break their incestuous ties. While most women do not commit
incest with their biological fathers, patriarchal marriage, prostitution, and mass
"romantic" love are psychologically predicated on sexual union between Daughter and
Father figures."[15] Religious institutions participate in this program as well by keeping
women in childish relationships with priestly Fathers, and a male God.

Although Anais Nin was raised Catholic, she left the Church in late adolescence. Nin's lack of belief in the Father God, like Emily Dickinson's, was directly
related to the abandonment by her father, but unlike the New England poet,
Nin's rejection of father-oriented religiosity did not cause her anxiety or meta-
physical wrestling with God the Father. Where Dickinson sublimated her rage
against her personal father and took it out on God, Nin freed her mind of religion
in order to follow what was of more interest to her—the intriguing pursuit of aesthetic, psychological, and sensual experience.

Nin may have successfully extricated her mind from Catholicism, but she
could not so easily free her body from the childhood abuse. When she turned
twenty, she married Hugh Guiler, a young man, stiffly proper, and solidly planted
on the lucrative road to a career in banking. His awkward, fumbling sexual inex-
perience met and combined with her sexual terror. The "gross" aspects of physicality revulsed and repelled her, and for years she simmered in the erotic
frustration of an unconsummated marriage.

The Divided Self

Like all the previous writers, Nin developed, in her teen-age years, a dual persona
in her writings: Linotte, a good and perfect girl, who dressed demurely and went

to Mass, the one she calculated that her perfectionistic father would love; and Anais, a sexually curious "coquette," a bad and "wicked" girl who paints her face and pretends she is an actress. In her marriage she continued to cultivate this divided self, this time the dual personae were predicated upon her parents' model: the good, faithful, attentive wife/mother and the exotic, sexually flirtatious, bad, whore/father. Clearly, her burgeoning sexuality both fascinated and scared her. Perpetually overheated with romantic fantasy and intensely seductive, she worked to channel all sexual feeling into aesthetics, clothes, and furniture, as well as her diary writing. She continued to forestall any sexual intimacy, the fleshy reality of which felt disgusting and terrifying. When she finally broke through the barrier of sexual terror, the carefully cultivated and controlled dual personality splintered into a hundred pieces, each reflecting shard becoming a different sexual persona.

When she was twenty-seven, Anais Nin met Henry Miller, a Brooklyn novelist, whose raw vitality and earthiness initiated her into an intensely literary and passionately sexual affair. It was a highly charged union fueled by their opposing personalities—"delicate and violent"—and their mutual love for and dedication to writing. Anais documented the most frenzied years of her lifelong relationship with Henry Miller in her diary, an edited version appearing during her lifetime. The unexpurgated version was posthumously published and filmed as *Henry and June*.

With Miller, Nin was launched into her career as a sexual woman. She would spend almost the remainder of her life engaged in an intricate pattern of sexual seduction with many men and some women. Her approach to all relationships was based on what she would refer to as her "genius for loving." In the early years, she was particularly skilled at seducing the men who were her "father figures," men of importance in the world, scholars, psychoanalysts—John Erskine, Rene Allendy, Otto Rank. But she also consistently sought out other men, men who seemed to emanate a kind of dark and twisted eroticism, the more hidden side of her father's obsessional sexuality. She found her father's sensual sadism in sensitive and artistic men like Antonin Artaud and her gay cousin, Eduardo. And all the while she kept the marriage to Hugh Guiler going, complete with dinners, entertaining, vacations, and an active, though always strained, sexual life.

During her years in Paris, she frequently complained about the demands that her life made on her—having sex with Miller in the morning, the analyst Allendy in the afternoon, and husband Hugh at night—yet she seemed to welcome the almost psychotic fragmentation as the condition and price for her creative life. "An artist," she says "is born with a mania to complete himself, to create himself. He is so multiple and amorphous that his central self is constantly falling apart and is only recomposed by his work."[16] One could seriously question the origin of the mania: Was it her innate artistic temperament or the manic drive to repair the injury done by her abusive father? Mostly she believed it was the artist's fate. Yet, as she, herself, once acknowledged: "Father betrayed me and I split . . . into a million small relationships."[17] Aware of how the drive for sexual seduction was implicated in her creative life, she observed: "Every act related to my writing was connected in me with an act of charm, seduction of my father. . . . In my dreams at night I did not achieve a work of art and present the world with it, but I lay naked in bed (with an invisible lover) and all the world could see me."[18] She also used her diary as if it *were* her sexuality, offering its intimacy to certain chosen others to read, often as a prelude to an affair. In this way the diary, like her own body, passed through many hands.

In her early fiction, Nin documented the effects of her father's abuse. Her descriptions are familiar to us now when sexual abuse has been named and claimed for the devastation that it causes. When Nin was writing, Freud had already submerged childhood sexual abuse into the realm of adult fantasy and wish fulfillment, so Nin did not directly name her own abuse. But reading her fiction today, we recognize all of the unmistakable signs of childhood sexual trauma: the dissociation, the encapsulation, the feelings of unreality, the sensation of being split and fragmented, the seeking for love mixed with the desire for revenge, the terrible difficulty with physical intimacy.

In "Children of the Albatross,"[19] the young woman, Djuna (Nin), remembers her childhood as a time when she "had been split into two pieces by some great invisible saber cut." Although she was now a young woman, living on her own, she still felt, like any woman who has been abused as a child, "cut in the middle of her body." The division manifested as a distinctly different inner and outer persona, one part relating to the world, the other in a desperate search for safety and self-protection:

> In the external world she was the woman who had submitted to mysterious outer fatalities beyond her power to alter, and in the interior world she was a woman who had built many tunnels deeper down where no one could reach her, in which she deposited her treasures safe from destruction and in which she built a world exactly the opposite of the one she knew.[20]

This need for an elaborate labyrinthian safety is a clear sign of trauma as well as an image of extreme psychic isolation.

As Djuna begins to make her life as a dancer, she inevitably meets men who want to love her. Her ballet master approaches her, simply, respectfully, yet passionately, and the erotic energy that is released sends her spinning. When he asks her to be his partner on the road, she reaches tentatively toward the possibility: "Hadn't she been the woman in quest of her body once lost by a shattering blow—submerged, and now floating again on the surface where uncrippled human beings lived in a world of pleasure . . . ?"[21] Yet, because of her unhealed early trauma, she cannot accept this simple man's invitation. "There is something broken inside of me. I cannot dance, live, love as easily as others."[22] She was sure she would sabotage the whole affair, break her leg, cause some disaster.

In her mind Djuna travels back to her adolescence spent in an orphanage where the only man in the place, the Watchman, dealt out privileges, gifts, and permissions to go out at night. (Although Nin makes the abuser in her story the Watchman, this phantom figure quickly merges with that of father.) She describes the strange feeling of being "special" that being sexually abused can sometimes give the victim: "The one he chose felt endowed immediately with greater beauty, greater charm and power than the other girls. He was appointed the arbiter, the connoisseur, the bestower of decorations."[23] The Watchman chose Djuna, and in this paternal role he possessed a will "she did not even question, a continuation of the will of the father."[24]

Now however, Djuna was released from all that: she was a young woman with her own life to live. But even though "Djuna thought the figure of the Watchman was long since lost, she would hear echoes of his heavy step . . . she still had the feeling that she might be overpowered by a will stronger than her own, might be trapped, might be somehow unable to free herself, unable to escape the demands of man upon her."[25] And although she was no longer helpless, "the echo of this helplessness was so strong that she still dreaded the possessiveness and willfulness of older men."[26] This is a powerful description of what adult survivors of childhood sexual assault feel. The abuse invades and intrudes on all later attempts at intimacy in the form of flashbacks, uninvited memories, giving the past an uncanny and unwanted vitality in present time.

In "Children of the Albatross," Nin uses a metaphor that symbolizes the kind of encapsulated dead space that sexual trauma creates in a woman's psyche. In her story, Nin uses the house, a common metaphor for the self in dreams, as an image for Djuna's inner life. The house that Djuna lives in has twelve window faces. "But one shutter was closed and corresponded to no room. During some transformation of the house, it had been walled up."[27] Djuna had chosen this house "because of this window which led to no room, because of this impenetrable room, thinking that someday she would discover an entrance to it."[28] Djuna worked to create this house so that it would be reflective of her rich and beautiful inner world: "rooms of flesh and Chinese lacquer, sea greens to walk through, inside of me there are lighted candles, live fires, shadows, spaces, open doors, shelters and air currents. Inside of me there is color and warmth."[29] Yet the perfection of her artifice and the one shuttered window kept people at bay. The house was like a myth, a dream. People stayed away—"None came near enough." And she realized: "There were houses, dresses, which created one's isolation. . . . which appeared to be made to lure but which were actually effective means to create distance."[30]

Djuna's dilemma was clearly an expression of Nin's own predicament—the impasse of a woman with a divided self. One part, traumatized and sealed off, "closed hermetically into muteness;" the other lonely, desperately desirous of contact: "one intent on creating trap doors of evasion, the other wishing someone might find the entrance that she might not be so alone."[31] The "shuttered window," the sealed off trauma, interfered with her ability to grow, to truly love. "It was enough for a man to possess certain attributes of the father—any man possessed of power—and then her being came alive with fear as if the entire situation would be re-enacted inevitably: possession, love and desertion. . . ."[32] Every authoritarian step announced the return of the father and danger, for the father's last words had been: "I will come back."[33] And for that event, one part of the woman waited, arrested in motion, frozen in place, while the other still felt the wound and mistook the pain she felt for being alive, the pain warning and guiding her.

In this remarkable short story, Nin reveals the intricacy of the traumatized psyche—the multitude of masks, disguises, evasions, and defenses raised to deal with the fundamental problems of autonomy and intimacy that are the inevitable adult sequels to childhood abuse. As Nin so clearly shows, Djuna remains a prisoner of her childhood, held captive by the unrecovered trauma. Nin was to write and rewrite Djuna's tale, a repetition in many variations, a telling and retelling of Nin's own abuse.

Nin's quest for an intimacy that would open the "shuttered window" of her trauma and release its hold on her drove her to engage in a great number of relationships. All of them were characterized by a desire for deep communion, and all were haunted by her fears of abandonment. Her intense drive to break into life, to break through the barrier of sexual terror, to fully enter the world of passion, was reckless. Although she herself felt (and acted at times) fearless with one man, there was always a need to rush back to another for protection. She sought out powerful men, particularly psychoanalysts, who offered her the care and nurturing she desired. By idealizing certain men, she buried the effects of the abuse and, in the name of love, she worked to gain her identity as a woman.

One of those men whom she invested with the protector role was her first analyst, Rene Allendy:

> As soon as life terrorizes me, I think of him—I need him. The femaleness in me needs him. I need man. And men have been so protective to me—so good even when they were weak—that I need them forever, that I confess this need, this dependence on man, that in return I give the woman's only gift: love, love, love.[34]

Later, in a conscious willful assertion of her womanly powers and in a desire to relive her trauma by reversing it, she would seduce Allendy and he would, in turn, become the weak and needy one, the pathetic one needing her strength and vitality to support his sagging masculinity. Allendy's failure as an analyst to fend off the seduction, to interpret it for the trauma-related behavior that it was, kept the "shuttered window" of Nin's abuse closed.

During this period of her life, Nin was also struggling with herself as a woman artist. The woman and the artist, she felt, were two opposing and contradictory forces—a notion that was highly supported by the culture, particularly the culture of psychoanalysis which was directed towards helping Nin make an adjustment to herself as a woman. By contrast, Henry Miller, who was also cognizant of the division in Nin between woman and artist, supported the artist part, although he was also the major recipient of Nin's "womanly" generosity:

> Henry is so wise about me and my work—*he is good to the artist*—concerned because he thinks I am too womanly, that I give too much time to the house, to him, to others that I evade the final big task of my art, that I circumvent it with the journal—that he doesn't believe in forcing the end of the journal, but that one problem is simply displaced by another and that the art should overshadow the journal. The Journal is an escape from my art problem. . . .[35]

It is Nin, however, who is confused and ambivalent. Sensing her artist-self to be masculine in nature, she tries reveling in "pure" womanhood. That is, in providing Miller with everything he needs to write—"no anxieties, not even interruptions"—and getting her satisfaction by "subordinating everything to Henry's work," feeling joy in his "heavily loaded desk" while he is "writing extraordinarily well—amply—deeply." All the while she tells herself, "I don't believe the artist in me is in danger because, certainly, what I give Henry returns a thousandfold." She goes on to write: "Of course, I have not worked. I have been swimming in my contentment as a woman. Danger, danger, I suppose. But Henry is watching out. And after all, as a woman, purely a woman, I have been so rarely happy with this fullness."[36]

Except for Miller, Nin describes her lovers, the ones she has "loved so passionately and consistently," as "mental, patient, controlled, Saturnine, cold men."[37] She sees clearly "the darkening, stifling influence of Saturn" on these men and, as a true Daughter of Saturn, she declares, "I defeat Saturn by my tremendous luminosity and joy."[38] Later, however, she will feel possessed by her protean efforts to awaken and illumine these men.

> I have been obsessed by the potentialities, the mysteries of unflowered lives, of the secret obscurities and heavy inert weight of Saturn! . . . this pain of recurrent difficulty of bringing my half-alive men out of their caverns has aroused in me paroxysms of fury, despair, and tenacity. The desire to illumine chaos; to create out of chaos; to lift masses; to tackle mysteries, elusiveness, inertia; to arouse and conquer passivity—all this has caused me my greatest pain and and my greatest joy. . . .[39]

She imagines herself as some lonely yet magnificent priestess of Aphrodite performing her hieratic functions:

> I walk like a lamp-lighter; I push ships into the open sea, I unearth precious objects; I rub the patina off dark paintings; I tune, attune, bring forth, mold, bring out, ignite, support, sustain, inspire; I plant seeds; I

search caverns; I decipher hieroglyphs; I read the eyes of people—
alone—alone in my activity.[40]

Sleeping with the Father

Anais Nin's unexpurgated diary of 1932–1934, which she entitled *Incest*, documents one of the most intense periods of her life. Having just turned thirty, Nin
was simultaneously married, having a passionate literary and sexual affair with
Miller, and sexually exploring elsewhere. She was hungry, not only for repair to
sexual injury, nor just for sexual experience as such (although there is that), but
more for an experience of a truly embodied life, which she imagined primarily as
sexual in nature. It was as if she believed she could be brought out of her dissociated state and thrust more deeply and fully into realistic life through the avenue of
sexual experience. For Nin, realism was sexual, her desire for "this taste of earth . . .
a revenge upon the high spheres. . ." At one point she described her journal as " a
manual of love, passionate love, fleshly love, understanding love, pitying, maternal,
intellectual, artistic, creative, nonhuman . . ."[41] One of the most shocking aspects
of this time in her life was her renewed relationship with her father.

As she makes plans to meet her father in Chamonix during the summer of
1933, he writes her a letter infused with sexual innuendo.

> I dream of our escape toward the sun and of having you completely to
> myself for a few days. We both deserve that heavenly joy. Our heart,
> scorched at every flame, will burst joyfully into flower. The good seed will
> send forth strong, healthy shoots under the ardent warmth of our resusci-
> tated souls. Fugitives from a painful past, we come to each other to reforge
> our broken unity. . . . The gods will never have known greater happiness.[42]

With some presentiment she writes, before meeting him: "Father's letter,
Father's coming visit, they lie like a flower in the pages of a book. In the center of
my book, my journal, my life. My first idol."[43] This meeting comes in the midst
of her deepest sexual awakening. She has met him only once in the twenty years
following his abandonment of his family. In July 1933, Nin spent a momentous
nine days together with her father at a hotel in southern France.

When she first saw him, her father presented himself as an elegant, ordered
persona: handsome, refined, genteel, aristocratic—yet ultimately narcissistic. She
immediately assessed him and thought: "My Double! My evil Double! He incar-
nates my fears, my self doubts, my faults! He caricatures my tendencies. Something
human and warm in me fights, fights against his coldness. I seek the *differences*."[44]
Yet she found more similarities: "I look at my Double, and I see in a mirror."[45]

As a woman now, she saw in her father, the mask of coldness that terrorized her
as a child: "The tense will, the criticalness, the severity. How as a child I had the
obscure terror that this man could never be satisfied." Reflecting back on her own

development she wondered ". . . what this sense of my Father's exactingness contributed to my haunting pursuit of perfection. I wonder what obscure awareness of his demands, expectations of life, moved me to the great efforts I made."[46] And she felt regret for the past: "I regretted the years I did not know him, learn from him. I was proud, and I suffered from not being up to his ideal when I came from New York. I felt unprepared. I feared disappointing him. Together with forgiveness, there was much of the need to give Father the best in me. When I felt strong, I felt the time had come. But if I had been humble I might have learned from him."[47]

Yet when they meet, he was suffering from a paralyzing lumbago, surely a psychosomatically created condition which does not escape Nin's scrutiny: "He appears cold and formal. . . . He conceals his feelings. His face is a mask."[48] His mask and coldness, she found, cover a narcissistic humiliation about his infirmity, his stiffness. She noticed how the physical rigidity manifests in his behaviour and compares herself: "I could see in him a more rigid pattern. At certain moments I can yield, do without everything. His life is more molded than mine."[49]

The *senex* (old man) father has a hardening of consciousness which manifests in his body as lumbago, while his psychological stiffness permeates his existence as an inflexible set of structured demands. A true saturnian man, her father displayed a "chronic" temperament, overly concerned with time, the clock, and elaborate systems of order—fussing over his room, what he eats, his clothes, his daily schedule. At first these appeared to Nin as admirable qualities, revealing a kind of self-control, but were later recognized by her as rigidly established habits that exerted authoritarian control over others. His demands for structure served only to bind and fetter her spontaneity. In her journal account, she describes her father's compulsive need for order, an arranged universe: "A demand for punctuality. A need of order, like a carapace around the possibility of disorder, destruction, self-destruction."[50]

When she met her father at age thirty, Nin had already played out many sexual scenarios, always exploring the possibilities and potentials for sexual freedom.

> My life has been one long strain, one herculean effort and struggle to rise, to surpass in everything, to make myself a great character, to create, to perfect, to develop—a desperate and anxious ascension to efface and destroy a haunting insecurity about my own value. Always aiming higher, accumulating loves to compensate for the initial shock and terror of my first loss.[51]

Yet when she found her father, she felt she no longer needed him; rather, she sensed, it was he that needed her. Yet she recognized in his need a lover of the same dimensions as herself:

> I have found my father, the god, only to discover that I do not need him. When he comes to me, he who has marked my childhood so

deeply, I am already woman, and I am liberated of the need of Father and god. I am so absolutely woman that I understand my Father the human being—he is again the man who is also the child. . . .[52]

She was not there to punish him for the past. Instead, she imagined she was there as an agent for *his* liberation. "Now I have become what I am alone, and only then do I make the gift of myself."[53]

> My Father comes when I have lived out the blind, cruel instinct to punish; he comes when I have gone beyond him; he is given to me when I don't need him, when I am free of him, . . . My Father comes to me when he is no longer the intellectual leader I craved, the guide I wept for, the protector which the child in me leaned on. He created a child and failed to inspire in her anything but the terror and pain of life, as God does, and I have outgrown the terror and the pain. Today I am preparing to liberate my Father of the pain and terror of life.[54]

In her mind, and undoubtedly in his, the liberation can come only through sexuality. "When my Father and I truly meet, after twenty years, it is not a meeting but a realization of the impossibility of meeting on earth except as man and woman, in the completeness of sex."[55] That she was playing with incredibly high stakes seemed clear to her. Yet the price was worth it. Despite the tremendous risk, she truly believed she would psychologically triumph, separating man from God, getting a human father and a God. But most importantly, getting herself free of both of them:

> The Father I imagined, strong, cruel, hero, tormentor, is soft, feminine, vulnerable. With him God, too, becomes human, vulnerable, imperfect. I lose my terrors, my pain, the sacrilegious passion. I find a Father who is sacred. I find sacredness. I may, as Henry says, "reconciliate" myself with God, too, because I am free.[56]

In the center of her journal, *Incest*, Nin wrote "First Day of Father Story." As she sat in the hotel room with her father, he shocked her with details about his life with her mother. The mother, whom Nin believed to be puritanical, bourgeois, secretive about sex, became in the father's telling, sexually voracious, crudely unkempt and unwashed, primitive in her jealousies and desires. Nin herself was quintessentially clean; her lovers, she said, were always amazed she had no odors, no smell other than her delicate perfumes. Miller claimed her small bruises gotten from their more vigorous love-making emitted the smell of rose petals.

In one of the most astounding parts of her journal, Nin documents the sexual consummation with her father. Her description of the confluence of natural and unnatural feelings creates a monumental tension—tenderness, violence, passion, repulsion, desire, joy, yielding, resistance, guilt—all flowing together. Despite seeing her father's joy, his ecstasy, Nin unsurprisingly felt poisoned by the act.

> I was not free to enjoy the splendor of it, the magnificence of it. Some sense of guilt weighed down on my joy and continued to weigh down on me, but I could not reveal this to him. He was free—he was passionately free—he was older and more courageous. . . . I went to my room, poisoned."[57]

She goes on to explain:

> This man's love, because of the similitudes between us, because of the blood relation, atrophied my joy. And so life played on me its old trick of dissolving, of losing its palpableness, its normalcy. The mistral wind blew and the shape and savors were destroyed. The sperm was a poison, a love that was a poison.[58]

But, this poisoning effect did not keep her from continuing with him for nine days.

When she finally came to the moment of their parting, she felt "keen pangs of regret," knowing that she must end it completely if she were to keep up the beautiful illusion of perfection: "Fear of disillusion, fear that I should break physically, be less beautiful, less than all he expected. A flight from the most precious experience at a certain moment, always Trop pleine."[59]

Writing to her father after their meeting, she tells him what she has gained from their encounter.

> All the discoveries I have made about your life and about you correspond to what I so deeply wanted them and you to be. I realize that I searched dimly for them in others, but you, only you, fill a great void that I found in the world. . . . I always wanted to go away, to leave the world behind. When you came back, reality became beautiful, completely satisfying. I broke the imitation, the dream—the artificial, congealed, dead world.[60]

Despite her effusiveness, the effect of the "poison" was systemic. Later she would write in the journal: "I want to go to (Otto) Rank and get absolution for my passion for my Father."[61]

Nin sought out Otto Rank as her second analyst. She had already read Rank's important works on the artist, the double, incest, and the father, and she felt she was a ready-made subject for him, having lived out what he had only written about. Rank immediately appealed to her because he was concerned with the artist, he spoke in mythological terms, he told her she was in the process of creating herself. As their first meeting came to an end, Rank asked her to leave her diary, which she carried with her everywhere, and in which she had just written before visiting Rank. Although she was frightened by his request, she submitted, because she liked the feeling of demand and surrender.

Rank had just moved to Paris after extricating himself from Freud's inner circle. His heterodoxy was to claim that the birth trauma, not the oedipal conflict, was the primary source of neurosis. His interest in artistic creativity and his preference for dreams and their literary and mythic amplifications made him the ideal therapeutic partner for Nin. In the second session, however, Rank made two dramatic demands: first, that she give up her diary-writing, which he perceived as her way of controlling reality, and second, that she live separately from her husband during analysis. Nin, with the approval of Hugh, did what Rank required, with her secret slight adjustment being that Miller take an adjoining room to the one which she had rented.

The analysis with Rank was meant to be short and intensive. For three months, Nin stopped writing in her diary. Their work together was positive, encouraging, touching on all the important issues, yet missing the deeper import of her early childhood sexual abuse. After Freud abandoned his "seduction" theory of neurosis—his early belief that all neurosis stemmed from a precocious sexual event—all other psychoanalysts followed suit. It would be fifty years later before the full import of Nin's early trauma would be recognized for what it was and the implications of it acknowledged. Yet the analysis, which lasted for five months, helped her see the connection between her feelings for her father and her creativity: "Whenever I feel sadness about Father, I write. When I yearn for him, I write. When I feel regrets, I write."[62] The analysis, along with her simple daily creative life with Henry during that time, worked their changes on her. One of the most profound changes was to be her pregnancy.

It appears that after the meeting with her father, in the midst of her analysis with Rank, while she was living with Miller, she became pregnant. Having been convinced she could not conceive, she did not immediately recognize her condition. It is likely that she still suffered from a severe dissociation to be so out of touch with her body. When she was already two and one-half months along, she finally realized what was happening

Although she was convinced the pregnancy was Miller's, she made sure that Hugh thought it was his. Her father, upon hearing of her condition, commented in true narcissistic fashion that she was now worth less as a woman.[63] The concatenation of events which follow are truly mind-boggling. Realizing that she wanted to be out of her stifling marriage to Hugh in order to set up a new life with Miller, she determined to abort her pregnancy. Since she saw Miller as an irresponsible child himself, she realized he was not capable of supporting her, much less a child. He had even told her he didn't want the child, and so she felt she had no choice. Yet, it was not just Miller's reluctance that forced her hand: Nin herself was terrified of the possibility of having a child. Like the classical Greek Aphrodite, Nin had little desire for the life of Demeter, the joys and woes of actual motherhood had little appeal for her. Although she was frequently possessed by the need to mother all the men in her life, including her father, the thought of real mother-hood left her cold—it was not possible, she was meant, she thought, to be a mis-tress, not a mother. Exhausted from being a "mother" to everyone, the prospect of actually becoming one was basically repugnant to her. As a patriarchal priestess she declared, "I want to live only for the love of man, and as an artist—as a mistress, as a creator."[64] So she contacted a *sage-femme*, a midwife trained in the arts of abort-ing, who gave her potions to end the pregnancy naturally.

While she took the medications and waited for their desired result, she again turned heavily towards Rank, deciding to use her great psychic powers to become an analyst in order to financially support herself. In turn, Rank was entering a period of his life in which he wanted to live more creatively and spontaneously, released from the demands of his writing and his practice. He was, indeed, look-ing for promising pupils who would carry his work forward. Anais Nin was one of his last two patients.[65]

Still pregnant, waiting for the "natural" abortion to occur, Nin set out to seduce Rank. They began their affair in June; she was now almost five months pregnant and still passionately in love with Miller. Yet in some bizarre twist of imagination, she made out that Rank was truly the "father" of the child, that his psychoanalysis had created her pregnancy. Her descriptions of their affair have a particular poignancy. Her portrait of Rank, this old man who looked to her like a "sad crab," who wanted so much to live outside the prison of his intellect, is terribly distressing, as he forgets his analytic vows and throws himself on Nin, crying, "You, You, You!" Yet again she managed to seduce the analyst, and yet again the analyst had been seducible.

Killing the Mother

During her affair with Rank, when she was already six months pregnant, Nin went to a regular doctor who told her the *sage-femme* had accomplished nothing, the child growing in her was alive and normal, she had milk in her breasts. She made another attempt to abort it. Her account of ending the life of the child she was bearing is sad, terrible, comic, grotesque, an experience of racking pain, and religious awakening. It is one of the most vividly written descriptions in women's literature of the physical, emotional, and spiritual consequences a women faces when she chooses to abort.

As she began preparations for the operation that would lead to the abortion, Nin had a telling conversation with the "child not born yet": "You are a child without a father, just as I was a child without a father. You are born of man, but you have no father."[66] She went on to identify the child part of herself, "the ghost of a little girl forever wailing inside, bewailing the loss of a father," with the unborn child. This ghost, she said, would haunt the life of the unborn child with its own needs. And then there was also the problem, she says, of the father who is, himself, a child and who would resent the unborn child's needs and demands. And, in a complete identification with the unborn child, she makes her final case:

You would be abandoned, and you would suffer as I suffered when I was abandoned by my father, who was not a father, but the artist and the child. It would be better to die . . . it would be better to die than to be abandoned, for you would spend your life haunting the world for this lost father, this fragment of your body and soul, this lost fragment of your very self. *There is no father on earth.* The father is this shadow of God the Father cast on the world. . . . It would be better if you died inside of me, quietly, in the warmth and in the darkness.[67]

By merging the image of her own abandoned child-self with that of the unborn child, she accomplished two things: It permitted her to proceed with what now appeared to be a "mercy killing" of the actual child, and it allowed her to finally end the haunted life of her ghostly, abandoned inner child.

There ensued an intense drama of physical torture, rage, fury, and fear which lasted for hours as she tried to eject the dead fetus. Finally an animal instinct and wisdom took over and she connected with her body in a way that allowed her to finally push the dead baby out. Against the wishes of the doctor and nurses in attendance, she insisted on seeing it—it was a little girl. "It has long eyelashes on its closed eyes: it is perfectly made, and all glistening with the water of the womb."[68] Initially she felt nothing but hate for this thing that almost killed her, yet later she felt great sadness and regret. As she considered her "first dead creation"[69] she realized that along with the child she had killed the human mother part of herself as a "sacrifice to other forms of creation." Her destiny was cast now, it was to be solely one of mistress. Against all her intellectual rationalizations, the image of the abandoning father again appeared as the real culprit: "I love man as lover and creator. Man as father I do not trust. I do not believe in man as father. . . . In man the father I feel an enemy, a danger."[70] The narcissistic and abusive father had extorted a most precious price.

Nin was thirty-one in the summer of 1934 when she aborted. That fall she made plans to go to New York to be with Otto Rank and become an analyst, which she did for a while. Although she believed that psychoanalysis saved her life and remained a fervent devotee, she could not sustain the rigors of psychoanalytic practice. Her first love was still writing. Her affair with Miller had cooled after the move back to New York, although they would remain lifelong friends, and she continued to have many other affairs, both long and short. From mid-life until her death in 1977, she continued her practice of living a divided life by having and maintaining two marriages—keeping her life as Mrs. Hugh Guiler in New York City while living as Mrs. Rupert Pole in southern California. This arrangement was known only to herself and a few select others, not to the husbands.

The Return of the Hetaira

In 1932 while Nin was moving daily between her lovers in Paris, Toni Wolff, a lover and companion to C. G. Jung, was developing her fourfold structure describing the archetypal experiences of the feminine principle.[71] Wolff laid out her structure in the form of a cross—on one arm the Medial Woman stood in opposition to the Amazon, on the other, the Mother stood in opposition to the Hetaira. Following Wolff's analysis, there can be no question the archetype Anais Nin was embodying was that of the Hetaira.

The original meaning of the word Hetaira meant a companion to men, but in later usage was thought of more in terms of concubine. The nature of the woman's companionship with men was not strictly sexual: it had a spiritual or creative potential as well. In her diagram, Wolff put the Hetaira archetype in opposition to the Mother. Like the goddesses Demeter and Aphrodite, the Mother and the Hetaira are driven by totally different desires. But in women's psychology if one is dominant, the other remains active (and usually troublesome) in the unconscious. Although Anais Nin consistently identified herself with the Hetaira courtesan archetype, she struggled for most of her life with a demanding and almost overpowering maternal instinct.

Nor Hall seems to have Anais Nin in mind when she describes the aphroditic fluidity of the Hetaira in *The Moon and the Virgin*. According to Hall, the Hetaira does not respect boundaries set by social roles; neither the socially accepted roles and rules of relationship regarding husband, teacher, priest, son, employee, nor even father, are of interest to her. Although she is usually oriented heterosexually she does not limit herself. Women are also included in her romantic repertoire. Her erotic fluidity flows easily and quickly over such protective boundary lines. In this sense she is felt as threatening to the established order of things and, in her own mind, as revolutionary. Her ability to disturb and disrupt the social ordering of relationships earns her fear and admiration.[72]

A woman dominated by the Hetaira archetype possesses the powerful medicine or pharmakos of Aphrodite which can kill or cure—she can bestow great insight on her chosen partners, but she can also blind them to their limitations. As Hall notes, the Hetaira "either enhances her partner's perception of himself or herself by exciting the psyche to new insights or she imprisons another by convincing him or her of some illusory talent, or latent potential, which would lead to losing a sense of what is and is not real about oneself."[73] Nin was famous for both of these abilities. And she occasionally became confused. Was Henry a good writer, or was it all trashy "street talk"? Did Rank's ideas really empower or did she merely inflate him so he would be a thrilling lover? The real danger, however, for a woman under the influence of the Hetaira, especially one who has had childhood sexual abuse, is that she herself easily loses touch with what is real, the sentient earth, the sensate body. And that is a danger that Nin continually experienced, fought against, and sought to repair.

The cure Nin found later in her life was to surrender more and more to her creative self, to her own potential. As she became older, her connection to her writing slowly began to replace the obsessive relationship to others. Throughout

Nin's diaries, one senses her growing hunger for an essential work. Beginning with her first diary entries, she was embarking on a relationship with herself that would last. Although she was convinced she had "a genius for loving," in the end it was the "genius" of her own work that compelled her.

It is clear that each of these literary Daughters of Saturn had fathers who were brilliant and prominent in the world and that they figured heavily in their daughter's psychological, creative, and spiritual development. Although a father's early interest and encouragement would seem to be the most important factor in a women's creative life, in the lives of these women it appears to be the opposite. These accomplished and gifted fathers did not act as mentoring, encouraging, teaching fathers, but rather were distant, closed, unavailable men. In fact, the father's emotional or physical absence, his lack of validation, affirmation, authentication seems to be one of the key factors that drove these women's creative process. Whether she is trying to reach him, please him, fight him, sleep with him, or destroy him, the father appears not as an enabling figure, nor even as an obstacle, but rather as a void into which these women threw their creative efforts.

Each of these women grappled in their adult lives with the troubled legacies their fathers left them with. Working out their unfinished father relationships with the men in their lives, with the culture and institutions of the fathers, and with God, each daughter found radical ways to meet and overcome the obstacles that their father relationships represented to their lives as creative women. Dickinson lived her whole life in her father's house, but she steadfastly refused marriage and religious conversion. Hilda Doolittle underwent psychoanalysis with Freud, although they had what she called a permanent "argument implicit in their bones." Sylvia Plath sought her dead father in her poet-husband and in her poetry, where she ended up assassinating him. Anais Nin slept with her father when she was thirty years old, committing incest in order to break the destructive spell his abuse and abandonment had on her as a child.

These four literary Daughters of Saturn did not receive much if any assistance to help them wrestle with the legacies of their personal fathers and the pressures of their cultural fathers. They did not have the benefit of understanding that their lives were lived within the cultural context of their gender. Nor did they have access to the enabling reality of the sisterhood of women to support and empower them. Yet despite their struggles, each of these women managed to find her own unique strategies to live a creative life.

·VI·

The Second Gate: The Threshold

Gerda Lerner articulates two necessary requirements if a woman is going to be able to self-define; the first is being, at least for a time, "woman-centered"; the second is stepping outside of patriarchal thought.[1] In my scheme of things, both these actions are inextricably related—to become "woman-centered" in our culture is a radical move which can be done only by finding the edge of patriarchal thought and stepping over it. Undertaking these two requirements means crossing the Threshold.

In all initiations, crossing the Threshold signals a rite of separation. This passage demands preparation, purification, and sacrifice. The Threshold indicates the moment of "sacred entering" and, according to van Gennep, it is the door that is "the boundary between the foreign and domestic worlds . . . between the profane and sacred worlds. Therefore to cross the threshold is to unite oneself with a new world."[2] This crossing over may be accompanied by an emotional or spiritual crisis. And as we make the step across, we always run the risk of an encounter with the "Guardians of the Threshold." These energies can be helpful or demonic.

I have noticed in my own life and in that of other women that whenever a woman goes to step more fully into her life, she is met by powerful forces which she must be willing to confront. Whether they are manifestations of the woman's own fear and reluctance, or whether they are truly autonomous energies that wait at the doorstep, one thing is for sure—the "Guardians of the Threshold" demand something from us, a fee for the privilege of entering. At the door, invocations must be said, prayers and offerings must be made, sacrifices must be willingly done. In some traditions, blood is smeared on the doorpost. Only when we approach the Threshold with such awareness of the spiritual possibilities and dangers can we be assured of safe passage.

In stepping across the Threshold, a woman steps out of the constructs of patriarchal thought. What is patriarchal thought? It is the "objective," emotionless, "scientific," and religious discourse on which Western civilization has been built. The ideas, treatises, and laws which imply Truth, and claim authority, spoken in a paternalistic voice. Patriarchal thought is premised on dualism and separation—between women and nature, man and woman, humans and animals, body and soul, mind and emotion, matter and spirit. It is the essence of Descartes' proclamation, "I think therefore I am." Patriarchal thought is male-centered, hierarchical, with male experience used as the norm and standard. In particular this thought has much to say about woman, who she is and what she can or cannot do: she has no soul, her sex is dangerous, her clitoris inferior, her moral judgment undeveloped. She has no capacity for making great art or music, her writing is "feminine," her thinking is woolly, her perceptions unfounded.

Each of the four literary Daughters of Saturn took her step across the Threshold in her own way. For Emily Dickinson it meant crossing the threshold into the privacy of her bedroom where, in the total isolation of that space, she faced the full force of her creative daemon. For H.D. it meant crossing the line of conventionality by having a child out of wedlock, loving another woman, and creating a lifestyle that could accommodate both; for Plath it meant standing on the rim of her own madness while writing the best poetry of her life; for Anais Nin it meant entering into a multitude of relationships that put her on the verge of psychological disintegration, and writing about them.

When a woman crosses the Threshold, she begins to learn that she is not "this or that" as the cultural definitions of her gender have proscribed for her. She may be a woman stepping into what Emily Dickinson referred to as her poetic "wickedness"; she may be seeking, not heaven as the Christian religions have proclaimed it, but, "haven" as the poet H.D. described it. Or she may be a woman rising out of the ashes, "eating men like air," as Sylvia Plath imagined her.

This step is not done without trepidation. And, if the woman is heterosexual, one of the most compelling fears, one of the hardest risks she faces is "loss of communication with, approval by, and love from the man (or the men) in her life." As Gerda Lerner reminds us "No thinking man has ever been threatened in his self-definition and his love life as the price for his thinking."[3] And yet, that is one of the prices we must be willing to pay. Even if a woman chooses other women, her choice may feel like crossing a threshold. Morgan Farley writes that falling deeply in love with a woman was a profound threshold experience, a penetrating awakening into herself "because this woman's love and desire for me broke me open and made it impossible for me to live as I had lived. I had to leap from one world into another to meet her: from innocence into extremes of experience, from safety into enormous risk."[4] This step of leaving the father's house[5] and crossing into a woman-centered world cannot be taken without consciousness, courage, and determination.

The Threshold is a liminal place, a crack between the worlds. Unlike the

Awakening out of the Belly of the Father which seems to happen because of an external motivating disaster, crossing the Threshold is a step made in full consciousness. It is not truly necessary: one may live a good life without having made it. Maybe it is not even right for everyone. But it is an essential step for the woman who would be creative, for the woman who would take up the pen, or paintbrush, or begin to move her body in new and undefined ways. For the woman who wishes to express herself, it is surely a step full of risk—you may remember your own name. And there are no promises.

In my own life, the Threshold experience took a number of years and had several parts. The first part came with the decision to deepen my commitment to art by entering into graduate school at age thirty-eight; the other was to undertake a long period of celibacy, followed by loving another woman at age forty-two. All of these experiences were intertwined in some way, the one and the other, moving me closer to my own self, helping me to "remember my own name." Standing on the brink of each of these decisions, I knew that they were what would give me entrance into a new life. I could not fall into them with my eyes closed, I had to consciously choose them. I sensed in some way that my whole life up to that point had been moving me to these edges and I could not stand forever on the verge, I had to step across each threshold into the new life. And I knew, having once chosen, my life would never be the same after I had stepped over the edge into some other way of being. What was sacrificed was any claim I had to "normalcy," to conventionality, to acceptability in the culture of the fathers. What I gained was the sense that my life was now in my own hands, even though I had no idea where it would lead me. I felt I was entering uncharted territory, what I now call the Wildzone.

Part Three

The Wildzone

·VII·

The Women Are Singing

We use the word "wilderness," but perhaps we mean wildness. Isn't that why I've come here? In wilderness, I seek the wildness in myself—and in so doing, come on the wildness everywhere around me because, after all, being part of nature, I'm cut from the same cloth.

—*Gretel Ehrlich*[1]

I am not an animal or a tree, I am the thing in which the trees and animals move and grow, I am a place.

—*Margaret Atwood*[2]

These places of possibility within ourselves are dark because they are ancient and hidden: they have survived and grown strong through that darkness. Within these deep places, each one of us holds an incredible reserve of creativity and power, of unexamined and unrecorded emotion and feeling.

—*Audre Lorde*[3]

Women of the Wild: The Rites of Separation

In their study of tribal cultures, social anthropologists Shirley and Edward Ardener located a cultural space they named the women's "wild zone." It is where women go to define themselves because, as they point out, "where society is defined by men, some features of women do not fit that definition."[4] For the Ardeners, the women's "wild zone" is a place that is not perceived or known by men and thus men do not know what happens in the women's "wild zone." This notion of a place where women go to find themselves is what I call, after the Ardener's model, the Wildzone.

The Wildzone is a separatist place, and although that frightens many women off, as Catherine Keller has said: "No one changes a world, a culture, without practicing modes of subversive retreat from it."[5] Separation from the known culture is an integral part of any male initiation process and is practiced throughout the world. When women undertake separation, however, it is generally regarded with fear and suspicion.

In my understanding, the Wildzone is where we must go to reclaim all that has been banished from us. All that we, as women, have been taught is dangerous, disgusting, ugly, nasty, unfeminine exists in the Wildzone. Our access to the power in our bodies, our sexualities, our breasts and buttocks, our bellies and our blood, our hair, our freedom to move, our freedom to speak, all can be found in the Wildzone. Although the Wildzone can be located spatially, as a geographical place like "the wilderness," it is more than that. It is, as Gretel Ehrlich says, "the wildness in myself"—experiential as well as imaginal, that we seek.

The Wildzone is where women's culture gets created.[6] It is where women find the ground they can stand upon. It is always symbolic and has its own secret language which only women know. Although most women's visits to the Wildzone are temporary and women remain incorporated into the dominant culture, the knowledge and experience of the Wildzone give women self-definition, an understanding and knowledge of each other as sisters, a common language, and a sense of self and each other outside the dominant culture's definition.[7]

The Wildzone is the place where we get our bodies back. A woman will literally change form in the Wildzone, she will carry herself differently, move her body in a distinctive way, feeling her muscles as well as her softness. She will breath from her belly. She will speak, and her voice will come from a place deep in her body.

The Wildzone is where a woman will learn to use her mind. It is where we can stretch out to the furthest reaches of our imaginations and find that the false hierarchical Great Chain of Being breaks down and all things are deeply connected. The Wildzone is the "beyond," the new ground beyond the boundaries of patriarchal prescriptions. It is full of chance, risk, and potential. It is suffused with magic, and mischief. The Wildzone is full of being, streaming, yes-saying. And it is where we learn to say "NO!" which, as Emily Dickinson reminds us, "is the wildest word we consign to language."

Each of the literary Daughters of Saturn tracked into the Wildzone, where she thought and imagined her way out of the confines of patriarchal prescriptions. For Dickinson, the Wildzone was her bedroom with its lock on the door, where she found the strength to renounce marriage and traditional religion for the sake of her wild mind. For H.D., the Wildzone was her relationship with women which provided her with a maternal shelter and ignited and inspired her poetic voice. For Sylvia Plath, it was the liminal space she occupied as an unattached woman in "the still, blue, almost eternal hour," the hour before dawn in which she wrote the poems that made her famous. For Anaïs Nin, the Wildzone was her diary, the one place she could record the full range of her innermost truths.

In the Wildzone, we begin to move deeply into our bodies, revive our instinctual knowing, find our "wildish" nature. We learn again how to sniff, scratch, trot, listen, growl, protect our young, and roll on the grass. The Wildzone allows us to expand our imaginations into what Mary Daly calls the "mystery of our history," remembering our lost wisdom. The Wildzone is where we find the Wild Mother and learn our Mother Tongue, a new/old way of speaking. It is where we can remember our name. The Wildzone is where our dreams come from. It is both a real and an imaginary dimension full of divination, prophesy, and ecstasy. It is an undivided place where we can consider the multiplicity of our natures.

The Wildzone gives what the Daughters of Saturn long for—space. As we have seen, daughters swallowed by their fathers and the culture of the fathers struggle intensely with issues of space. The need for clear, clean, open space in which to breathe, to grow, to stretch and spread our bodies and minds, where there is room enough to include relationship with all parts of ourselves as Susan Griffin describes:

> Space filled with the presence of mothers, and the place where everyone is a daughter. *Space which does not exist without matter.* The place where she predominates. *The space which is never separate from matter.* The space shaped by the movements of white-haired women and ringing with the laughter of old lady friends. The world seen on the faces of middle-aged women. The place filled with the love of women for women. Space shaped by the play of the littlest girls.[8]

The way to the Wildzone is not a super-highway, it is more like an animal path, known only to the species, used for a while, and then rerouted. Like cunning Gretels, women have left a trail of crumbs for anyone who would follow them. Unlike the fairy tale, women are purposefully on their way to the witch's oven, the bread oven, earth oven, the place of transformation. For women today going into our "wildness" means entering a new dimension of space and time, feeling our connection to all living things, and learning to live our lives from that place of knowing.

Diving Deep

Since the Greek myths arise out of a patriarchal imagination, clearly they can take us just so far. Recently women have begun to search their dreams and imaginations in earnest for images, stories, and metaphors looking for a new mythology, one that can inspire, strengthen, and energize us as women. Marija Gimbutas's archaeomythology of the goddess-worshipping cultures of Old Europe, certain contemporary works of fiction, feminist revisioning of fairy tales, and other efforts to recover lost archetypes, like the Wild Woman, have been most successful.[9] One of these new stories is Margaret Atwood's novel, *Surfacing*, a fictionalized tale of a woman's spiritual quest which begins with a search for her father and takes her deep into the territory of the Wildzone.[10]

In the beginning of the novel, the unnamed woman protagonist is returning home to the Canadian north because her father has been reported missing. The postcard she received said in broken English, "Your father is gone, nobody can't find him." Although her mother had already died some years ago, her father, a botanist, remained living in the family cabin. She is going back with friends and her lover to look for him.

The cabin is not easy to get to. She must rely on her memory of natural markers—one of her father's policies was camouflage: "he had picked the most remote lake he could find" to build their family cabin on. This father who preferred to be in hiding, both physically and emotionally, was now the object of her search.

Inside the cabin she finds all her father's books. He was, she remembers, an avid proponent of *techne* and *logos*. Finding his technical books, she recalls how "he believed that with the proper guidance you could do everything yourself." His serious books proclaimed the power of reason: "He admired what he called the eighteenth-century rationalists." The garden is still there, as it was in her childhood, as are the bluejays her mother used to feed, although they are wild and wary now, refusing to sit on her outstretched arms.

In the cabin she finds some recent papers that her father has left behind. At first glance, these crude drawings of hands, a human figure with tree branches or antlers protruding from its head, convince her that he went mad, bushed, from living alone too long in the isolated cabin. While rummaging she comes across some old scrapbooks, hers and her brother's, filled with drawings they had made as children. Her brother's are filled with violence, monsters, war scenes, explosions; her own were "page after page of eggs and rabbits, grass and trees, normal and green surrounding them, flowers blooming, sun in the upper right-hand corner of each picture, moon symmetically in the left." She had forgotten she had ever done these pictures, evidence to her now that at an early age she had dissociated, encasing herself in sugar-coated fantasies and denial.

Studying the strange drawings left by her father, she realizes that they are actually pictures of rock engravings left by paleolithic natives—he had been researching them—and with this realization she understands that he is not still on the island, gone crazy or mad, but that he is dead. Further study of another antlered figure drawing along with a map with a tiny red X tells her where his body might be and she goes to look for him.

During her search, deep into the island wilderness, she comes upon a horrifying sight:

> I smelled it before I saw it; then I heard the flies. The smell was like decaying fish. I turned around and it was hanging upside down by a thin blue nylon rope tied round its feet and looped over a tree branch, its wings fallen open. It looked at me with its mashed eye.[11]

The dead heron, the beautiful, graceful bird totem of the island lakes, has been gratuitously killed by someone. Her rage turns outward toward the "Americans," the crass, wanton destroyers of natural land and wildlife, the ones who come to the pure Canadian wilderness as tourist hunters and fishers and pollute it. But gradually she feels her own complicity in this murder, "sticky as glue, blood on my hands, as though I had been there and watched without saying NO or doing anything to stop it." Then another memory starts to take shape just below the surface.

When she finally finds the spot where the X was marked, she realizes that because of the dam the image she is looking for is underwater and that to find it she must dive down to it:

> It was there but it wasn't a painting, it wasn't on the rock. It was below me, drifting towards me from the furthest level where there was no life, a dark oval trailing limbs. It was blurred but it had eyes, they were open, it was something I knew about, a dead thing, it was dead.[12]

What comes flooding back to her is the memory of an illegal abortion, one she never chose but was talked into. She remembered that after it was over, she thought, "I was emptied, amputated; I stank of salt and antiseptic, they had planted death in me like a seed." It is this "death" she had forgotten, submerged, repressed. Now she thought how that tiny new life had been "hiding in me as if in a burrow and instead of granting it sanctuary I let them catch it. I could have said No but I didn't: that made me one of them too, a killer. . . . Since then I'd carried that death around inside me, layering it over, a cyst, a tumor, black pearl. . . ."

What began as a search for her missing father opens into something much bigger. She starts to look for some gift, some token, a note, a message, a will, something he would have left just for her. By diving deep she had found, by way of her father's drawings and map, not only her own memory, which would allow her to feel again, but also a spiritual reconnection with the land and the original inhabitants, the native people who made the rock engravings: "The Indians did not own salvation but they had once known where it lived and their signs marked the sacred places, the places where you could learn the truth." But, she realized, she hadn't actually found these engravings because they weren't there. What her father had been looking for and found were "new places, new oracles, they were things he was seeing the way I had seen, true vision; at the end, after the failure of logic." It was also her father's dead body she found submerged in the water. He had indeed fallen in while searching for his images, the "dark oval" of an eye that had looked up at her was the camera still around his neck. As she leaves the spot she makes a thank-offering to the spirits of the place: "The gift had been greater, more than a hand or an eye, feeling was beginning to seep back into me, I tingled like a foot that's been asleep."

With the gift from her father firmly understood, she begins to search for what her mother might have left her. In the old scrapbooks, she finds a drawing she had done as a child, "a woman with a round moon stomach: the baby was sitting up inside her gazing out." She recognized the drawing as her own, they were her early "pictographs" which her mother had saved for her. Like the rock-engravings discovered by her father, they contained archaic messages from the past, but she would have to "immerse myself in the other language" in order to understand them. "Not only how to see but how to act." She must learn her mother tongue and feel the powers of her body.

The night before the boat is scheduled to pick them up, she takes her lover out in the grey-green dark of the rising moon. She is naked and barefoot, she lies down on the damp earth with him, and she thinks "He needs to grow more fur." They make love and she conceives—"I can feel my lost child surfacing within me, forgiving me, rising from the lake where it has been prisoned for so long . . . it buds, it sends out fronds." She decides that this time she will give birth squatting, on dry leaves. "The baby will slip out easily as an egg, a kitten, and I'll lick it off and bite the cord, the blood returning to the ground where it belongs; the moon will be full, pulling. . . . it will be covered with shining fur, a god. . . ." In the morning she gets into her canoe and disappears while the others, her lover and her friends, board the boat that has come to take them back to civilization. They are forced by her absence to leave her on the island.

Pregnant and alone, she embarks on her own vision quest. Lying in the bottom of her canoe she is given a revelation, through the memory of the dead heron, of the great cycle of life in which she also participates—life, death, and regeneration:

> Through the trees the sun glances; the swamp around me smolders, energy of decay turning to growth, green fire. I remember the heron; by now it will be insects, frogs, fish, other herons. My body also changes, the creature in me, plant-animal, sends out filaments in me. I ferry it secure between death and life, I multiply.[13]

She can't get back into the cabin, because it has been padlocked shut so she breaks a window to get in. She makes one last plea to her parents to be there with her and when they don't appear she is besieged with a fear that will go away only when she is outside. She understands that there are powers operating now and that she'll have to listen carefully. She asks at last, "What sacrifice, what do they want?" When she knows for certain that "everything from history must be eliminated," she goes back into the cabin and performs a ritual purification of all the past and her human connections to it. She burns all the books, including her art supplies from her illustrating job that prostituted her creative talent. She smashes glasses and plates, throwing what she can't break on the floor, and she uses the big kitchen knife to slash "once through" all the remaining clothing, coats, bedding, and blankets. Taking only a rough blanket to cover her "until the fur grows," she exits the cabin and goes to the lake where she immerses herself and peels off her clothing, leaving her "false body" floating on the surface of the water. She digs vegetables out of the garden with her bare fingers, she defecates on the ground, scratching the earth over it like an animal. She has become an animal, a part of the land, part of the landscape. She sleeps in a lair of dry leaves and dead branches.

Then the powers will not even let her into the garden, they will not allow her to put her feet on the path, anything that has been touched by humans is forbidden. She is forced to go deeper, to forage in the wilderness away from the cabin for her food. She enters into a final stage of transformation as the boundaries that separate her from nature melt away—"I lean against a tree, I am a tree leaning." In this state of wildness, she has a vision of her mother standing in front of the cabin, her hand stretched out feeding bluejays—"She doesn't move, she is feeding them: one perches on her wrist, another on her shoulder." As she moves closer to the apparition, her mother disappears as the birds fly into the trees. She looks up at the birds "trying to see her, trying to see which one she is; they hop, twitch their feathers, turn their heads, fixing me first with one eye, then the other." Her mother feeds the bluejay, her mother *is* a blue jay—the barriers between the worlds dissolves. Then she has another vision, this time of her father. She feels that a creature who has wolf's eyes is watching her, his seeing is totally impersonal, he does not approve or disapprove, but sees her only as part of the landscape. Then, in an instant, he shape-shifts and becomes a fish jumping in the water.

Given these final messages, she comes back into human form. She can walk again on the paths, can re-enter the cabin, and eat a tin of beans. The message she has received is "To prefer life." Looking at herself in the mirror, she recognizes that her natural woman would look like a madwoman to the "civilized" world, her "face dirt-caked and streaked, skin grimed and scabby, hair like a frayed bathmat stuck with leaves and twigs. A new kind of centerfold." Recognizing the vulnerability of this woman, she decides "This above all, to refuse to be a victim . . . give up the old belief that I am powerless." She dresses herself in her old clothes but takes with her "the primeval one," the small life in her belly. And it is to this new life that her own life is committed as she makes the choice to re-enter civilization.

Atwood's novel does not tell us how this woman will survive in the world, only how she has transformed herself in the Wildzone and learned the powers of life, death, and regeneration. With the gifts given by her parental spirits and by finding her own profound connectedness with the earth and the powers of her own body, she has found the key to her life.

Surfacing begins with a contemporary woman's search for her missing father. But the turning point in Atwood's novel comes when the woman looks at herself in a mirror and sees the transformation of a lost and tired daughter of the patriarchy. The change is one that looks like regression: the woman who looks back at her is a raging fury, a woman gone back to the earth, full of raw, primitive, vital energy, her true, stripped-down self. The veneer of civilization, of adaptation, of persona has been dropped and the woman touches the "wild" in herself. From that point on she is permanently changed.

The unnamed protagaonist in Atwood's book finds that her reconnection with maternal and paternal energy happens on many levels—personal and transpersonal. By conceiving a child she knows she will bring to term, she partakes of her mother's capacity and power to merge into nature and finds her own ability to connect with the earth—"I am not an animal or a tree, I am the thing in which the trees and animals move and grow, I am a place." Her father, she understands now, had the shamanic oracular and prophesying powers of shape-shifting and seeing. She realizes that because she has submitted to the demands of her initiation these gifts now belong to her as well. They are her true inheritance, gifts that her father could not give her while he was alive. Only after his death and through her efforts to find him are they released.

Remembering the Wild Mother

In Atwood's novel, when the woman protagonist is stripped of all cultural identity, when she is deeply and fully rooted into the natural world, her mother appears to her as a Mistress of Animals, a woman who talks to the birds, a woman who *is* a bird. This mother, although she has some identifying attributes of her personal mother, is really the woman's Wild Mother. In the Battlezone of patriarchal culture we have seen how, for the Daughters of Saturn, a strong connection with the mother was missing. In the Battlezone, mothers frequently are seen as victims or operate as enforcers of the culture and are not available as encouragers and supporters of their daughter's wildness. In women's quest for a new mythology, one figure stands out as most important, the Wild Mother.

The Wild Mother is the mother who has not been victimized and oppressed by the patriarchal social system. The Wild Mother is maternal and sexual, nurturing and fierce. She can be found living at the edges, away from the taming forces of civilization, outside the margins of patriarchal scripts. She lives in our dreams where she appears to women as the goddess in her many manifestations, a Metis, a Witch, a Sorceress, a Shapeshifter, a Spinner, a Black Madonna, a Wise Woman or a Spider Woman, a Shamaness—all images that evoke female power. She may appear from the animal world, as in Atwood's novel, where she is a blue jay. Or she may show up as a manifestation from nature, as a large tree under which a woman can take shelter. But the Wild Mother is not overly comforting. She is the opposite of the sweet, protective, "milk-teeth" mother everyone would hope for their baby, their new life. The Wild Mother is much more demanding, even stern, or cold in her requirements. Sometimes the Wild Mother appears in women's dreams as the earth itself. A woman who is an artist dreamed:

> I have been drawing a white silhouette of a woman with three horizontal parallel black marks on her face. I don't know why I draw her. A friend comes in and shows me the front page of the newspaper. "Look

what they have found," she shouts. I look at the headlines "11 FT. TALL WOMAN FOUND IN NORTHERN MAINE" Underneath the headline is a photograph of the same woman I have been drawing.

The scene shifts suddenly—I am now very low to the ground. I am very close to a large head (at least twenty feet tall) of an old woman. She has long white hair, a very weathered face and she is strong and beautiful. As she rises out of the earth. She is saying wise words—I don't know what they are but I feel she is speaking with the wisdom of the ages. It is very dark and I can only see the left side of her face and hair. The right side is in shadow and out of my line of sight.

Another abrupt change of scene—I am very low—possibly in the earth looking out and up at a HUGE woman's head towering above me. She is further away from me than the wise old woman. The woman's head rises out of the earth like a powerful volcano and great slabs of earth are wrenched up where she has forced her way through the crust. This image is in color, mostly reds, oranges and earth tones. This woman is ANGRY!! I'm glad I'm at a safe distance. The air around her is filled with the red glowing heat of her words which sound like a deep boiling growl: "Some pens are one pointed. Mine is double pointed. Mine is born of fire and heat!!!!" Then she erupts with an angry earth-shaking scream that I could actually see come out of her mouth and into the air.

Oftentimes dreams like this one work as forceful diagnosticians, telling us in no uncertain terms what ails us, on the personal and the collective level. Dreams may offer startlingly accurate symbolic information about the nature of our dis-ease, sometimes providing a missing context, a hidden diagnosis that unlocks the door to understanding. Some dreams, like the one above, seem to point to the existence of what dream-tender Stephen Aizsenstat calls the "World Unconscious," a realm of our psyches where animals, the things of the world, even the earth, herself, appear on behalf of themselves. The "World Unconscious" uses our mind's "visionary faculty" and the messages it attempts to relay to us through dreams and poetic visions seem necessary not only for *our* personal healing but for *their* collective survival as well.[14]

The Wild Mother, as she appears in dreams and other manifestations, is the mother who existed before the patriarchy. She is our true, original mother and many women sense her existence. In the dream quoted above, the Wild Mother appears with two apparently different faces: one is calm and wise, the other erupts out of the earth, ablaze with her cryptic but urgent message. The Wild Mother has not been fragmented into specialized functions like the Greek goddesses. She is maternal and sexual, virgin and mother, loving and full of wrath: she contains in one image a multiplicity of female capacities.

The dream ends with a peculiar proclamation about single and double-pointed pens. It seems that the powerful earth woman has some things to say or write with her double-pointed pen dipped in fire and heat. We can be certain that she does not abide a divided life and will be speaking to us in the "Mother Tongue."

The Mother Tongue

Language has been used and misused to oppress women, to call us names, to contain us in certain categories, to explain our desires, and to confine our passion. In the Garden of Eden, Adam was given the right, by God, to name things. And with this divine entitlement, men have been doing so ever since:

> They write, of their authority to accord names, that it goes back so far that the origin of language itself may be considered an act of authority emanating from those who dominate. They say that they have said, this is such or such a thing, they have attached a particular word to an object or a fact and thereby consider themselves to have appropriated it. The women say, so doing the men have bawled, shouted with all their might to reduce you to silence.[15]

But women are not merely passive victims in this process of naming. We have also been able to seize words and metaphors that exhilarate and liberate our imaginations—particularly our embodied imagination. This is not a casual pastime; it is a critical pursuit. As Luce Irigaray says: "If we don't invent a language, if we don't find our body's language, its gestures will be too few to accompany our story. When we become tired of the same ones, we'll keep our desires secret, unrealized. Asleep again, dissatisfied, we will be turned over to the words of men—who have claimed to 'know' for a long time. But not our body." She exhorts us: "Get out of their language. Go back through all the names they gave you. I'm waiting for you, I'm waiting for myself."[16]

One way that women have imagined themselves into another language is by bringing language back closer to the body, especially the body of the mother. It is at the breast that we learn the power of language, our Mother Tongue.

> The child's gradual acquisition and use of language reflects the dynamics of the early mother-child relationship which revolves, logically around food and nurture. Language, we think, is first used as a response to the child's sense of separation from, or hunger for, the mother: the word is both an acknowledgment of loss and an instrument of power.[17]

The Mother Tongue as it is imagined and written about is a language that arises out of a woman's hunger for the mother's body, her cycles, her rhythms, her sensuality. We need this language because it loosens, lightens, and warms us. It is a language that can speak of our bodies and their multiple pleasures, a language that leads us out of stagnation, blockage, and paralysis and towards creative action.

Dreams: Poetic Memory

One way we can enter the Wildzone and begin the process of remembering the Wild Mother and our Mother Tongue is through our dreams. Much of women's history and tradition has been lost to us, not recorded, burned, erased. How do we know who we are if we don't have our memories? How do we remember the Wild Mother? How do her stories stay in our memory? Tribal cultures have their oral traditions through which memory passes down the generations, creating a body of knowledge and wisdom on which the culture can draw. I believe if we began to listen carefully to the dreams of women, we would get back our memories, our traditions. Dreams are powerful messages from the deep wisdom of the psyche. Some say dreams are presented to us by God, by the Great Dream Weaver, the Riddle Mother, the Guiding Self. The indigenous Naskapi believe they come from the Great Person, the soul in its active state. Wherever dreams come from, the belief that they influence and inspire is as old as dreaming itself.[18]

Recent research shows that women's dreams differ from men's—a difference arising in part from our physiological make-up, but also from our differing experiences and responses to our cultural environment. Perhaps these factors cannot be completely assigned because dreams also contain a large dose of mystery. If there is truth to the notion that dreams have more to tell us than just the personal residue of an individual's daytime experiences, it seems important that we attend to the dreams of women. Sharing our dreams by telling them or encoding them in visual or verbal images is one way to remember. The personal iconography of a dream becomes, in the hands of an artist or poet, a gift to our collective memory. Dreams are important for our survival as women, as Susan Griffin reminds us:

> This above all, we have never denied our dreams. They would have had us perish. But we do not deny our voices. . . . And even if over our bodies they have transformed this earth, we say, the truth is, to this day, women still dream.[19]

Dreams can take us to the Wildzone. Dreams are often memorable, impressing us with images of unsurpassed beauty and strangeness. Images that could never occur in the natural, everyday world astonish us in the night, increasing our daytime ability to imagine, giving us a wider, deeper appreciation of what is possible. Dreams help us to remember, both in the sense of remembering what has been forgotten, but also in reconnecting with what has been lost to us in our waking lives, putting us back into contact with levels of consciousness that can release us from our mundane amnesias. In dreams we remember that we can breath underwater like whales, we can fly through the air with the birds, we meet or even become angels or aliens. In dreams we move through landscapes never before imagined, we live in mansions of unparalleled richness, or find ourselves in dreary shacks; we anxiously grope for exits in dark labyrinthine corridors, or we suddenly come upon a tiny, secret door in a closet. We may meet grand lovers or fend off dark intruders; we may reunite with the dead or lose our precious babies. Animals come to our aid bringing their deep instinctual knowledge and wisdom to bear on a situation. A fox flashes in the woods, a bear lumbers through, an eagle streaks the sky, an owl lands on our shoulder. In dreams the natural world responds and we feel the earth quake or see the tidal wave coming, or glimpse the dark funnel of a tornado heading our way in the distance. Dreams are evocative and sensate, full of body and feeling—we undergo, we are afflicted, we endure, we open. As dreams pull on all possible and impossible imagery, so, too, our response to them draws on all levels of our being—biological, psychological and spiritual.

There seems to be an urgent necessity in women to return in some way—to remember, recollect, and reunite ourselves with what has been lost to us. One way we can do this is by working with our dreams. In this way, making poems or art from dreams becomes a ritual for remembering and renewal. By reaching deeply into the dream, each woman can revitalize those images that have been lost to our collective waking memory. Working with our dreams, we enter empathically into their realm, to feel and intuit, to resonate and reflect, upon the images and their meanings. In this way, we render something back to the dream source. We are all—artists, poets, dreamers—born from Memory, the mother of the Muses, who comes to us with her visions of the night.

"In Dreams Begin Responsibilities"

Dreams are not only glimpses into the most intimate corners of our particular psyche—they are an impending invitation into the multidimensional depths of the Wildzone, which may begin with our personal experiences but quickly drops down into the collective and archetypal realms—the unconscious deeps. There the lost, rejected, unadmitted, unrecognized, unknown, or undeveloped realities of our existence await us.

Certainly dreams have the power to startle us with vivid, shocking images sometimes breathtakingly beautiful and sometimes bizarre. Deep in the night, we call out in our sleep, our heart pounds; we wake up sweating or in tears or even sometimes laughing. We may have been visited in the night by visions of astonishing power and beauty, images that heave us onto the sands of morning, our mouths agape in wonder. But by the time we wake up to our daytime life, these images quickly fade from our awareness like wisps of smoke. Yet we may find we are haunted throughout the day as the memory of the dream's images reappear like flashes of a surreal movie overlaying our waking activities. And we might ask ourselves: What do these visions of horror or beauty or strangeness want from us, what do they have to do with us or what do *we* have to do with them? Why are we so moved—sometimes feeling more strongly in our dreams than we do in our waking lives? How is it that we are brought to tears, to shouting, to feelings of deep sadness or great joy by these visions in the night?

It is shocking to find that the deep psyche, whose presence we are barely aware of, is vibrantly and inescapably alive, inhabited by strange landscapes and creatures whose agenda seems independent of our conscious will. Suddenly the ordinary everyday self is thrust into another kind of ruling order. As a psychotherapist who works with my own and other's dreams, I find I move continually in wonder, awe, and trepidation at the power of dreams to move and reveal, to diagnose, instruct and prophesy.

Maybe you have learned over the years to watch your dreams, even to write the most compelling ones down in a journal, or have found yourselves telling another at the breakfast table "Listen to what I dreamed last night!" Maybe you have learned to let the dream images live and inform your daily lives. Maybe you have even devoted tremendous time and energy into bringing the images into full dimension. If you do this, you may find yourselves wondering, listening, questioning, pondering. Living with a dream is like lifting a veil or a curtain. Freed of our usual language, we respond to a visual imagery that may have been our earliest mode of thinking. What is revealed may startle or surprise us: we often are told things about ourselves that we never knew, or are reminded—again—of something we have always known but, for some reason, keep forgetting in the amnesia of everyday living. In the night world of the dream and the day world of imagination, the doors of repression are opened part way. The conscious self is always under pressure from the unconscious to open that door, and dreams are the way the unconscious works at us often with a power more persuasive then we can imagine. Some images get dreamed over and over, and finally insist on being used. The *images* insist on being used.[20]

It is at this point, when our awareness has been touched so profoundly by another person, plant, animal, energy field, or even an alien, that the ethical imperative of dreams comes into play. It is not enough just to dream, to remember dreams, to honor them in a passive way. Dreams call us to action. It is not enough to watch the dreamworld as if it were our personal nighttime television news program reporting on events at home and abroad. Dreams ask that we engage ourselves fully, they plead, beg, badger, console, irritate, soothe, shock, surprise, anger, terrorize, and push us into awareness. The images *insist* on being used. They often demand tremendous courage from us. To truly attend to the Dreamworld in a deeply honoring way means taking the dream seriously in our waking lives.

Dreams are important for women especially because they give us access to deep wisdom. In this way we become more fully connected not only with ourselves, but with each other and the world around us. We can even enter into the kingdoms of other species. Animals can appear in our dreams and lend their energies, wisdom, and medicine to our struggles. But the animals, plants, or even the earth can also be speaking to us about themselves, and like the Australian aborigines we learn that we are living and participating in a great web of life called the Dream Time.

Dreamquesting

For the past several years, I have co-led a canoe trip with Anne Dellenbaugh, a Maine guide who leads wilderness trips for women. We call our trip a Dreamquest.[21]

At the end of summer, a group of women gather together to set out in canoes on an eight- or nine-day journey up a long-fingered lake in a remote region of Northern Maine. The women, most of whom have never met before, come together for this period of time to dedicate themselves as a community of women who go into deep nature to dream dreams for individual healing, for collective healing, and for healing of the planet. We make the lake and its shore our wilderness home. It is August; the weather is warm.

During these days and nights, we paddle our canoes, set up camp on the beaches, make delicious food, sleep in tents and dream. We share our dreams by telling them, drawing, and enacting them. At night around a blazing driftwood fire, we deepen into ourselves.

As the days go by, the dream-language enters into our day-time speech and the dream world and the waking world move closer together until they become almost seamless, one and the same. We learn to recognize and know each other by the concerns of our dreams, by the animals, spirits, and symbols that inhabit our dream life.

The first night around a large driftwood fire, a woman shares her dream. We do not know it then, but this dream will set the tone, like a prayer, for the whole trip and the images will continue to move in many women's lives for the months that follow.

> There is a group of women in the wilderness. A mother bear comes to the women for help. She has lost her cubs. We are to look for the cubs and whistle when we find them. A whistle comes. We see one cub in a tree, the other is being attacked by a mountain lion. The mother bear swipes the lion with her paw and the cub drops out of her grasp, dead. The mountain lion retreats. We ask, shall we bury the dead cub? The mother bear indicates to us that it is "useless, useless." The mother bear then asks the women to come and feel her breath. A shy woman is afraid. A stern woman takes the shy woman's hand and places it on the bear's chest. We all feel the bear breathing. It is the bear's gift back to the women for helping her.

In this dream, the women are being instructed and gifted by an animal. Once upon a time we knew to make images of animals out of clay and bone and stone.

We painted them on cave walls: horse and elephant, deer and bison. We made masks and danced them, letting our bodies take on their movements: snake and water bird, hedgehog and toad, deer and dog, bear and bull. We prayed to them for their wisdom.

> Animals were once, for all of us, teachers. They instructed us in ways of being and perceiving that extended our imaginations, that were models for additional possibilities. We watched them make their way through the intricacies of their lives with wonder and with awe. . . . They reminded us of the grand sweep and diversity of life, of its infinite possibilities. The connection of humans with totemic animals was an essential need to ally ourselves with the power and intelligence of non-human life, to absorb some of the qualities bestowed by the evolutionary process on other creatures.[22]

The night that we worked with Kathryn's dream, Susan dreamt a dream with the instruction:

> Sing a song for Kathryn.
> Put the bones in the circle
> And the Goddess will come.

She is told in the dream that "The Song for Kathryn" is made up of a combination of strong out-breaths followed by rattling. The rhythm goes—two out-breath beats, followed by three rattle beats—a five-count rhythm.

Waking in the night from this dream, Susan got up out of her sleeping bag to get a pencil to write the instruction down. She stepped outside of her tent. The lake was like a silver mirror, the night foggy, and utterly still. As she opened her pack to get her materials, she heard two distinctive, long out-breaths. She thought it was her tent-mate, but soon realized it wasn't. She was hearing the same breath and rattling rhythm she had heard in her dream. She listened, and it was there again. She became frightened, feeling a chill run up her spine. She looked into the woods, thinking someone was there making this sound but she saw no one. She remembered the shy woman in Kathryn's dream and tried to quell her fears. When she couldn't stay outside any longer, she made her way back into the tent to write. Then tears began to fall down her face. She knew she had heard the bear breathing and the wise woman playing her rattle, and she felt overwhelmed with wonder as her sleeping dream became a waking dream. She knew that the next night she must lead us in this ritual.

The following night we gathered around the big driftwood fire for the evening ceremony. We brought drums, rattles, whistles and sticks to make our music. We sang many songs and then Susan instructed us. We sang a chant, "Shamu, Shamu-ya" over and over again, calling the spirits to be with us. We were given bracelets made of white deerskin that we tied on each other's wrists, binding us together. Then Susan gave us the rhythm of the chant for "The Song for Kathryn" as it came to her in the dream. We began with the five-beat breath and rattle series, doing it over and over and over until at some point the rhythm broke open into a free and living thing. It grew in volume, changed in shape, twisted and turned, we breathed, we whistled, we moaned, we rattled, and drummed. And all the time the breaths kept coming. Sparks from the fire flew up into the black sky and our spirits sailed out into the night with the Wild Mother, riding on her rhythms, her song, and we let her carry us out.

The next morning we packed up, taking our leave of the place that had given us such a deep connection to Her. We were quiet, the only sound was the water's shush against the paddle as our canoes moved us up the lake to a new site. We carried our experiences of the Wild Mother with us as we went; she was part of us now.

Our last night on the lake, the wind blew incessantly, stirring up everything, making every action difficult, creating chaos. It blew all night, the trees bending and whipping from its force, the waves slashing against the shore. Each woman enfolded in her tent, a small bundle of fear and hope, felt buffeted by the powerful breath of the south wind. The breath of the bear mother, I think. We have to really feel her. In the morning the rains finally came, the breaking of the waters, strong and hard, and the wind rolled around to the east and then to the north, sweeping the sky clear and clean with its motion. The sun came out and the lake sparkled with tiny lights.

By the end of our time together, we had woven our stories, dreams, hopes, and fears together in such a way that we had formed a powerful net of care and responsibility towards each other. Although we knew we would go off into our separate lives, we would not return as the same women. We had some new knowledge to take back with us.

·VIII·

The Elemental Daughters of Saturn

On the Dreamquest we moved through water, built fires, slept on the earth, were moved by the wind. We came into touch with these primal energies. Our ritual to the Wild Mother invoked the elements of Fire, Earth, Air, and Water and through their powers the captive Wild Mother was liberated in us.

Each of the Daughters of Saturn—Hestia, Demeter, Hera, and that other Daughter, Aphrodite—has her originary impetus in the elemental energies of Fire, Earth, Air and Water. Taking these goddesses back to their elemental beginnings means moving them deeply into the symbol systems of Old European Neolithic goddess-worshipping cultures. Before they were swallowed and subsumed into the patriarchal pantheon of Greek religion these goddesses were the energic forces of the body and the natural world. There we can still connect with the full force of their elemental powers.

1. HESTIA AS ORIGINAL FIRE

In the Wildzone, Hestia is the keeper of the fires. One of the major symbols of Hestia is the circle, a circle wherein the fire is held. When the circle of women gather around the fire, there is Hestia. She is the boundary keeper, she helps keep the circle closed, contained, safe—virginal—in the sense that the integrity of her space is preserved.

For the Greeks, Hestia's fire was the hearth fire in the center of the family home. For women who make their home in the Wildzone, the hearth can be located, as it is in the Russian poet Anna Ahkmatova's poem "At the high fire in the forest's heart . . .":

You have come by a hard road
To be lit up by this fire.

Your eyes have grown dull, your tears cloudy,
Your hair is grey.

You don't understand the songs birds sing
Anymore, nor stars, nor summer lightning.

Don't hear it when the women strike
The tambourine; yet you fear the silence.

I have come to take your place, sister,
At the high fire in the forest's heart . . .

And one went away, ceding
The place to another, wandered
Like a blind woman reading
An unfamiliar narrow path,

And still it seemed to her a flame
Was close . . . In her hand a tambourine . . .
And she was like a white flag,
And like the light of a beacon.[1]

In this poem, Akhmatova acknowledges what a hard road a woman has to travel in order to reach this place of fire. The journey drains and ages a woman. She has been living in the Battlezone of Culture: her eyes are dull; her hair is grey; she has lost touch with the simple, beautiful things of nature, birdsong, stars, summer lightning. The woman has been made mute from her suffering, yet she fears the silence, and so she finds her way to the Wildzone, to the fire and the music of the tambourine. The poet, with the white flag of her poems, beckons to other women as "the light of a beacon," giving them a blaze of hope.

A circle of women dancing around a fire in the night is an ancient thing. Anyone who has done it knows what primal memories are evoked. Even if we have never actually done it, we sometimes dream it. How many dreams have I heard which begin with the words: "I am in a circle of women, it is dark, there is a fire. . . ."

Fire is used for heat and warmth. It also is used for cooking. The hearth is also the heart, the fire in the heart. In physiology the first artery off the heart goes back to the heart; it is the coronary artery. The message from the body is "Feed yourself first." Metabolism creates energy. When we are really working hard, using our full creative capacities, we say we are "cooking."

Hestia knows how to feed the fire. She knows the fire needs wood to burn. Being a fire-tender is an art—how to start a fire, how much wood to use without wasting, how to keep the flame steady, hot, radiating without consuming. So too, does each woman need to know what ignites her, what gets her going, heats her up. A woman needs to have the right materials at hand to be able to feed her own fires, to keep her fire from smouldering or going out.

Sexual Fire: Choosing Celibacy

I have noted earlier how, in the Greek version of the myth, Hestia chose celibacy, and how in the Battlezone, celibacy or sexual closure may be a woman's only refuge from an abusing culture. Since women's sexuality has often been considered as belonging to others, celibacy has not been a choice, but rather has been dictated to women. Historically, a woman who was unmarried was expected to be chaste. And women recently widowed were expected to be respectfully celibate for a period of time. Women who have chosen convent life are also under the vow of celibacy. Outside of these instances, there are very few cultural situations where a woman can be celibate and keep her self-worth. The celibacy of older women is, of course, culturally expected, but the chosen celibacy of a younger or middle-aged women is suspect. Except for a few socially accepted circumstances, celibacy is not a culturally sanctioned choice for women.

In the Wildzone, however, choosing celibacy can be an empowering decision for a woman. When a woman declares herself celibate by choice, it is basically a radical act. By choosing herself, she is taking charge of her own sexual energy. She may be a woman recovering from sexual injury or she may just be a woman who is feeling the need to reclaim that part of herself, needing her energy for other endeavors. Whatever the reason, a woman who chooses celibacy belongs to no one except herself. For that reason chosen celibacy can be subversive of the existing order.

Creative Fire

As Clarissa Pinkola Estes says, "A woman must be willing to burn hot, burn with passion, burn with words, with ideas, with desire for whatever it is that she truly loves."[2] It is this kind of creative fire that women need to feed.

Emily Dickinson understood that the fiery heat upon which a poem was forged was awesome. She challenges the reader of her poems:

> Dare you see a Soul at the White Heat?
> Then crouch within the door —
> Red — is the Fire's common tint —
> But when the vivid Ore
> Has vanquished Flame's conditions,
> It quivers from the Forge
> Without a color, but the light
> Of unanointed Blaze.[3]

Dickinson as poetic blacksmith forges out of the white heat intensity poems of light. Her fire is both self-creative and purifying. As Gilbert and Gubar describe it, Dickinson is a prophet of "Imagination whose brain is a furnace in which gross materials of life are transformed into both the products and the powers of art."[4]

As Dickinson's poem shows, Hestia's fire can be used for purification, especially mental purification. Virginia Woolf describes this kind of fire:

> And let the daughters of educated men dance round the fire and heap armful upon armful of dead leaves upon the flames. And let their mothers lean from the upper windows and cry, "Let it blaze! Let it blaze! For we have done with this "education.""[5]

One imagines these mothers and daughters burning away the "dead leaves" of all the books that have falsely educated women as to their place in the world. This is an especially liberating fire. Many women-created rituals have used the purifying forces of fire to free themselves of unwanted and unnecessary "scripts."

There is another kind of fire that appears in women's imagination and in women's dreams. This is the fire at the center of the earth, volcanic, lava, liquid fire. If a woman can manage it, this fire, like molten magma, can be used to create a new earth.

2. DEMETER AND PERSEPHONE: SISTERS OF THE EARTH

> This earth is my sister; I love her daily grace, her silent daring, and how loved I am how we admire this strength in each other, all that we have lost, all that we have suffered, all that we know: we are stunned by this beauty, and I do not forget: what she is to me, what I am to her.
>
> —*Susan Griffin*[6]

The earliest figurative representations of Demeter and Persephone show them as two conjoined female images—one standing for the above, one standing for the below—embodying two parts of a whole consciousness. Their combined mythology follows the seasonal cycling of life, death, and rebirth expressed within a maternal paradigm. Charlene Spretnak, in her version of the Demeter and Persephone story, imagines Persephone's descent to the Underworld not as abduction, but as a calling from the dead that she must honor: "The dead need us, Mother. I will go to them." Demeter resists, but finally, in her wisdom she relents, saying: "I understand why You must go. Still, You are My Daughter and for every day that You remain in the underworld, I will mourn Your absence."[7] As the Homeric "Hymn to Demeter" relates it, Demeter's mourning affected all crops, trees, and plants, and the earth became barren. But Spretnak tells it from a woman's perspective:

> Demeter was consumed with loneliness and finally settled on a bare hillside to gaze out at nothing from sunken eyes. For days and nights, weeks and months She sat waiting.
>
> One morning a ring of purple crocus quietly pushed its way through the soil and surrounded Demeter. She looked with surprise at the new arrivals from below. . . . Then she leaned forward and herad them whisper in the warm breeze: "Persephone returns! Persephone returns!"
>
> Demeter leapt to her feet and ran down the hill through the fields into the forests. . . . Everywhere Her energy was stirring, pushing, bursting forth into tender greenery and pale young petals. Animals shed old fur and rolled in the fresh green grass while birds sang out: "Persephone returns! Persephone returns!"
>
> When Persephone ascended from a dark chasm, there was Demeter with a cape of white crocus for Her Daughter. They ran to each other and hugged and cried and laughed and hugged and danced and danced and danced. The mortals saw everywhere the miracles of Demeter's bliss and rejoiced in the new life of spring. Each winter they join Demeter in waiting through the bleak season of Her Daughter's absence. Each spring they are renewed by the signs of Persephone's return.[8]

Every woman, at the deepest level, understands like Adrienne Rich that "Probably there is nothing in human nature more resonant with charges than the flow of energy between two biologically alike bodies, one of which has lain in amniotic bliss inside the other, one of which has labored to give birth to the other."[9] Does the memory of these resonant charges, this *jouissance* between mother and daughter, get lost in the onslaught of patriarchal culture? Or does it go "underground?" Intuition suggests that the reunion between Demeter and Persephone, between mother and daughter, which results in such a florescence revolves around keeping *jouissance* alive in the most adverse conditions.

Jouissance, a concept from Roland Barthes developed by the French Freudian revisionist, Jacques Lacan is a word derived from the French *jouir*, a slang word meaning "to come." But rather than limiting it to a genital sexual meaning, Lacan offers *jouissance* to women as a fully sensuous way of being, a way of being beyond the imposed and institutionalized domination of the phallus. And, the question arises, where does a woman's capacity for *jouissance* come from? And more to the point, where does it go? Does a woman's *jouissance*, her sexual joy, arise out of an ancient memory of mother-daughter love? Is not the mother's body our first experience of warmth, softness, holding, safety, comfort, pleasure, joy? Whenever a woman experiences bodily pleasure, does her body not seek or recall in some way the body of her mother? Is not the mother's body implicated and evoked in all of our body-events? What do we do with the body's memory when, as daughters, we are required to shift our allegiance from mother to father and then, as women, are oriented toward the body of a man? Do we forget? Can we hold on to the truth of the body that does not lie? Can we include the mother's body in our body's knowledge of pleasure?

Adrienne Rich has written in a poem entitled "Sibling Mysteries" that daughters were never so much "brides of the father" as of the mother, and then "true brides of each other / under a different law."[10] What Rich is talking about is the deep capacity that women have to love each other "under a different law"—that is, not under the law of the father, the patriarchal culture, but under the law of the mother, the law that rules the love between sisters, daughters, and women. In the Battlezone of patriarchal culture, we are taught to mistrust this love, to compete with each other, to separate ourselves in all the many ways. We are taught to be suspicious, to be afraid, to despise the idea of women loving each other. This kind of thought does a great injury to us as women. It keeps us away from each other as a source of energy, empowerment, and shelter.

From the perspective of women's culture, the myth of Demeter and Persephone is not simply a mother-daughter enmeshment myth. Although Demeter feels tremendous loss when Persephone goes to the Underworld, she understands that her beloved daughter must do what she must do. She does not engulf her daughter or attempt to stop her even though she knows Persephone's absence will cause her pain. She understands the necessity, not of separation, but of differentiation. She offers Persephone what every creative woman wants and needs, maternal shelter.

As Spretnak's version tells us, the reunion of Demeter and Persephone results in a great florescence, a re-flowering of the world. What better image to help us remember the potential of woman-to-woman identification for creativity. The blossoming that arises out of a woman's capacity to go into her deeps, her unconscious, even her depression, to attend to the dead, and then return with the wisdom from that place is the meaning of the Demeter-Persephone cycle. Their reunion, the joining of upper and lower worlds, results in a burgeoning maturity.

Reconnecting the Mother-Line.

There is another aspect of the Demeter and Persephone myth that is a survival from pre-patriarchal times. In the myth, old Hecate is the only one who hears Persephone cries. Hecate joins Demeter in her search for Persephone. There is a deep remembering of matrilineality encoded in this aspect of the myth, a knitting together of the thread that passes from grandmother to mother to daughter—the female lineage. Remembering our mother-line with all its joys and sufferings helps us to reconnect with women's history.

The mother-daughter stories that have passed down the generations of women are a great resource, bearing important messages for us to remember. One woman in her mid-life dreamed a dream of deep reconciliation with her mother.

> My mother and I are going to plant some trees. There is one tree in
> particular, an evergreen tree. I've neglected it, not watered it, it is almost
> dead. We take it and discover that if we cut it, clip off the outer edges
> that are brown and dead, it will be all right, it will have retained its same
> shape. The soil we are going to plant it in is very dry, parched, like clay.
> I go to get a bucket full of beautiful rich soil. There is a bed there and I
> fall asleep. When I wake up I realize I am saying, "Mum, Mother.

She says that she had not uttered these words since she was a small child, always
preferring to call her mother by her first name. Hearing herself call out "Mum,
Mother," she felt the full feeling implications of the dream and its message of
mother-daughter love.

In her poem, "Demeter," written for her daughter, Genevieve Taggard names
some of Demeter's teachings:

> In your dream you met Demeter
> Splendid and severe, who said: Endure.
> Study the art of seeds,
> The nativity of caves.
> Dance your gay body to the poise of waves;
> Die out of the world to bring forth the obscure
> Into blisses, into needs.
> In all resources
> Belong to love. Bless,
> Join, fashion the deep forces.
> Asserting your nature, priceless and feminine.
> Peace, daughter. Find your true kin.
> —then you felt her kiss.[11]

Although it names only Demeter, Taggard's poem combines all the goddess's
functions—Demeter's art of the seeds, Persephone's dying out of the world, Hestia's
endurance, Aphrodite's dance on the waves, Hera's imperative to join, Athene's
assertion of feminine wisdom, Artemis's fashioning of the deep forces—making the
poem's command a true charge from the Great Goddess. Sealed with a kiss.

Baubo

There is another aspect of the Demeter myth that belongs to women's culture. In
the midst of her deepest grief, Demeter has made her way to the women's well.
She has not eaten; she is unbathed. Women gather round her, sensing her loss
and sorrow. But they do not pity her. Instead they send Baubo, a special woman
who knows how to tell "dirty" stories. Baubo lifts her skirts, wiggles her behind,
shakes her breasts. And Demeter begins to laugh. She probably tells Demeter

some story about the vicissitudes of penises—the ups and downs. Baubo is earthy; she is raunchy. She causes women to belly-laugh. Baubo has been represented in little sculptures which show a woman's head perched on a vulva with legs. Baubo's humor comes from between her legs; her vulva experiences are hilarious.

In the Battlezone of patriarchal culture, women spend so much time protecting their sexuality from unwanted intrusion that any opportunity to let loose is highly welcomed. There is nothing quite so liberating as the times when Baubo makes her appearances.

On one of the Dreamquest canoe trips, our group of women had been paddling hard all morning. Around lunchtime we pulled onto shore where a great outcropping of granite met the water. The lake was deep enough to dive into, and the water felt deliciously cool after the long paddle. Women stripped their clothes off and dove, and swam, and bobbed around in the water. Eventually we all made our way to the generous warmth of the granite slabs, where we laid around like seals. Then someone began telling a story, a few women laughed, a small rippling sound. The stories got earthier, the commentary funnier, the laughter deeper, until finally we were all shrieking with laughter, rolling around, with huge guffaws, howling, and carrying on. None of this is particularly exceptional, the jokes not worth repeating. But the experience is actually rare for most women. The conditions of safety and trust necessary for a woman to "let loose," let her guard down, let herself go—go into the sheer joy and release of earthy laughter are not conditions usually found in our day to day life. If we do find them, we know they are precious. Laughter that arises from deep in our bellies is different from the stifled tittering and giggling that comes from high out of our throats.

3. HERA AND THE MOON CYCLES

> I will choose the tongue
> for my songs. I am
>
> a young woman still
> joining hands with the moon, a creature
> of blood and its the singing of the blood
> that matters. . . .
>
> —*Wendy Rose*[13]

Often a woman will feel she is "too big" to live in the confines of domestic arrangements—the house feels too small, the relationship too constricting, her work too confining. She longs to take to the wilderness, to let her energies expand. Only the mountains are big enough to contain her body, only the open water lets her sing out at the top of her lungs, only the night wind causes her breath to become full and deep.

On the Dreamquest we were instructed through Kathryn's dream to feel the bear breathing. In the ceremony the following night, we were told to breathe and rattle and the goddess would come. Days later we were paddling our canoes against a powerful headwind. That night we were swept into the chaos of the night wind, hoping our tents would hold and that we would remain on earth. The air, wind, breath, spirit, breathes and blows. We are moved by the wind. It is the dark of the moon.

In earliest myth it is the Great Goddess Hera who rules the lunar heavens. And it is her cycle of maiden, mother, and crone that is illuminated by the moon. The lunar cycle is embodied in her mythology and makes her linked to the Old European "Goddess of Regeneration," the Snake Goddess who sheds her skin, and the cow, whose gestation period is similar to women's and whose horns are shaped as cresent moons. As goddess of the moon cycle, Hera is also goddess of women's blood mysteries.

The correspondence between women's cycles and those of the moon are part of a deep rhythm of creativity. The interconnectedness between women, the moon, and planting has been recognized since ancient times. The moon was known to influence the ocean's tides, the push and pull of liquid in our bodies, and the living fluids in plants. Women who cultivated the earth understood that the moon, their bodies, and plantlife were bound together in some deeply important way. The sowing of seeds, transplanting, and harvesting was timed with the phases of the moon. In general, it was believed that the waxing of the moon is the best time for sowing seeds because as the moon grows, so will the plants. Some people still plant by the moon. So, too, do our sexual rhythms correspond to our moon cycle. Hera's lunar cycle is a deep metaphor for a woman's creative process.

New Moon

As Hera *parthenia*, a woman's creative energy is like the waxing moon. As the maiden, she is free to explore, to feel her new energies rise; she can move, be curious, nose around, discover. She can play. She is a young adolescent with a budding body. Her sexual and creative energies are still virginal, kept to herself, stored in her body. All of the eggs in a woman's body are there when she is born, the creative potential stored within her. Her blood time is yet to come.

In her earliest mythology there is a story of how Hera bathed in the Kanathos spring each year to renew her virginity, her freshness, her integrity. Charlene Spretnak, in her re-membering of Hera, tells this story:

> Hidden in the foothills nearby, the spring called Kanathos flowed secretly, silently from Earth's womb. Each year Hera appeared to the

Argive women at the spring. She bathed in the cool water and emerged
with Her virginity renewed once again—One-In-Herself, the Celestial
Virgin. The women received the blessing of Hera's grace and crowned
one another with wreaths of aster, blossoming with the Goddess'
starflowers.[13]

As this re-imagining of Hera indicates, Hera was also worshipped as the goddess of flowers. Girls in her service were known as flower bearers, and the
spring festival in her honour celebrated by Peloponnesian women could be
described as the prototype of our May Day. Later the Floralia, the festival of
the Roman goddess of flowers, Flora, took place between April 28 and May 3.
Later still, the Virgin Mary would take over all these functions, and May would
be her month.

One of my most cherished memories from late childhood is one where my
mother and I made May altars to Mary in my bedroom. We used the old cedar
chest covering it with scraps of silk cloth which had been sent to us by my aunts,
the nuns. The beautifully colored fabrics were remnants left over from the making
of priests' vestments. We also acquired, from somewhere, a two-foot-high plaster
statue of Mary which I determined was too pale. I took my paints and gave her
brilliant red lips and rouged cheeks, I also made her mantle a deep, almost nighttime, blue violet. I gave the snake she was standing on a couple of dabs of green
and a red touch to the apple in its mouth as well. My mother did not object.

For the month of May, this altar was in my bedroom. I gathered spring flowers to place on it, especially violets which I love. At night my mother and I would
say the rosary together: "Hail Mary, full of Grace." For these few moments in my
pre-adolescent years my mother and I meet. This ritual took place far outside the
realm of organized religion—the priest did not tell us how to do it, the nuns at
school never encouraged it. I didn't even know if other girls and their mothers
created this kind of altar. All I knew was that making the May altar in my bedroom changed me for that month. I was no longer the rebellious resister, the one
who frequently fainted in church in order to get out, the one who refused to identify with this woman who was my mother, whose life and religion felt so intensely
stifling to me. This May-time ritual was something just between us, no brothers,
no father, no priests. My mother and I seemed to be in some deep and abiding
agreement over this May-time honoring of Mary

This memory stays alive in me. On Mother's Day, when I am fifty years old, I
take a nap after talking to my mother on the telephone. It is May, my parents'
wedding anniversary, and we had been talking about her simple marriage ceremony, how she was pregnant with me, what she wore, what flowers my father
brought for her. It was one of those rare and precious talks that seems to come
out of the blue, unplanned, unrehearsed. When I sleep, I dream that we are
together, my mother and I, and that she is singing one of the songs that we sang
at the May altar: "Oh Mary we crown thee with blossoms today, Queen of the

Angels, Queen of the May!" I wake up amazed and moved and immediately call her back to tell her my dream. In her conscious mind, I know my mother has no recollection of Beltane, that glorious, ancient spring festival of fertility, but somewhere in her deep memory something remains, and in the May altar ritual of my childhood we find our place of remembering.

Full Moon

As Hera *Teleia*, the goddess's creative energy becomes Hera fulfilled. As a mature woman, Hera joins with other women as they move into their moon-time:

> The women of Argos left their homes and walked together to the Stream of the Freeing Water. They bathed and then gathered branches from the nearby lygos bushes, which they laid in a large circular bower. On this ring they sat throughout the day, each seated with the women of her mother's clan. With the blessing of the Goddess, the lygos encouraged the flow of their sacred blood that would complete the cleansing they had begun in the stream.[14]

In the fullness of her blood, Hera is capable of fostering and nurturing life, she is a woman possessed of her full creative powers. She is able to feed herself and feed others out of her own fullness and abundance. She is able to be responsible, not in the old, tired, draining way that many of us so often feel, but in a strong and fortified way. She blesses women's fecundity, however it may wish to manifest. Because she knows how to replenish herself, she is full of response—to all life. She knows how to support and bolster that which is full of life. As my friend Karin says, "She keeps making the space bigger."

Hera's Gifts: The Ring Ceremony and Self-Marriage

Many women who have entered into marriage while still psychologically undeveloped, or still suffused with adolescent dreams of romantic love, or clinging to some hope of fulfillment through traditional marriage arrangements, find themselves profoundly devasted when faced with a divorce. Oftentimes this divorce has come totally "unexpectedly." After years of accommodation to an ideal accompanied by daily denial of what she actually feels or wants, a woman who is delivered a divorce decree may feel the most acute abandonment, loss, and rejection. Long after the divorce has been settled, it may take her years before she can bring herself to remove the outward sign of her status, her engagement and wedding rings.

When she has played her sorrow, grief, fury, and depression out to its unredeeming end, a woman will sometimes spontaneously arrive at a surprising solution. She will be moved to go out and buy a ring for herself. This usually unselfconscious move stems, I believe, from an inner need to marry one's self.

Morgan Farley, in her long, ecstatic poem "Her Radiance Everywhere," writes of her mid-life awakening to loving a woman. The last section of the poem, "reflects the inner marriage, forged when the union in the world dissolved." This marriage takes place in the Wildzone:

red rocks, round moon
come be my witnesses
tonight I marry myself

here in this silence
where three deer stood still for me
I join one hand to the other in simple love

as I place the ring on my finger
moon says, marry your own fullness
rocks say, only that endures

no witnesses
but these
no family in rented formal clothes

midnight, the moon
burgeoning with light
spilling her radiance everywhere

I come home to
myself here
prodigal refugee lost child

I marry
the woman I am
ripe and tender and full of juice

oh I am the one
I have been waiting for
with such patient longing

this bride
cannot be bought
at any price

her hand is given
into the keeping
of her own steadfast heart[15]

As Morgan Farley's poem shows, to marry one's self is to become permanently bonded, in terms of fidelity, to one's own true self. A woman can make vows to herself, promises of faithfulness as strong, if not stronger, than the ones she feels have been sundered. To love, honor, and even obey the self gives a woman her own authority. Then a woman cannot ever be so utterly abandoned, because she will not be tempted to project the core of her being onto another. Whether she decides to partner again, to marry or not, is another choice. The important thing is that she has wedded herself.

I had created this rite of passage for myself at one time wearing for years a snake ring from Crete as emblem of my dedication to my female energies. It served as a reminder of my promise to myself to remain true to what I knew and felt. I have since watched other women spontaneously come up with the idea. Sometimes I will notice a new ring on a woman's hand after she has been divorced for awhile. One woman created a ring ceremony for herself by buying a South Sea Pearl and wearing it on her wedding ring finger after she cleaned it and blessed it in the sea. The ring symbolized her marriage to herself. Oftentimes a woman will "confess" that she couldn't believe how much money she had spent, but she just had to have this ring! Even though she may dismiss her motives in an attempt to trivialize, she knows this is an important gesture. The ring, a symbol of self-commitment, may also accompany a name change.

Sometimes a woman will resume her maiden name, other times she will name herself, choosing a name that represents her true self more clearly and cleanly then her "given" name. The new name confers power and identity. What is important here is that the name is one of her own choosing. These two cere-monies of self-marriage and self-naming are unauthorized by the culture we live in, but many women have found their way to them. These unsanctioned sacra-ments confirm a woman's sense of self, they serve to make her commitment to that self sacred. These are two of the gifts that Hera, as goddess of marriage, can bring to women.

The Waning Moon

The waning moon is the part of the cycle that corresponds to the Old Woman. In Hera's moon cycle she is *Hera Chera*, Hera the Widow. In her mythology this is when Hera disappears from the domestic scene and withdraws into her self. She is the Dark of the Moon, the Crone, the Wisdom Woman, the Elder. She is a woman whose bleeding has stopped. Although her creativity is no longer reproductive, it flourishes in other ways. And she still has her blood wisdom to dispense.

A woman in her late fifties, a prolific and successful painter, was searching for an image that would express a certain kind of mood she was feeling. In her imagination she saw a gnarled grape vine, pruned down to its essence. The image was compelling for her. That night she had a dream:

> I am sitting on what appears to be a throne surrounded by many young children (all girls) perhaps four to five years of age. They are lined up and pass by me in a procession. They halt only to receive a piece of lollipop that I have prepared. Around me there are boxes upon boxes of tampons. As each child reaches me I take one tampon out of its protective covering, dip it in a bottle of red juice and sugar and hand it to each child. As they walk off I keep thinking this looks like blood but I know I am giving them juice, not blood, so I feel very comfortable, loving and serene.

The woman dreamer is insistent that what she is giving to the young girls is "juice," not the blood of sacrifice and pain, the "curse" given to Eve, but creative "juice." She has become a teacher, she can pass on her wisdom.

In the waning moon part of her creative cycle, a woman may come into touch with the Crone, an eccentric, articulated self, who wears no cultural shackles. In this phase, the relationship between body and spirit changes place: the body, once the most important vehicle for wisdom, begins its process of turning into spirit. In the waning moon, it is the spirit's turn to carry the body.

4. WATER AND THE SACRAMENTS OF APHRODITE

> Until she rises as though from the sea
> not on a half-shell this time
> nothing to laugh at
> and not as delicate as he imagined her:
> a woman big-hipped, beautiful and fierce.
> —*Sharon Barba*[16]

According to her mythology, Aphrodite was born foam-risen and connecting. Birthing herself out of the severed phallus, she passes through the gate of the fathers, it is a birth passage to liberation. Nor Hall says, Aphrodite is about "becoming your own father, being self-generating, capable of independent thought and action, especially in the realms of love."[17] When the father's phallus explodes into foam, Aphrodite uses all its energy to make herself. She becomes self-seeding; finding her own phallic powers within, she has the capacity to self-conceive. Aphrodite is the essence of woman's self-becoming out of the father. The immense amount of creative freedom that springs forth is hers. This is the cure which Aphrodite brings to her swallowed sisters. The phallus and its powers are no longer projected "out there"—they are in her and of her.[18]

In ancient times the longing to be in touch with the mysteries of great Aphrodite was accomplished through her womanly representative, her priestess. It was the Sacred Prostitute who took the stranger into her arms and satisfied the need for physical and spiritual renewal. Both partners knew that it was Aphrodite who was blessing them and that it was she who was being served by their actions.

The role of Sacred Prostitute was undertaken by women as a devotional service to the goddess. Religious ceremonies of sexual union were performed as part of an honoring of the powerful life force expressed in sexual union. Ritual intercourse with a priestess of Aphrodite was the closest a person could come to being in touch with the goddess. Only a mortal representative of the goddess could bestow that kind of blessing, and intercourse with her was understood in these terms—as a rite of renewal and transformation.

A woman's role as priestess to Aphrodite has always been subject to potential reversals depending on who is in power—praise and worship of the goddess is easily threatened by misogynist political and religious takeovers. We have very few remnants to remind us of the ancient rituals of the Sacred Prostitute, but what there are confirm the holy powers of her knowledge.

From the ancient civilization of Sumer come the writings of a holy woman, Enheduanna (born ca. 2275 B.C.), a priestess of Inanna (the Sumerian Aprhodite), and a poet. In her long poem, "The Exaltation of Inanna," Enheduanna laments the falling away of the worship of Inanna and her own banishment and revilement as her priestess:

> Me who once sat in triumph
> he has driven from the
> sanctuary.
> Like a swallow in flight through a window
> he cast me, my life is
> consumed[19]

As enemies threaten the temple and drive her into the wilderness, Enheduanna sets up her great lamentation poem to her goddess, Inanna. It is a poem where the fates of priestess and goddess combine. When Inanna's worship is restored, both priestess and goddess reclaim their powers and the exaltation is proclaimed: "She was robed in womanly beauty. / Like the light of the rising moon, how splendid was her array!"

The poet and writer Deena Metzger imagines a return of the Holy Prostitute in contemporary women's lives. It was through intercourse with the Holy Prostitute, she says, that one came to the Divine. Access was both personal and transpersonal: "As the body was the means, so inevitably pleasure was an accompaniment, but the essential attribute of sexuality, in this context, was prayer."[20] Like a modern-day Enheduanna, Metzger laments the loss of this knowledge: "In a sacred universe, the prostitute is a holy woman, a priestess. In a secular universe the prostitute is a whore. In this distinction is the agony of our lives."[21]

Aphrodite's task, according to Metzger, is to commit oneself, in love, to the sacredness of sexuality and the body—"to accept the body as spiritual, and sexuality and erotic love as spritual disciplines, to believe that eros is pragmatic. To honor the feminine even where it is dishonored or disadvantaged."[22] In this way "we become world through love" an act that is both political and spiritual in its ramifications since "Nothing can change as long as we devalue the feminine, denigrate the body and disbelieve in a sacred universe."[23]

Lilith

Lilith is one name given to Aphrodite's energy. Originally Inanna, Aphrodite, and Lilith were all part of the Great Goddess, who ruled over women's sexuality and the sacred mysteries of life, death, and regeneration. In Hebrew legend, Lilith, the first bride of Adam, had insisted on her own independence. Above all, she would not agree to intercourse where the man was on top. Outraged by this enforced sexual hierarchy, she fled from Adam into another realm.

> Adam and Lilith never found peace together; for when he wished to lie with her, she took offence at the recumbent posture he demanded. "Why must I lie beneath you?" she asked. "I also was made from dust, and am therefore your equal." Because Adam tried to compel her obedience by force, Lilith, in a rage, uttered the magic name of God, rose into the air and left him.[24]

When the religious symbol system of the patriarchy took over, hierarchy between the sexes was established, the primordial female life force was banished, and in Lilith's place came Eve. However, like all attempts to repress female sexuality, Lilith was never really gone from the imagination. From her place in the wilderness, the ancient Hebrews believed that Lilith would reappear at night entering into a man's dreams with her dark eroticism, causing nocturnal emissions. She was the "night hag," a seductress, a stealer of semen and of children. Rules of conduct were laid down in order to avoid her evil and impure influence. A man was forbidden to sleep alone lest Lilith find him. Women were thought to be especially connected to her in their earthiness, their sexuality, their capacity for seduction. And so all women were feared—and hated—because of their secret closeness to Lilith. Many contemporary women are working creatively with the mythology of this patriarchal Jewish-Christian tradition, attempting to retell the old tale from the place of women's culture.

The Wild Mother as Lilith

The novelist, Elizabeth Cunningham, In her modern day fable, *The Wild Mother*,[25] tells the story of Ionia, a young girl with haunting purple eyes, who dreams at night of a woman who crests the hill to dance beneath the trees by moonlight. "The woman's hair was darker than the night and wilder than the wind. Her dance would begin gently and then slowly grow stronger until even the trees and the hills seemed to dance with her. Then she would stretch out her arms to the house. 'Ionia, Ionia,' she seemed to sing, but her voice might have been the wind's." When she awoke from her dream Ionia, would draw images of the woman dancing on the crest of a hill, with her wild black hair spread out against the sky.

Ionia lives with her father, Adam, a professor of alchemy, a grim and controlling man who once made his way into the Empty Land where he met and fell desperately, obsessively in love with a woman named Lilith, a direct descendant from the primordial Lilith, who still lived and for whom she had been named. Adam brought Lilith into his home in her wild state. Her nakedness only partially covered by coarse black hair, which fell below her waist: "This hair looked as though it had never been combed. It was full of leaves and here and there a wildflower." Her eyes "were purple in color, and in expression they were as wild and wary as any animal's."

Once Lilith entered Adam's remote home on the edge of the Empty Land, he began his program to tame and control her. In one of his many attempts to possess her and her knowledge, Adam "married" Lilith, although Lilith herself had no concept of such an arrangement. In fact, she had no knowledge of ownership, property, or any of the other laws that govern power between people. She had no conditioned "morality," and thus no shame. Her only law was freedom, her only need was to be in the Dance. Soon after giving birth to a daughter and a son, Lilith escaped from Adam and went back to her Empty Land, the woman's Wildzone.

Returning years later to Adam's house to retrieve her daughter, Lilith finds that Adam has set a trap for her with Ionia as the bait. In her absence he has built a wall around his house with a gate which only he can operate. When she tries to leave with Ionia, they find they cannot escape. Lilith tries the gate and, realizing she cannot open it, she "hurled herself at the gate, throwing her whole weight aganst it. Then she began to leap at the gate again and again, making high, frightened yelping sounds." Adam knew that his plan had worked. "She was in an enclosed space, his space. He could do what he liked." Yet having captured her, he became confused—the thrill of the chase was now lost to him. He no longer knew what he wanted from her.

As time went by, Lilith began to grow physically frail, although her essence was still strong. She slept naked outside against the wall. At least, outside at night, she could see the stars. She tells her daughter: "When I lie on the bare ground, I can feel the earth spinning, following its path in the Dance. I can see the moon waxing and waning in time with the Dance. In the melting snow and the greening grass, I see the eternal changes of the Dance, and, in the wind, I hear the music of the Dance. . . ." But it is not enough to sustain her: "I can watch the Dance but I am not in the Dance. I am out of my place; I am not following my steps. No living being then, mortal or immortal, can live long outside the dance."

One night Lilith told her daughter she was dying. She says: "The Grand Mother is immortal, though the men who fathered us were not. We, her daughters, are made immortal by the rites of the water of life." Cut off from the sacred water she will die. "Captivity will kill me; I am dying of it. I have no choice." Death, she explains, is a better choice anyway, since "it is considered dishonorable among my people, your people, Ionia, to suffer a captive existence." Then and there Ionia decides to go against her father's will. She makes a plan to enlist her friend Jason, her brother Fred, and her grandmother in an effort to liberate Lilith.

During a week when Adam is at a conference, they all attempt to dig a tunnel under the wall. When that effort fails, they enter Adam's study to find some clues. In a book on the *Mysteries of the Moon: The Making and Unmaking of Magic*, they learn the secret spells on how to break open the gate. On the night of the full moon, they all undertake a powerful moon ritual. As soon as the moon breaks over the horizon, Lilith sings a Mother Tongue song:

> Mysterious Moon,
> Raiser of wind
> Ruler of water Mirror of fire Mover of earth
> We the captives of one man's magic
> make supplication to your Majesty.

Soon all the elements invoked appear in their full powers, knocking the humans out of consciousness. As Lilith was singing, Ionia could see women appearing on the crest of the hill:

> a whole band of women danced in a circle around and around the three
> trees. As the singing grew stronger and the dance wilder, the hills began
> to rise and fall, rise and fall, as if they, too joined in the dance. . . . The
> earth trembled, and she felt it open beneath her. The women vanished;
> the hills vanished; the sky vanished, and she felt herself falling, falling
> into a deep, warm darkness.

When everyone came back to consciousness, they found that the gates had been blasted open by the magic of the moon ritual. Lilith asked Ionia to come with her to the Empty Land, her real home. But Ionia could not yet decide. She walked with her mother through the wall where the gates had been to the top of the hill. Then Lilith disappeared and was gone from sight.

When Adam returned, his uncontrolled rage at having been outdone reached its peak. Screaming at the children that he would kill them, he drove them out into the Empty Land alone in search of their mother. Ionia, her young friend Jason, her brother Fred, and the dog all take off over the hill in search of Lilith. Once they reached the crest of the hill, they were immediately transported to another realm of existence. After several days of wandering in the Empty Land, Ionia remembered that her mother had told her how to follow her inner wisdom. Following a herd of wild cows from whom they feed, they find her mother's hut, an earthen dwelling carved into the side of a hill with a pool of sacred water at its center.

When they were reunited, Lilith told Ionia that she would have to choose whether or not she would live in the Empty Land with her: "This is your country, Ionia, if you choose it. . . . The wilderness is for the wild." But Ionia was in deep conflict, for "man-children" were not allowed in the women's wilderness and she could not imagine separating from her little brother Fred, nor even her friend Jason.

On the eve of the Summer Solstice, Ionia and her mother gathered with the other women around a great sacred fire. Ionia "watched each woman as she entered the circle of light. There was one woman with hair like fire, another with hair the color of clouds or ashes, yet another with hair like light itself. Their skins were of many different shades, too. . . . In that light all their eyes were bright, all their bodies naked, and all seemed ageless in the human sense of the word." Into the center of this circle of women came the First Woman, massive in build, with long white hair and dark skin, like the moon on a dark night. On her head she wore a crown of dark leaves. She was the Grand Mother, and she invited Ionia into the Dance. But the Grand Mother also told Ionia that she must choose. "Are you wild or human?" she asked. Ionia was confused. To be wild meant to stay with her mother and the other women of the race of Lilith in the Empty Land forever. To be human was to go back home with Fred and Jason, and, someday, to die. After much deliberation, and a period of deep self-reflective solitude, Ionia chose to go back to her country and be human. With Lilith's blessing, she and the boys headed for home.

Over the summer months, with the children gone to the Empty Land, Ionia's father, Adam, had undergone a strange transformation. Alone in his empty house, without any human connection, he began to feel his own pain, suffering, and loneliness. In his isolation, he wept, he felt grief, he surrendered his ambition to control through knowledge. In disgust, he burned his alchemical manuscripts. Deep in sorrow, he found his mother's overgrown garden on the side of the house and he began to cultivate and grow things. Over time he went from a solitary, enraged, and controlling black magician to a simple man, a gardener, working and tending his small plot of soil.

When the children returned from the Empty Land, they came back to their country accompanied by Lilith. There, Lilith spoke to the woman, Eva, who wished now to be Adam's wife. Lilith agreed to the marriage and said to Eva, "my children, both of them, are human. I am wild. They need a human mother. Will you be the human mother?" Eva said "Lilith, I will be the human mother, but they will not forget their wild mother." And Lilith replied, "Let them remember." The human family reunited with Adam. Lilith went back to her sisters in the Empty Land.

The Return of Lilith

In her novel, Cunningham shows the tremendous loss and dislocation that we have suffered since Lilith went away into the Wilderness. Cunningham's tale describes Adam's attempts to trap and tame Lilith, to extract her wisdom and add to his knowledge, like Zeus swallowing Metis. In this way, men have sought for millennia to tame, control, and appropriate both nature and women, since in the patriarchal imagination the two are dangerously connected. Because women and nature have always been joined, women have been persecuted and nature has been exploited, her mysteries and treasures misused and co-opted. But Cunningham's story is truly a redemptive one. While Lilith remains in the Wildzone it is Adam who must undergo necessary changes. He learns to give up his need for control and his lust for obtaining and owning the secrets of female sexuality, and he humbly comes to respect the lessons of the mother's garden—the cycles of nature, the birth, death, and regeneration patterns of the goddess. Only then can he be reunited in harmony with his human family.

Lilith on Top

As the banished goddess, Lilith has lived for millennia in the desert Wilderness. But Lilith has always existed as a place of wildness in women's psyches. As Cunningham tells us, the Wild Mother cannot bear to live in captivity: she has to live in the wild. She is lawless, without the taming, molding, shaping regimens that govern and control our lives as patriarchal women. She appears to us in our dreams as a dark woman, heavily sexual, often disheveled, with abundant hair. Lilith also lives in our bodies. In Hebrew myth Lilith was banished because of her refusal to be "on the bottom" all the time. That embodiment of sexual hierarchy is what sent Lilith away. But Lilith is making her return in women's lives. Lilith on top means freedom of movement, she is in charge of her own sexuality, her orgasms. As my friend Karin says, "It's a wild place to be."

"She is the bolstering Other"

Cunningham's story of Lilith tells of the hunger and need the daughter has to remember, recollect, and be in touch with her Wild Mother. Although Ionia chooses in the end to remain human and not live forever in the Wildzone with her Wild Mother, at least she has been there once and has learned the Dance. She knows she has a choice and she brings her Wild Mother's knowledge back with her.

Lilith has been outcast and given a long and bad reputation, but she has a gift to bring us: the instinctual knowing that there are other ways to be, to think, to live, to move outside of patriarchal thought. Lilith, the Wild Mother, lives in a world outside of patriarchal social structure and definition, and her daughter needs to know her and remember her. As the poet Diane di Prima sees her, she is the "bolstering Other"; she not only supports our knowledge of wildness, she heightens and intensifies it with the force of her natural powers. She pressures us to the point of transformation:

> . . . Higher you climb
> the more she fills yr dream.
> She is the bolstering Other, backside
> of the coin. Underpinning of stage set
> you love. Whatever play you're doing.
> She is flying moon in the clouds
> on all the foggy coastlines of the earth.
>
> Where land touches water; where fire meets w/air
> where guts of earth burst out in coal, or diamond:
> is is flesh, it is flesh, it is Lilith. Interface.[26]

While Greek mythology has been content to leave Metis in Zeus's belly and Jewish-Christian religion has been happy to leave Lilith in the desert, it is Metis and Lilith and their daughters who continue to disrupt and upset by being indigestible wild women. We cannot rely on patriarchal traditions to teach us about her. It is up to us to remember the Wild Mother. As Monique Wittig tells us:

> There was a time when you were not a slave, remember that. You walked alone, full of laughter, you bathed bare-bellied. You say you have lost all recollection of it, remember . . . you say there are no words to describe it, you say it does not exist. But remember. Make an effort to remember. Or, failing that, invent.[27]

In *The Wild Mother*, Cunningham describes the Great Dance of the women which takes place around an enormous fire: "Silhouetted against its light, so that they looked like the shadows they cast, were women circling round and round the fire, sometimes with their hands joined, sometimes not. All the women had long hair that whirled around them as they danced." Only after Ionia participated in the Great Dance, becoming one of the circle of women, could she decide to make her return home.

·IX·

The Third Gate: The Return

a woman can't survive
by her own breath
                alone
she must know
the voices of mountains
she must recognize
the foreverness of blue sky
she must flow
with the elusive
bodies
of night wind women
who will take
her into
her own self

—*Joy Harjo*[1]

As anyone who has experienced it knows, the Return is the trickiest part of any initiatory journey. The fears and apprehensions that usually accompany the start of a big journey are nothing like what we face when we make the turn towards home. Anytime we venture out into something that takes us away from our cultural scripts and habits—a visionquest, a journey to a country that is foreign to us, a workshop that has expanded us, a spiritual retreat, a week in the mountains—we eventually find ourselves heading for home.

One of the last ceremonies we did on the Dreamquest trip was to make clay figurines that honored the great Dream Weaver. Women made dreamhouses with clay, stones, and leaves; a seated female figure shaped out of clay had a feather headdress and a shell vulva; a large sculpted hand held natural treasures collected on the trip. Each clay sculpture captured the essence of the woman's journey and her dreams. We placed them together on a great rock where they sat watching over our campsite for the night. In the morning each woman ceremoniously took her sculpture and found it a wilderness home: clay sculptures were left in trees, in rock clefts, at the shore of the lake, under bushes, on driftwood logs. The whole landscape was filled with our thanks-offerings to the place and the spirits of the place. This rite of honoring provided us with an important exit ceremony. We left our place of deep dreaming knowing that although the sculptures would dissolve back into the earth, something of our experience remained and we could always go back, in memory, to touch and remember what and where we had been.

On the last night of our canoe trip, a group of us sat dispersed on a rocky shore watching the sun go down. As the dark gathered about us, we faced in the distance the lights of the "civilized" world we were about to re-enter. Each woman sat alone with her thoughts. We were like a tribe of aborigines, I thought. We had, in our short time together, developed community, a pattern of life complete with rituals. We had lived outside for days, had become familiar with the patterns of wind and clouds, had watched the lake shift in mood, had seen the moon through a third of its cycle, had been dazzled by a monumental electrical storm. On the sand we had tracked the hoofprints of deer, moose, and the other creatures with whom we shared the lake. In our dreams these animals came and spoke to us. As the thin veneer of our civilized life fell off, our faces changed, our bodies moved in more natural ways, we felt stronger, more sure of ourselves, more alive. It seemed we could go on like this forever. We wanted it to last. Filled with this knowledge, memory, and desire we prepared to make our Return.

The Return can often be bumpy, rocky, disorienting. As we make our re-entry, we look at things through a different lens. What we always put up with now seems intolerable, the dead places in our lives tighten around us like an outworn carapace—jobs no longer have any juice, partnerships may seem empty and unfulfilling, our routine life feels deadly, we feel alone. We try to cling to what we experienced in the Wildzone, the insights, the depth of connection, the feeling of community, the sense of self, the pleasure of expansion. But the wisdom gained during the rite of separation in the Wildzone can easily get drowned out by the clamor of our daily lives. Women begin to learn the difference between being silenced by the noise of the Battlezone and being nurtured and held in the silence of the Wildzone. One woman recalls: "I craved the silence of the lake. The noises of the 'civilized' world were too much. I used to listen to classical music all the time but now I am aware that even those sounds prevent my hearing my own voice."

Another woman, who would face a diagnosis of breast cancer upon her return, remembered a moment when she was paddling hard into the wind with her canoe partner. She was afraid and didn't feel her arms were strong enough to continue paddling. When the wind whipped up, they began spontaneously singing old camp songs at the top of their lungs. She said: "I don't sing—or rarely do—but the wind was coming up and in some way its energy connected with the joyfulness we were sharing. *Something gave way in me . . .* and my paddling changed. I became the paddle with seemingly no effort at all and we began to fly across those whitecaps as if some energy outside of my arms was pushing the canoe. Then there was a quiet moment when we both realized what was happening." It was that silent moment that stayed with her during the many hard months to follow. Reflecting back, she said, "There is a language out there in the silence of the woods and water that I began to hear, to feel, the barrier to listening somehow disappeared that week."

Rituals of Incorporation

In rites of passage, there are ceremonies for the Return, they are called rituals of incorporation. On a body level, incorporation means digestion, absorbing, and assimilating that which has been taken in, letting it nurture and sustain. On a psychological level, incorporation means integration and integrity, mixing new material into one's psyche and having it become integral to one's sense of self. On the cultural level, incorporation means carrying back the knowledge and wisdom gained from the Wildzone and bringing it to bear on the way we live our lives. Ritual incorporation includes communal sharing and a distribution of gifts. I imagine this process as one of cultivation where the metaphor of gardening applies. The seeds of women's culture gathered and wildcrafted in the Wildzone are brought back into our everyday world. As each woman spades up the old earth, she plants her new garden with those seeds. From her own soil, she grows and harvests her creative efforts and offers them as gifts to feed the culture.

Part Four

The New Earth

X

The Women Are Speaking

Daughters, the women are speaking.
They arrive
over the wise distances
on perfect feet.
Daughters, I love you.

—*Linda Hogan*[1]

For the master's tools will never dismantle the master's house.
—*Audre Lorde*[2]

This above all, to refuse to be a victim. Unless I can do that I can
do nothing. I have to recant, give up the old belief that I am powerless and because of it nothing I can do will ever hurt anyone.
—*Margaret Atwood*[3]

Searching for the Father, Finding the Man

After a woman has encountered the elemental energies of the goddesses in the
Wildzone, felt the power of the Wild Mother in herself and the community of
women, she may return home, but she is walking on new ground. Feeling her own
strength as a woman, she may feel compelled to undertake a final search for her
father. A woman on this kind of mission begins to ransack her memory, rummage
around in the old stories, looking for something that will be of use in her creative
life. She may feel that something has been left unfinished, unsaid, undone, in relationship to her father. Because fathers are so good at hiding, a woman may suspect
that something important is being kept from her, something she wants and needs
from him, not approval or respect this time, but something deeper, more visceral.
Something like truth, the emotional and embodied truth of the man.

This kind of search for the man hidden inside the father is the subject of Germaine Greer's book *Daddy, We Hardly Knew You*.[4] Despite her international acclaim as a writer and feminist, Greer was still looking for something from her father. She says: "It is a wise child that knows her own father. I knew as I held my father's old hand in my own, its exact replica, and watched my own skull emerging through his transparent skin, that I am my father's daughter."[5] She easily found his genetic heritage in her own body—in "the cleft in the end of my nose, my receding hair-line, my lantern jaw, my large ears, my blunt fingers and my narrow chest . . ."[6] She recognized his high strung temperament, his tendencies toward nervous exhaustion and his "touchy tummy" as part of his physical bequest to her. But her search was for something more primitive than body, she was hungry for something more visceral from him. She was convinced she did not know the truth about his life and her quest for that truth turned into a hunt: "Bone of your bone, Daddy. You shall not escape me."[7]

For the first five years of her life, Greer knew her father only through a photograph enshrined on the maple sideboard in her childhood home. He had left his wife and infant daughter to join the Australian Air Force during the Second World War. When she and her mother went to pick him up at the train station after his military discharge, she couldn't find him. What she saw instead was a "distant speech-less wreck."

Only when he was finally dead did she begin to have some idea of the devastation that he had suffered and embark on her search for who this man really was. She was filled with unanswered questions about his life, where he had come from, who his original family was, what had happened to him in the war that had so destroyed him. She spent the next years tracking through dense underbrush to find him. He had skillfully covered his tracks and pulled down a "curtain of silence" around himself. She searched for three years, through England, Australia, Malta, Tasmania, and India. She scrutinized records and archives—genealogical, military, and civil—looking for clues.

Her five-thousand-mile quest was trailed by what she calls "the primal elder's curse." Like the demons always present at the threshold of consciousness, all sorts of threatening and demoralizing events pursued and attacked her: a clump of hair was inadvertently torn from her head; she lost her spectacles; a bird accidentally flew square into her windshield; she lost important letters, two rolls of film, all her photographs of her father, and the copy of her parents' wedding certificate. In her archival and genealogical quests, she met gatekeepers and key-holders of various stripes, some friendly and helpful, others cruelly inefficient and withholding. In a truly labyrinthine journey, she met myriad dead-ends and cold trails. While in India, the desperate Greer finally did a *puja* to the goddess Durga, to draw strength and to "do penance for defying the laws of life":

> Durga is time, the now, the immediate. By digging my father out of
> his grave I was flouting her. She is the lady of destruction, the queen of

cannot be. As I laid my head upon her stone wedge of a foot like an anvil, I accepted my destiny, the dharma of a woman with neither father, husband nor son. With Durga's help I could pass among the rakshasas of my father's night unscathed.[8]

She was looking for Reg Greer. She carried his last name, the name she had built her fame around, her patronym, her father's name. Although she found a massive Greer clan and traced them back to Scottish Kings of Ulster, she couldn't find him. It never dawned on her until much later in her search that he had lied about his name and his childhood, not only to her but to her mother when he married her, as well to the RAF. Although she had always believed he was absent when she was born, she found out from her research that he left for the Air Force when she was three. Did he run away? From his wife? From his troublesome daughter? She was face to face with the implacable truth of his abandonment; "he chose to leave us and go to the other side of the world" and she wonders "why a certain little girl mis-remembered that her father went to war early and stayed late, when he went late and left early."[9] She says, "I do not know why the time he was gone seemed to me so long, when in fact it was so short, except that I must have missed him very much."[10]

It was during the war years on the island of Malta that her father developed what the military doctors called "anxiety neurosis." Greer suspected that he became anorexic as a ploy to get himself out of an unbearable military situation. Along with his military cowardice, she discovered other unsavory things—including evidence that her father was a philanderer.

As she moved closer towards the truth of her father's life, she found herself turning into a kind of terrible creature. "Though I felt sad as hell, I did not feel merciful, I felt like hell, implacable, hard and bitter. My heart was wrung out, shrunken to a stone, I was exhausted without being sleepy, famished without appetite."[11] Searching for the father she hardly knew made her realize, "I hardly knew myself." Like Atwood's unnamed heroine, Greer found herself staring in the mirror after another sleepless night. What she saw was a Fury:

> My face was set, my eyes staring, the pupils fixed as if suddenly grown insensitive to light. My brows had collapsed over them like a No mask of unutterable severity. My top lip was drawn down in a rictus with harsh wrinkles like hooks at the corner. . . . "You're mad," I said to myself.[12]

The woman in the mirror incriminated her by saying that she had always known her father was not what he said he was, "You knew he was a fraud. Dammit, you treated him as a fraud." Ever more vicious in her truthfulness, she confronts the face in the mirror accusing her of tracking down her father not because she loved him but because she hated him—"He rejected you and you hated him." This brutal self-confrontation continues until she realizes that the abusing face in the mirror has suddenly turned into the physically abusive mother of her childhood.

What Greer learns during her search is that the man she had fantasized she would find, the idealized father, "the brilliant refined young man with a great future and distinguished connections who just happened to lose touch with his family,"[13] was a poor foster child instead, one of twenty-five children taken in by a working-class woman named Emma Greeney and her husband. This is the truth her father had hidden from and lied about for his whole life.

In her search for her father, Germaine Greer eventually found out who his real parents were:

> On September 1, 1904 in a mean house in Middle Street, Launceston, my grandmother gave birth to a boy. She gave him the name Robert Hamilton, and because she was unmarried he bore her own surname, King. The name Robert Hamiltion was probably the name of the child's father, for neither name ran in her own family. . . . Robert Hamilton King was my father.[14]

As Greer notes, in saying this she now knew more than her father did. Relinquished as an infant by his mother, who was a domestic servant, her father had become a ward of the state. He was subsequently boarded out, taken in by Emma Greeney, never officially adopted, nor actually fostered, thus not even paid for by the state. He lived with Emma Greeney and her husband until he was sixteen, at which time he took off with a vaudeville group. As a young man, he had managed to banish this humble upbringing and the fostering of Emma Greeney from his mind, a fact that Greer can hardly reconcile much less forgive.

What did Germaine Greer get in return for her years long search? The truth. Did it serve her, did it help her understand herself or her father? Was she given a more open heart, a more compassionate way of being? The answers to these questions are left highly ambiguous. Greer is no proponent of the maxim, "The truth will set you free":

> There is a change—and I am poor. I cannot speak to Daddy any more because I know he lied to me. It was not the war that destroyed his love for me, but his charade and my censorious, scrutinising nature. . . . He was good company, but not for me. I was never his boon companion, but a full-on pain in the neck. In finding him I lost him. Sleepless nights are long.[15]

What Greer had to sacrifice in her search for the man hidden behind her father was her fantasy of finding the high-class man with the privileged background, the hoped-for inheritance, and the longed for closeness and intimacy. At the end of the story, she leaves us with her feelings of emptiness. Finding this father was not fulfilling, and she herself questions the wisdom of the pursuit. Nor was she given even a modicum of new love for her mother, a woman described in scathing terms by Greer as grotesquely shallow, self-absorbed, and a bit addled. She was not given the gift one would expect or wish for from facing the truth. Or maybe, since Greer is still alive and well, the gift will come to her later.

There is a secret gift embedded in this story, however, placed in the dedication of the book. The inscription reads: "To the memory of my three grandmothers." The names include her maternal grandmother whom she knew as a child as well as the two grandmothers that she discovered on her search—her father's biological mother, Rhoda Elizabeth King, and his foster mother, Emma Wise Greeney. These women and the stories she uncovered about them, tales filled with the hard realities of the lives of two good women, are the legacy and boon that Germaine Greer reclaimed in her quest for the man who was her father.

The Death of the Father: Women's Work of Mourning

As the father approaches death, our interest in him may once again be heightened. If he has not died early or suddenly, we may rush to fill in the empty spaces as he ages and we feel his death approaching. Before Greer undertook her search for the truth of her father's life, one of her fantasies was that she would take care of him as he grew sick and old. As she portrays it, the fantasy is not of a father and daughter, but something more primal, more maternal, something embodied—an infant-parent pair:

> When he was old and frail and soon to leave this world, I nurtured a fantasy that I would have time and he would have time for me to nurse him, to bathe him and groom him and feed him and hold him close so that he did not find his way out of the world alone. I have done as much for total strangers but I was not to get the chance to do it for my father. He went so fast and so far away that I couldn't catch up.[16]

The daughter's longing to physically touch the father's body is one of the great unsaid longings. If the father has been "too touching," violating the daughter's love by literalizing his desire and abusing her sexually, this desire to touch the father will be mixed with rage and repulsion. But in many women's stories, there is clearly not enough touching. Instead, there is what Andrew Samuels calls "an *insufficiency* of kinship libido," not an excess of it. He notes, "Mockery, strictness, and plain uptightness are reflected in a (father's) lack of physical involvement from the time the girl is a little baby." He goes on to say that there is a need to rethink why this is so and to begin to imagine "an optimal erotic relation between father and daughter and, hence of the pathology of a failure to achieve that."[17] It is this healthy erotic relationship with the father that can be potentially liberating, allowing a daughter to find and follow her own path. It seems that this embodied connection is what many women long to feel when a father is near death.

There is no more searingly radiant and courageous vision of a father's death then that told by Sharon Olds in her book of poems called simply *The Father*.[18] In these poems Olds reaches into that vast unspoken territory of father-daughter erotic love. Olds had written of her father many times before, in terror, passion, pain, and desire, but these poems about her father's death and dying drive right into the heart of embodied love.

The poems start as her father begins his long and torturous dying process while she participates in his care. In the beginning the poet imagines her father's death as her own pregnancy: "He knows he will live in me after he is dead, I will carry him like a mother. / I do not know if I will ever deliver."[19] As he moves towards death, she feels his dying in her own body—"I sense every inch of him moving / through me toward it, the way each child / moved, slowly, down through my body."[20] She makes her love poems out of the most intimate and intolerable physical images, the catheter bag, the cup of spit-up mucus, hair, sweat, skin, the accretion of the body's wretched progress towards its inevitable endpoint. As her father's body deteriorates, she notes how he gets shinier, more radiant until at last his final breath goes out.

In her last poem, "My Father Speaks to Me from the Dead,"[21] Olds imagines her father speaking to her from the other side. It is a long love poem in which he names each of her body parts and how he loves them. He instructs her to look at her hand and move it and to understand that in that movement he lives in her as "matter" and that the movement is love. What Sharon Olds reveals in these poems is the primal truth that our fathers are first and foremost implicated in our physicality, our connection to them is biological, the divine connection is located in matter. All the rest is built and constructed on that reality.

How our father's die, the circumstances, the words, spoken and unspoken, how the body is touched or left untouched, greatly affects us. We may long for the final blessing, the intimacy and closeness denied during the lifetime, the precious "I love you," the special look or gesture that would acknowledge the bond. Or we may feel relieved of the struggle, glad for the end. If there has been suffering, physical or emotional, the death itself may be a blessing. But when a father dies, we may still be left with more questions than answers.

As she sat at her father's deathbed, writer, Sally Cline, thought:

> You have spoilt me and misunderstood me. You have made me laugh and irritated me profoundly. I have always felt uneasy anywhere near you. I have hungered for affection throughout my childhood but I have never wanted you to touch me physically. I have spent nineteen years in a house with you, and I do not know who you are.[22]

As Sally Cline's message to her father reveals, if we have not been able to touch the father in a real and physical way, we cannot know him. The enormity of risk in that touching is what Sharon Olds' poems are about. The prohibition against physical touching because of the incest taboo can only be broken by the daughter in her search to know her father as a man, a vulnerable human like herself. Otherwise, like Cline, the question "Who are you?" may continue to haunt the daughter and the woman she has become.

It is interesting to note how many women have written about their fathers as a way of completing their grieving process. It is almost as if the death of the father releases the daughter from the pact of silence and lets her touch into the man. The death of Greer's father left her in such a state of unknowing that it sent her on a discovery mission, later to be published as her book of that search. Certainly Olds' poems are written as a memorial to her father. It is through his dying and her poetry that she came to know him and could speak of her love for him.

The death of Yael Dayan's father compelled her, too, to write a book in order to speak of what they had shared together as daughter and father. In her passionate and painful memoir, *My Father, His Daughter*, she recalls the deep and complicated relationship she had with her famous father, Moshe Dayan, one of Israel's foremost military leaders. Her book is a palimpsest where the intimate and highly nuanced daughter-father story is recorded over the broad sweep of historic and mythic tales surrounding the military hero. Yael, an acclaimed Israeli novelist, was moved to write her daughter-father story immediately after her father's death in 1981. His premature death had left her emotionally raw and ripped open, the powerful bond between them gaping and incomplete. Writing was her way to stitch together the sundered tie, helping her to put closure on this most compelling relationship of four decades.

She begins the book with the death of her father:

> I have seen many dead faces. Tranquil or accepting, amazed or tortured, childish or wrinkled. My father's conveyed angry frustration, as if he didn't mean it to happen quite then, and for the first time ever was caught unaware, deprived of the last word. Those things unsaid and unaccomplished hovered there, almost palpable. The furious aura has haunted me ever since.[23]

Immediately after his death, almost as a ritual of mourning, she undertook the writing of her memoir. She made it clear from the outset that she was not writing about her father as a public man, but instead she was writing about the man who was a father to an only daughter. As she says, her father had had two wives, two sons, many lovers, many friends (and enemies), but only one daughter. Only she could write the story of the complex intimacy that they shared as daughter and father.

This book, too, is written in part as the conclusion to my relationship with my father, the last word, so to speak in a long, difficult conversation. The writing of it has let me be with my father while understanding more fully my struggle to be free so I could truly feel my love for him.

My father died of an aortic aneurysm at age seventy-eight, after three days in the hospital. In the several years before he died, we had found and enjoyed a new kind of communication. Although he could still be emotionally difficult, the years had mellowed him, the frustrations and unfulfillment he had so long lamented were replaced by a kind of acceptance and a quiet sense of accomplishment. Until he entered the hospital a few days before his death, he and my mother had lived for thirty-five years in the last house he had built in the old neighborhood.

Since he had occupied such a prominent place in my psychological life, I had always dreaded the idea of his death. Fortunately by the time it came, I was ready. We had even joked together one time about how we hoped we had completed our assignment together this lifetime because we didn't want to go through "this" again. When it came, his dying was as natural as can be expected in these days of medical technology.

Although I was the first-born, I was the last to arrive at his hospital room where he had just died. There he was in the bed, all tubes and devices gone, all evidences of effort removed, only small tape scabs remaining. His beautiful white hair was a little yellow, but his face was very sweet and peaceful. My mother, brothers, sisters, and I encircled his bed and for an amazing hour or so we held hands and wept and laughed, and told stories, remembering events both painful and funny, telling our dead father all the things he wasn't supposed to know while he was living, all the secrets we had kept from him because in life he was so emotionally reactive. The sound of our weeping and laughing had a rhythm to it, rising and falling, loud and soft, a tribal tribute to the life we had all shared together. We stayed in the room while we wrote his obituary feeling very attuned to what he wanted us to say—and again the sound of laughter and tears came and went. I was the last to go out of his room, and as I kissed his forehead I held on to the metallic bars of the hospital bed and cried one last time, deeply and completely.

The memorial we created together as a family was a celebration of my father's life. My father would never have wanted a standard funeral: it was against his religion, the religion of nature, the garden, the seasons. It was done in the Catholic Church, officiated by a young priest who was willing to cooperate with our need for something unorthodox. There were over 200 people at the service. My brother read the passage from Ecclesiastes: "There is a time for all things under heaven, a time to be born and a time to die. . . ." And I read a poem by Tennyson that my father used to recite by heart—"Let there be no mourning of farewell when I embark. . . ." Then each of us brought up to the sanctuary something from his life—my brothers brought his carpenter tools, the ones he had used to build our home; my mother brought a basket of vegetables just harvested from their garden; we brought photographs from his childhood, his old track medals; a full display of all the things that were meaningful in his life. With the community of neighbors and friends, we sang and really celebrated this man who was our father. I could not have asked for a fuller more gratifying end to my forty-seven year relationship with him.

Claiming the Inheritance

What a father bequeaths to his daughter, in his lifetime or after he is gone, is telling. The bequest is almost always a mixed one, material and nonmaterial, gifts and curses. My father's will was simple, everything was to go to my mother. The only material objects I own that came directly from him are a large wooden cedar chest with brass fittings that he had made when he was seventeen and a small wooden plaque with a seed packet of forget-me-nots appliqued to its surface and an inscription to me on the back. Along with all the memories, one of the biggest blessings he left me with were my brothers and sisters. We would carry on where he left off, we would do our best to cleanse the family tribe of its addictive tendencies, its depression, its base of melancholy; we would raise our children, write our books, counsel, build, and contribute to the community using his legacy of pain, frustration, endurance, humor, intelligence, and hard work as our material.

Not all deaths are as easy as my father's, nor are the legacies so easily gotten. When Germaine Greer's father died impoverished, suffering from arteriosclerosis, penned up in a half-way house for incompetents, she was "left not so much as a cuff-link or a fountain pen, or a book with his name in it." Her name was not even mentioned in his will. It is hard to imagine the level of suffering this caused her. Her bitter drive to find the truth of her father's life must have been fueled in part by the paucity of what he had left behind. Yet, as Greer's example demonstrates, no matter how much or how little we are actually left, we seem to be compelled to make something out of it.

In her memoir, Yael Dayan writes of the deep pain she felt when she heard that her father's will made no provision for her. Everything that her famous father accumulated in his lifetime was left to his second wife, nothing of value for his children or grandchildren, nor any tribute to his long-suffering first wife of thirty-five years. By way of explanation, his second wife had told her, "He was so proud of the fact you needed nothing and were independent."

Dayan's attempt to come to terms with the love, respect, hurt, bitterness, and disbelief in relationship to her beloved father who left her without a visible inheritance was to write the book, *My Father, His Daughter*. At the end she writes: "My father was born in the spring and died in the fall. This is the cycle of fruit-bearing trees. Against the basic laws of nature, while the tree itself is gone, its roots are not dead, and it continues to bear fruit."[25] Her children and her own continued writing were the fruit born out of her painful lack of paternal inheritance.

Susan Griffin, in her lyrical work, *A Chorus of Stones*, recalls the deep stream of melancholy running through her father and his history. A true Saturnian father, "He had the loneliness as of a man who seems in solitary confinement even when among others."[26] When she was in her early fifties, she went on a search for the true story of his suffering. What she found was not only his, but the hidden suffering of others as well: "For perhaps we are like stones: our own history and the history of the world embedded in us, we hold a sorrow deep within and cannot weep until that history is sung."[27] In singing our history, we are released into grief. Only when we can weep can we feel free. It is out of this mixture of loss and gain, grief and gratitude that a daughter must learn to construct her womanly power.

The Construction of Women's Power

Because we live in a patriarchy where power traditionally passes down from father to son, or, as in the myth of Saturn, the son castrates the father to achieve his power, we have few stories of how power passes from father to daughter. One of the only myths that portrays the daughter-father relationship in terms of a transmission of powers can be found in the Sumerian cycle of Inanna poems. This series of poems which traces the initiations of the Goddess Inanna, Queen of Heaven and Earth, is truly remarkable. In particular it presents us with an almost unheard of daughter-father story.

As a young woman who has come into her fullness, Inanna undertakes a journey to visit her father, Enki, the God of Wisdom and Waters. Enki is a big Shaman, the Creator of Humankind, the Fertilizer of the Land, and Organizer of his Creations. He is a Magician and a Master of Ritual and Incantation.[28] The interaction between this father-figure and his young goddess-daughter, Inanna, centers around the handing over of power, what the Sumerians call the *me*, the knowledge of the workings of the world of social relationships, the natural world, and the cosmos.

Before she sets out on her journey, Inanna leans against an apple tree and beholds and celebrates her "wondrous vulva." Acknowledging her own beauty and power as a woman, she then sets sail by herself to Enki's city of Eridu, a place where the fresh and salt waters meet, where the Tigris and Euphrates rivers and the Persian Gulf converge.

Enki knows that Inanna is approaching and tells his servant to prepare for her coming, offering butter cakes and beer at the holy table, the table of heaven. And, in one of the most unusual daughter-father statements found in literature, he says "Treat her like an equal." When Inanna arrives she is treated with great respect and she and Enki begin to drink beer together, lots of beer. As mythologist Diane Wolkstein has noted in *Inanna, Queen of Heaven and Earth*, in this interaction, Enki becomes generous, and offers the treasures of his kingdom, the *me*, to his daughter. "Enki, swaying with drink, toasted Inanna" saying "In the name of my power. In the name of my holy shrine! To my daughter Inanna I shall give the high priesthood! Godship! The noble, enduring crown! The throne of kingship!"[29] In an unprecedented display of daughterly entitlement, Inanna replies, "I take them!" In the poetry, all of the *me* are recited by Enki and after each accounting, Inanna states, "I accept them." The last of the *me* given by Enki is "the making of decisions." "Then Inanna, standing before her father, / Acknowledged the *me* Enki had given to her."[30] "My father has given me the me," she says, and she recites again the long list of powers. Inanna quickly uses the gift of decision-making as she gathers together all the *me* and sets sail for her own city of Uruk.

When Enki wakes up from his drunken stupor, he questions his servant about where the *me* went. The servant replies, "My king has given all the *me* to his daughter, Inanna." Enki turns dark and sends the servant after Inanna. Upon reaching her, the servant says she must return the *me* to her father, she must not disobey his "words of state." Inanna is outraged. She cries out: "My father has changed his word to me! / He has violated his pledge—broken his promise! / Deceitfully my father spoke to me!"[31] Despite her sense of betrayal, it is clear she has no intention of giving back what she has been given.

Upon hearing her refusal, Enki sends a series of demons after his daughter, "the wild-haired *enkum*-creatures," "the fifty *uru*-giants" the "fifty *lahama*-monsters" the "sound-piercing *kugalgal*, the *enunun*, the watchmen of the Iturungal Canal." But Inanna defends her treasures through the strength of Ninshibur, her faithful female servant, a symbol of her own "inner spiritual resources." As Diane Wolkstein points out, "By defeating Enki's magic creatures, Inanna acquires their corresponding shamanic powers. When she returns to Uruk, she enters as the heroic, shamanic queen."[31] But there is more to the story then just the wresting away of her father's powers for the sake of her community. When Inanna lands and the *me* are at last unloaded, suddenly more *me* appear. These new *me* belong to the women:

> Inanna brought the *me*:
> She brought the placing of the garment on the ground.
> She brought allure.
> She brought the art of women.
> She brought the perfect execution of the *me*.
> She brought the *tigi-* and the *lilis*-drums.
> She brought the *ub-*, the *meze-*, and the *ala*-tambourines. . . .[32]

With her powers installed in her holy shrine, Inanna takes her rightful place as queen. She has brought the inheritance from her father to her people and she has added on to it a few gifts of her own.

Taking the Power

Like the goddess, Inanna, contemporary women are working to claim and reclaim their powers from their personal fathers and the cultural fathers. One of the first things we learn in this process is how our power has been taken away from us. Even if a woman's father is dead, he may still exercise control over her. One woman on the Dreamquest had had a terrifying dream about fighting with her father over the loss of her power. She dreamed of a man who is in control, a man who seems to have too much power. He leads a group of people around a corner into a dark alley and there is no questioning him—everyone follows.

> A young woman is there, holding a child. She has long, dark curly hair and looks foreign. She looks sad. The man has her lying down on a table and he begins to kill her. He cuts her open from her chest down through her stomach with a large knife or cleaver. He is cutting into her spleen. She looks horrified, sad, and resigned to what is happening to her. No one is stopping him. He has total control and is pure evil. I can't stand it and I pick up a large pair of tweezers. I stick them into the man's face and stomach. He is all soft and gooey. I am surprised. I tell everyone to run.

Reflecting on this dream, the woman says: "The man looked very average. The distinctive thing about him was his complete control over everyone and everything. In that respect he reminded me of my father." The table the woman was stretched out on looked to her like an altar. She thought this crude operation was, in fact, a sacrifice. The spleen was associated in her mind with anger and the immune system. The tweezers, the only weapon in sight, were what she, herself, uses in her work in the laboratory. She uses them she says, "to pick up and hold things I don't want to touch or that may be harmful." In the dream she was surprised that when she poked the man with the tweezers, the man's insides were not vivid red but soft, white and grey indicating that a putrefaction process had already begun.

Working on her dream, a group of women decided to create a Dream Theater. Patty agreed to take the role of father, the role of the dreamer was taken by Kaye, another woman agreed to be the sacrificed woman, while the rest of us gathered our energies together to support the process: As the woman dreamer, Kaye took up a big stick to represent the tweezers. The following is one woman's recording of the dialogue that ensued.

> "Father": Put down that stick!
>   Stop talking to me like that
>   Sit down and behave yourself
>   Act like a lady
>   You speak to me only when you are spoken to
>   I am the father—you do what I say or I will kill you.

With the support of the group of women gathered in around her, Kaye, as the daughter, responded:

>   I will not be quiet
>   I will not sit down
>   You pay attention to Me.
>   I have important things to say to you.
>   You hurt me. You hurt other people. You don't have
>   any idea of how to use power in a way for good. I

> HATE how you treated me and used your power
> to hurt me.

The Father answers back:

> I am your father.
> You cannot speak to me with these words or in that
> tone of voice. You should respect me and keep your
> voice to a whisper, if you speak at all.

This gave Kaye, the daughter, the opportunity to let her voice out, to make it strong and loud, clear and firm.

> NO! MY VOICE IS BIG AND STRONG AND I WILL USE IT TO TELL YOU
> THAT YOU HAVE NO POWER OVER ME. I PULL THE PLUG ON YOU. I
> RE-CREATE YOU IN A NEW IMAGE!

Kaye commanded the Father to leave and we did a hands-on healing for the woman who played the sacrificed, cut-open woman in the dream. All of the dream characters took themselves out of their roles and we shared what we had experienced.

Following the enactment of the dream, the work of the dream theater unfolded further when Patty created a three act (Re) Creation bringing the whole process to a healing conclusion for all.

> Act One of (Re) Creation:
>
> I thank you for teaching me about the *mis*use of POWER. From you I learned about how to use power to control others through fear. I learned how to keep myself separate from others. I learned how to use power to hurt and destroy. I learned that I needed as much power as possible and that I should take it or get from others in whatever ways possible . . . (mother script: especially through indirect and manipulative ways.)
>
> From you, I learned that power and how power is used makes a difference in people's lives. I thank you for this teaching and I release you.
>
> Act Two of (Re) Creation:
>
> I welcome my power back into my life.
> I welcome my willingness to claim and use my power.
> I release my fear of having my power.
>
> Act Three of (Re) Creation:
>
> This is how I am willing to have you in my life, because you are a part of my life and cutting you out is like cutting out a part of myself. I am

willing for you to remind me that I am a part of you that, like you, can be active and powerful.

I want you to hear and understand that I intend to use my power in very different ways. I intend to use my power to listen to myself, to speak my voice, to recognize injustice, to have my anger and all my other feelings. I intend to use my pain to set limits for you and for how I intend for you to speak to me.

I deserve words of encouragment and support. All other words will come out of your mouth as a whisper and be drowned by the sound of the rushing stream before they ever reach my ears.

I deserve words that remind me that I am wonderful, special, unique, beautiful, incredible, marvelous, and powerful—a woman with important things to say. All other words will come out of your mouth like a wisp of smoke to be carried away by the wind before they ever reach my ear.

I deserve words that remind me of my power and creativity and that encourage me to use my power in ever wiser and more compassionate ways. All other words out of your mouth will be like brittle leaves that are consumed instantly by the fire in my belly.

You bring me strength and power and I claim it as mine for use as I will.

You are limited in your access to me. You must wear a Bright Red outfit that has an audible alarm so that wherever you are present, I will be instantly aware of you. I will build a safe space for you, where you can read or draw or sleep, where you will be safe.

In this space you will not have access to any other part of me. You are limited to this space at all times. I will return you to this space immediately if I ever find you outside this space.

I call on all those parts of me that were ever hurt or damaged by this abusing father self, this part who knew power but not how to use it.

Things are different now. Things are safe. I invite you back. I am here, to listen to your pain and to use our power for your healing.

Work and Love: 'Whom Do You Serve?'

Freud imagined that the meaning of life could be found in work and love and that psychoanalysis was a way to clear the obstacles to achieving satisfaction in those areas. But for women something else must be added—the answer to the question, "Whom do you serve?" It is not enough to claim our power as women: we must be able to use our powers consciously, knowing where and how our energy is spent, on what, on whom, for what purpose—both in work and in relationships.

A woman poet whose father has been dead for many years had been struggling in her own life with his legacy. He had, she felt, worked himself to death in order to provide his family with financial well-being. This left her with an enormous difficulty in finding her right relationship to the issues of work and love. As she began to pursue a change in careers, she had a dream about burying the laws of the Father. The dream begins as she and a group of women are being told a myth by a male teacher. In the dream she takes on the role of "the most-conscious" son and she begins to bury the father's law.

> These laws were in the form of writings on clay tablets that were also like old grave markers like the ones in New England graveyards—from the time of intense patriarchal Protestantism. I bury the tablets in loose moist sand that is part of the breastlike sacred Tor in Glastonbury— the huge breast with the tiny Christian tower on top. And I bury them not in hatred, but with a sense that this stuff is extinct. It is appropriate that we bury it, but shallowly, so that we can retrieve, remember, and also at times honor these writings as part of our history. Some of the writings on the tablets are original, by an individual father, not handed down by a patriarchal god. In some way in the dream, it felt important also to honor this individual father's own writings, and thus not bury them irretrievably deep.

She recalls that although she is playing the role of the son in the dream, at the same time she is quite aware, of being in her own female body. Her body, she says, "feels able and strong and very satisfied as I bury the laws. And when I turn to say to the group, 'This stuff should be buried. It's like a dinosaur; it's extinct,'" "I am very clearly not playing the role of the son, I am myself."

The dream ends with the male teacher telling the end of the myth, which judges the youngest son as BAD for burying the laws, precisely because he is doing it with a great deal of consciousness, not in the heat of newly discovered and unprocessed feelings. She says, "The son is angry, but it's the kind of anger he can stand in, that gives solidity, that is backed up by thought and understanding." In working with the dream she sees that there is still some part of her that buys the cultural judgment, transmitted by a male teacher, that to bury the father's laws is BAD—bad like in an overtly controlling and moralizing tale, like in very simplified, black and white thinking. But she realizes that "I feel too good, too right, too satisfied in my own body about burying the laws. Its feels like the dream ends with me being about to turn to the other women to see if they give me support."

This dream left her with a great deal of excitement but also the feeling that in her conscious life, the strength and ability to bury the laws of the father at times feels very far away. Despite her doubts, she says, "The dream seems to have ushered in a slowly growing sense that this is absolutely necessary if I am to live my life according to my own authority."

Transformation of the Father

Like many dreams, this woman's dream is more of an announcement of what is to come: she senses its rightness but knows she has not grown into the fullness of its message. Sometimes a dream will reveal an image of what has already been accomplished. In the initial stages of writing this book I had a dream:

> There is a rather repulsive looking stocky man with a bullet-shaped head who is sitting naked with his legs open. His genitals are only vestiges, partially there. It seems that a woman has bitten them off some time ago. He had retaliated against her and had to spend seventy years in jail. Then I see he has become transformed into another man, very refined, with silver hair, chiselled face and soft, deep brown eyes which are moistened with tears. My dreamer looks upon him with deep compassion and thinks how beautiful he has become and how much he has lost of life because of all those years in prison.

Although this dream was quite strange to my waking mind, as I worked with it I began to see that it was setting the stage for this book. Then the dream was shocking because of its message. It seems to be a woman's version of the Saturn myth—the castration, the banishment, the transformation. My personal associations with the bullet-headed man was with a story I had recently heard from a friend of mine whose daughter had been terribly injured by a hit-and-run driver. It turned out that the driver, a man whose last name was Savage, was associated with another cruel and reprehensible event. Many years ago he had been parked in a car with a woman, a prostitute he had hired, and in the process of performing fellatio she had bitten his penis. He murdered her, then and there, by beating her to death. He had been given a rather short prison sentence and so years later he was again the perpetrator of this terrible car accident.

My psyche took this story to a very deep level and hooked it up to the writing of this book. In the dream I saw the man had been castrated by the teeth, not of the son, like in the Greek myth, but by the daughter. Now this man had emerged from prison, his coarse crudity refined, after the enforced introversion and introspection of seventy years, as in biblical terms where seven times seven indicates a very long time. And I, the dreamer, am changed as well—I have moved from feelings of hatred and repulsion to mourning and compassion.

With the mystery of this dream message I began to understand the implications of the Saturn myth and its dynamic of transformation as it applies to daughters. In the Greek myth, Saturn, the overtaking son, castrated his father and sent him to the netherworld of Tartarus. In my dream Saturn was castrated by a woman. He was then sent to prison for seventy years for killing her. His transformation came from the decades of incarceration where the pressure of solitary confinement created a womanly alchemical process whereby his crude matter had been turned, not to gold, but to silver.

On a personal level this dream reflected back to me my own years of incarceration, years where my creativity was imprisoned, years of being unable to speak, the years when I had been swallowed by the overbearing influence of my personal father as well as the cultural fathers. When I emerged in my forties from a seven-year period of celibacy and a psychological process of extricating myself out of the Belly of the Father, I had full access to my creative powers. I had learned the lessons of severe limitations—not only how blocks to my creativity were formed but also how training, discipline, solitude, and constraint were necessary for bringing a creative work into a form. But the price of the imprisonment was big—I had lost much in those years, I had no biological children; this required a period of mourning. Eventually as my dream shows my compassion flowed toward the silver-haired dream man who had sacrificed a lot of life's pleasure during his imprisonment.

On the positive side, Saturn is thought to be deeply associated with agriculture, as the god of fertility, the earth, and the harvest where his castrating sickle becomes transformed into a harvesting tool. The celebration of Saturn in the ancient Roman tradition is called the Saturnalia, and it is celebrated at winter solstice, the time of the night sun, place of darkness and death, when the sickle of the moon is in its lowest position. The dream recounted in the beginning of the book, the one I had in my mid-forties while sleeping in my childhood bedroom, showed a numinous father Saturn sitting on a threshing machine accompanied by the music of the spheres. I believe now that the dream presented itself to me ten years ago as an announcement, so I would and could do the labor of writing this book.

The transformed Saturn does not swallow his daughter appropriating her creative energy. Instead, he teaches his daughter the lessons of agriculture, the patience of planting, the work of cultivating, the joy of the harvest that comes after a great deal of concentration, focus, analysis, and renunciation. The transformed Saturn is also known as Sal Sapientiae or Sal Saturn—the bitter salt of wisdom.

Incorporating the Father: Forming the New Earth

When my father died in August 1987, we divided his ashes between us, brothers and sisters, west coast and east coast, half to the Pacific, half to the Atlantic, according to my father's wishes. Despite the fact that he was born and lived his whole life in the Middle West, he enjoyed the idea that his ashes would be cast into these two great bodies of water meeting somewhere south of the equator. It appealed to his sense of the dramatic. When the time came for me to perform the ritual dispersal of ashes, I wound my way along the black, jagged rocks at Pemaquid Point, on the coast of Maine. Feeling the wind tear at my clothes, the sea roiling and churning glass green to grey, the cold of early November, my birth month, austere and bleak, I wondered for a brief moment if my father, who so loved the sun, the lushness of the midsummer garden, would not feel terribly out of place in this harsh New England landscape. But somehow it fit. The two of us facing and learning the lessons of the north: the cold, bitter, melancholic remoteness a reminder of his Saturnian aspects, and myself as a daughter of Saturn.

In the split second before I flung his ashes into the sea, I spontaneously put some in my mouth. A part of me was taken aback in shock not knowing what I had done, another part understood well the necessity for this rite of incorporation. I had tasted this man's melancholy for years. I had once rejected him and all he stood for. Now was my chance to begin something new, out of the ashes. . . .

> Let the old man lie in the earth
> (he has troubled men's thought long enough)
> let the old man die, let the old man be of the earth
> he is earth,
> Father, O beloved
> you are the earth,
> he is the earth, Saturn, wisdom,
> rock, (O his bones are hard, he is strong, that old man)
> let him create a new earth,
> and from the rocks of this re-birth
> the whole world must suffer,
> only we
> who are free,
>
> may foretell,
> may prophesy. . . .
>
> —H.D.[33]

·XI·

The Daughters of Saturn as Muses

In this process of cultural transformation, the role of the artist is crucial. The Goddess is a Muse, "mother" to art as well as vision. The artist's revisionist mythmaking is "revolutionary . . . for her art is a creative act that helps establish a new cultural tradition.

—*Susan Stanford Friedman*[1]

For millennia our cultural myths of creativity have been myths of male primacy. Theological and artistic creativity have been premised on the male as prime mover such as, "In the beginning was the word." These are some of the laws of the Father which a woman must bury if she wishes to enter her creative life.

One way women have been taught to divide themselves from their own creative authority is embedded in the idea that women's power to create comes to them through the agency of a male muse. It is not a psychological "fact," as C. G. Jung would have it, that women's creative essence comes to life through the inspiration of an animus, some known or unknown masculine spiritual energy. Jung's concept of the animus is an invention made to explain a psychological strategy used by women attempting to create in a patriarchal context. By contrast, his equivalent notion of the anima, as a man's source of creative inspiration, is an idea describing a phenomenon of the soul. These are two different categories of experience—hardly the same, and definitely not symmetrical in value.

Although many women artists have claimed a male muse, it appears that they almost always do so for reasons having to do with what the culture has allowed for men (or disallowed women), not because there is some basic psychological rule under which we live and create. In her essay on Emily Dickinson, Adrienne Rich suggests that "a woman's poetry about her relationship to her daemon—her own active, creative power—has in patriarchal culture used the language of heterosexual love or patriarchal theology."[2] If male poets have projected their inspiration as feminine, women poets have learned to project their creative power as masculine.

Who then, inspires a woman to write? In this last section, I wish to consider the ways in which the mythic Daughters of Saturn may enter our creative lives as muses. In my re-mythologizing of these goddesses as muses, I imagine that each of them brings her particular wisdom and inspiration to bear on a creative work. In the Battlezone, the goddesses according to Greek myth operated as separate, opposing, and fragmented female powers. But re-mythologized as goddess-muses, they may work together in a process of interdependent sharing, each lending her sacred energy, her elemental powers, her own complexity, diversity, and possibility to the work. In such a web of connectedness, Hestia's solitude does not clash with Aphrodite's passion for intercourse, and Demeter's maternal shelter does not deny Hera's desire for the cycles of death and rebirth. As mother, lover, sister, friend, each goddess-muse brings forth her particular strengths granting women the power to create new culture. As critic Susan Stanford Friedman reminds us in the above epigraph, "The Goddess is a Muse, 'mother' to art as well as vision."

The goddess-muse is not always or possibly ever a cozy, tea and biscuits visitor. As the poet H.D. describes her, she is more often a fierce companion with a powerful command:

> why must I write?
> you would not care for this,
> but She draws the veil aside,
>
> unbinds my eyes,
> commands,
> write, write or die.[3]

The essayist Hélène Cixous, in her long essay, "Coming to Writing,"[4] says that she never wanted to write, did not feel strong enough or "right" enough to write, in fact, she felt like a mouse. But, "one day I was tracked down, besieged, taken. . . . 'Writing' seized me, gripped me, around the diaphragm, between the stomach and the chest, a blast dialated my lungs and I stopped breathing. Suddenly I was filled with a turbulence that knocked the wind out of me and inspired me to wild acts. 'Write.'"[5] She goes on to describe her puny resistances which were countered by the forcefulness of her attacker. "An urge shook my body, changed my rhythms, tossed madly in my chest, made time unlivable for me. I was stormy. 'Burst!' 'You may speak!'"[6] She questions, "Who is attacking me from behind?" And the answer comes to her: "A joyful force. Not a god; it doesn't come from above. But from an inconceivable region, deep down inside me but unknown, as if there might exist somewhere in my body another space. . . ." This joyful force will not let her be. The nature of its fury demanded "Let me through, or everything goes!"[7] Once she surrenders to her, the implacable powers of the goddess-muse offer a woman strength for the work.

Hestia and Creative Solitude

As a goddess-muse, Hestia enters a creative work at the first and the last. One of the hardest things for many women who wish to enter their creative lives is taking the time and making the space in which creative work can happen. Hestia's symbol of the circle can give a woman a sense of centeredness. With Hestia as her guide, a woman can draw her energies in around her. As she works to mediate what the soul requires, Hestia casts a sacred circle, an inviolate and necessary boundary around a woman. In Hestia's creative solitude a woman can find her ability to concentrate and focus and thus she can begin her work, as Barbara Kirksey reminds us:

> Without Hestia, there can be no focusing on the image, and there are no boundaries to differentiate the intimacy of the inner dwelling and the outer world, for there is no psychic house to give protective walls. There can be no joyous feasts, no celebrations of life, no food for the soul.[8]

In her *Journal of a Solitude*, the writer May Sarton begins by calling her solitary life her "real life":

> That is what is strange—that friends, even passionate love, are not my real life unless there is time alone in which to explore and to discover what is happening or has happened. Without the interruptions, nourishing and maddening, this life would become arid. Yet I taste it fully only when I am alone here and "the house and I resume old conversations."[9]

It is Hestia that ensures the sacred space where, in creative solitude, we can give birth.

Demeter and the Need for Maternal Shelter

Unlike the heterosexual love paradigm or the childbirth metaphor, the notion of maternal shelter provides a different kind of metaphor for what is needed if a woman's creative process is to proceed. As goddess-muse, Demeter provides maternal shelter for Persephone when she acknowledges Persephone's need to go into her "deeps," into her unconscious. She knows Persephone is called to the Underworld because she has work to do there. Demeter lets her go, but not in a submissive, passive way. She actively holds a space for Persephone. She holds it even at the expense of her own comfort, even when she is in pain. By holding the space for Persephone, Demeter provides a maternal shelter which allows her daughter to go into realms that Demeter does not know about. Demeter does not hold Persephone back. She provides an opportunity for her daughter to follow her intuition, her desire, wherever it may lead.

Persephone is able to take this living knowledge with her. Even though she is going without Demeter, she possesses the feeling of being held in a good inner space. Demeter's maternal shelter provides an indispensable sanctuary, an expandable womb space which is required to incubate all forms of creativity.[10]

Sometimes "maternal shelter" is a blessing provided in our lives by a nurturing partner, or a mentor, or therapist, sometimes it appears simply as a place, a room of one's own, or the work itself serves as a holding and sheltering container. However one finds it, Demeter's maternal shelter provides the necessary safety and nurturance, an ambience conducive to exploring the depths and coming back with what was found there.

In a deeply Demeterian mode, Cixous writes:

> Writing: as if I had the urge to go on enjoying, to feel full, to push, to feel the force of my muscles, and my harmony, to be pregnant and at the same time to give myself the joys of parturition, the joys of both the mother and the child. To give birth to myself and to nurse myself, too. Life summons life. Pleasure seeks renewal.[11]

Hera's Creative Cycles of Death and Rebirth

I have shown how the ancient cycles of Hera correspond to the cycles of the moon. When Hera appears to a woman as the goddess-muse, she brings her lunar wisdom along. The new moon appears as the slim light of a creative thought, gestating itself until it reaches fullness. Then the energy begins to fade until the moon itself cannot be seen. As any women who writes knows, a creative idea undergoes many of these lunar cycles of creation and destruction before it can stand on its own as a living work. The woman writer learns to bear this death and rebirth process within herself until she can, at last, deliver something whole and alive. Sometimes it feels like undergoing the torments of the flesh. I, myself, had many dreams of operations, especially on my third eye, while I was working on this book. I also had dreams of death. Cixous comments on the process: "First she dies. Then she loves. I am dead. There is an abyss. The leap. That someone takes. Then, a gestation of self—in itself, atrocious. when the flesh tears, writhes, rips apart, decomposes, revives, recognizes itself as a newly born woman . . ."[12] She goes on to describe the visceral life and death struggle which the goddess-muse Hera, "our most dangerous and generous mother," presides over for it is lunar Hera who is the one who mediates these great forces:

> [She is] the one who gives us . . . the staggering wish to come out, the desire for both extremes to meet, enter into and reverse each other, and day doesn't come after night, but struggles with it, embraces it, wounds it, is wounded by it, and the black blood and the white blood mingle;

and in the same way, life emerges crawling from the entrails of death that it has lacerated, that it hates, that it adores, and it never forgets that death doesn't forget it, that it is always there, never leaves it. . . .[13]

Cixous goes on to say that we move towards and away from "Death, our double mother" through the process of writing and that writing itself is a way of mourning. "And I say: you must have been loved by death to be born and move on to writing."[14] Understanding the deep wisdom of Hera's cycles of death and rebirth can help a woman to meet the challenge of creative work and to find it exhilarating. "When you have come to the end, only then can Beginning come to you."[15]

Aphrodite's Passion for the Work

In order to sustain the labor necessary to produce a creative project, one must develop a passion for the work. In this way, Aphrodite's influence can be a great blessing. In Aphrodite's mythology there is a complex association between gold, honey, speech, and sexual fluids which provides a deeply sexual metaphor for a woman's creative juice. There is never anything quite like an unimpeded creative flow. Cixous asks, "When my being was populated, my body traversed and fertilized, how could I have closed myself up in silence? Come to me, I will come to you. When love makes love to you, how can you keep from murmuring, saying its names, giving thanks for its caresses?"[16] Whether it comes as a stream of words or a surge of erotic energy, the goddess-muse Aphrodite brings her gifts of honeyed speech. "And this language I know, I don't need to enter it, it surges from me, it flows, it is the milk of love, the honey of my unconscious. The language that women speak when no one is there to correct them."[17] This is the gift of Aphrodite as muse.

·XII·

The Fourth Gate: Possibility

I dwell in possibility.

—*Emily Dickinson*[1]

we know no rule
of procedure,

we are voyagers, discoverers
of the not-known,

the unrecorded;
we have no map;
possibly we will reach haven
heaven.

—*H.D.*[2]

I know the bottom, she says. I know it with my great tap root:
It is what you fear.
I do not fear it: I have been there.

—*Sylvia Plath*[3]

I may not become a saint. But I am very full and very rich, and I
have a great deal to write about.

—*Anais Nin*[4]

Possibility

We have lived and died through many eras of impossibility. A few women, against all odds, were able to resist the great silencing and give voice to the struggle. We are the beneficiaries of their efforts. It is up to us now to make the impossible possible. Every woman has a story to tell, a story we need to hear. As Helène Cixous reminds us:

> We are much more than what our own name authorizes us and obligates us to believe we are. We are *possible*. Anyone. We need only avoid closing up the parentheses in which our "why nots" live. Thus, I am a person who begins a long time before me, with the first molecules, and who continues after me and all around me. However, and by chance, I am a woman, and I belong to the human race. Oh yes, I am human and also a woman.[5]

What the goddess, Inanna, gains when she takes the powers from father Enki are the whole collective powers of society—politics, oratory, crafts, trades, farming, sheepherding, the raising of families—the whole hierarchical caste of king, priest, warrior. But, as the poem cycle reveals, when Inanna lands in her own city, she steps out as queen onto her own ground. At that precise moment, other powers appear—powers the father could not give because he does not have them to give. These are the powers she earned by courageously facing the demons and bravely undergoing her ordeals. They are her womanly powers, the ones that will make the flow of all power go in the right direction.

As in the story of the goddess Inanna, whatever creative work a woman may undertake, these womanly powers will now be her guide. Her creativity is no longer driven by the personal or cultural fathers. Her work becomes a self-chosen task of cultivating, the making of a womanly contribution to the community, something for the common good, in whatever field she chooses. This is a woman's power to create.

Notes

Preface

1. Yael Dayan, *My Father, His Daughter* (New York: Farrar, Straus & Giroux, 1983).
2. Susan Griffin, *A Chorus of Stones: The Private Life of War* (New York: Doubleday, 1992), 8.
3. Adrienne Rich, *Of Woman Born: Motherhood as Experience and Institution* (New York: W. W. Norton & Co., 1976), 245.

Introduction

1. Juliet Mitchell, *Psychoanalysis and Feminism: Freud, Reich, Laing and Women* (New York: Vintage Books, 1975), xiii. Female psychology per se was not Freud's central concern. Out of a monumental body of work only two papers are devoted completely to this topic: "Female Sexuality" (1931), Standard Edition [hereafter SE] (Lodon: Hogarth Press, 1953), 21: 223–43; and "Femininity" (1933), SE, 22: 112–35. The rest of his writings on the subject are incorporated into other essays.
2. Sigmund Freud and Joseph Breuer, *Studies on Hysteria (1893–1895)*, SE, 2: 19–181.
3. Ellyn Kashak, *Engendered Lives: A New Psychology of Women's Experience* (New York: Basic Books, 1992), 60.
4. Sigmund Freud, "Female Sexuality" (1931), SE, 21: 229.
5. The "absent father" phenomenon has been explored primarily in terms of its effect on boys. Two recent books that look at fathers and their influence on children and families are: Stanley H. Cath, Alan Gurwitt, and John Ross, eds., *Father and Child: Developmental and Clinical Perspectives* (Boston: Little, Brown & Co., 1982) and Stanley H. Cath, Alan Gurwitt, and Linda Gunsberg, eds., *Fathers and Their Families* (Hillsdale, N.J.: The Analytic Press, 1989). See also Alix Pirani, *The Absent Father: Crisis and Creativity, The Myth of Danae and Perseus in the Twentieth Century* (London: Routledge, 1988) and Alexander Mitscherlich, *Society Without the Father: A Contribution to Social Psychology*, foreword by Robert Bly (New York: Harper Perennial, 1993). These current traditional psychoanalytic texts still proclaim the importance of the father for the daughter's "sense of self and in her feminine identity." (*Fathers and Their Families*, 191.) In writing about the daughter, a recent psychoanalytic text notes that while some fathers prefer having daughters, "most have a preference for sons"

(192) and this preference bears out cross-culturally. The text goes on to note that "There are only five societies that are considered daughter-preferring societies" (192). Only one of these is "American": The Tolowa Indians of Northwest California (192).

6. Since the second wave of feminism, the incesting father has been the topic of many books. Among the most influential are Florence Rush, *The Best Kept Secret: Sexual Abuse of Children* (Englewood Cliffs, New Jersey: Prentice Hall, 1980); Ellen Bass and Laura Davis, *The Courage to Heal: A Guide for Women Survivors of Child Sexual Abuse* (New York: Harper & Row, 1988). The landmark works of Judith Lewis Herman, *Father-Daughter Incest* and her recent *Trauma and Recovery*, deal with the prevalence and impact of sexual abuse and other traumas on daughters and women.

7. Suzanne Fields, *Like Father, Like Daughter: How Father Shapes the Woman His Daughter Becomes* (Boston: Little, Brown & Co., 1983). From the title itself we can tell who is the active agent, who has the possessive pronoun. The image on the jacket cover visually underscores her point. On the cover is a picture of what we assume to be a father and adult daughter at an outdoor café. They are dressed exactly alike in dark suits, blue tailored shirts and bow ties. They both wear glasses and both are reading newspapers with big grins on their faces.

8. Adrienne Rich, "Split at the Root: An Essay on Jewish Identity," (1982) in *Blood, Bread and Poetry: Selected Prose 1979–1985*. (New York: W. W. Norton & Co., 1986), 100.

9. Adrienne Rich, "Sources" in *Your Native Land, Your Life: Poems* (New York: W. W. Norton & Company, 1993), 15.

10. C.f. Lynda E. Boose, "The Father's House and the Daughter in It: The Structures of Western Culture's Daughter-Father Relationship," in Lynda E. Boose and Betty S. Flowers eds., *Daughters and Fathers* (Baltimore and London: Johns Hopkins University Press, 1989).

11. Adrienne Rich, *Of Woman Born: Motherhood as Experience and Institution* (New York: W. W. Norton & Co., 1976), 33.

12. Ibid.

13. Gerda Lerner, *The Creation of Patriarchy* (New York: Oxford University Press, 1986), 238–39.

14. The late Marija Gimbutas, an internationally renowned archaeologist from University of California at Los Angeles has pioneered a massive interpretation of the iconography and symbol system of the Great Goddess as she appears in the Neolithic period of Old Europe. Her books and articles provide a solid scholarly and interpretive foundation for looking at and understanding the Great Goddess, her images, her religion, and the culture that worshipped her. Marija Gimbutas, *The Civilization of the Goddess: The World of Old Europe* (San Francisco: Harper & Row, 1991). *The Language of the Goddess* (San Francisco: Harper & Row, 1989). *The Goddesses and Gods of Old Europe: 7000 to 3500 B.C. Myths, Legends and Cult Images* (Berkeley and Los Angeles: University of California Press, 1983).

15. Lerner, 239. For a recent analysis of American women and their relation to power see Naomi Wolf, *Fire with Fire: The New Female Power and How It Will Change the 21st Century* (New York: Random House, 1993).

16. Lerner, 234.

17. Ibid.

18. Ibid.

19. Ibid., 239.
20. Ibid., 240.
21. Anthropologists see the incest taboo as a founding principle of social organization, what Levi-Strauss calls the "rule of the gift," allowing families and tribes to exchange women through the institution of marriage, insuring trust and stable mutual relationships, the ultimate guarantee of security. Phyllis Chesler and other feminists have argued that the incest taboo also acts to reinforce the male-dominated culture: "Women are encouraged to commit a surrogate form of incest as a way of life, as opposed to marrying our fathers, we marry men like our fathers . . . men who are older than us, have more money than us, more power than us, are taller than us . . . our fathers." Phyllis Chesler, "Rape and Psychotherapy," in *Rape: The First Sourcebook for Women*, ed. Noreen Connell and Cassandra Wilson (New York: New American Library, 1974), 76.
22. Fields, 5.
23. Rollo May, *The Courage to Create* (New York: Bantam Books, 1975), 22.
24. Ibid., viii.
25. I wish to thank Patricia Rushton for her insightful work, "Women's Courage to Create: The Relationship of Trauma to Creativity," Santa Barbara, Pacifica Graduate Institute, unpublished ms., 1993.
26. For a Jungian perspective on how the father influences the daughter's creativity see the works of Linda Schierse Leonard and Marion Woodman. For a psychoanalytic object relations perspective see Susan Kavaler-Adler, *The Compulsion to Create: A Psychoanalytic Study of Women Artists* (New York: Routledge, 1993).
27. Yael Dayan, *My Father, His Daughter* (New York: Farrar, Straus & Giroux, 1983), 81.
28. Edward Ardener, "Belief and the Problem of Women," in Shirley Ardener ed., *Perceiving Women* (New York: John Wiley & Sons, A Halsted Press Book, 1975), 2. For a feminist literary criticism based on Ardener's notion see Elaine Showalter, "Feminist Criticism in the Wilderness," in Elaine Showalter ed., *The New Feminist Criticism: Essays on Women, Literature and Theory* (New York: Pantheon Books, 1985). For another perspective on Ardener's idea of the Wild Zone, see Ursula K. Le Guin, "Woman/Wilderness, 1986," in Ursula K. Le Guin, *Dancing at The Edge of the World: Thoughts on Words, Women, Places* (New York: Grove Press, 1989).
29. Jane Lazarre, *On Loving Men* (New York: Dial Press, 1978), 177.

Chapter I: The Devouring Father

1. Sharon Olds, "Saturn," in *The Gold Cell* (New York, Knopf, 1991), 24.
2. I have excerpted this version of the myth from Hesiod, trans. Richard Lattimore (Ann Arbor: University of Michigan Press, 1973).
3. Raymond Klibansky, Erwin Panofsky, and Fritz Saxl, *Saturn and Melancholy: Studies in the History of Natural Philosophy, Religion, and Art* (New York: Basic Books, Inc., 1964). This work is an exhaustive look at the centuries-long cultural tradition which links Saturn with Melancholy.
4. Ibid., 247.
5. Juliana Schiesari, *The Gendering of Melancholia: Feminism, Psychoanalysis, and the Symbolics of Loss in Renaissance Literature* (Ithaca, N.Y.: Cornell University Press, 1992), 7.
6. Ibid., 9.

7. Robert D. Romanyshan and Brian J. Whalen, "Depression and The American Dream: The Struggle with Home," in *Pathologies of the Modern Self: Postmodern Studies on Narcissism, Schizophrenia, and Depression*, ed. David Michael Levin (New York: New York University Press, 1987).

8. For a feminist look at how the culture of the 1950s impacted women's life decisions see Brett Harvey, *The Fifties: A Women's Oral History* (New York: Harper Perennial, 1993). Thanks to Pat Reinke Mepham for bringing this book to my attention.

9. Bruno Bettelheim, *The Uses of Enchantment: The Meaning and Importance of Fairy Tales* (New York: Vintage Books 1977), 205.

Chapter II: The Silent Daughters of Saturn

1. Mary A. Hill, *Charlotte Perkins Gilman: The Making of a Radical Feminist 1860–1896* (Philadelphia: Temple University Press, 1980), 149.

2. Susan Griffin, *A Chorus of Stones* (New York: Doubleday, 1992), 286.

3. Judith Lewis Herman, *Trauma and Recovery: The Aftermath of Violence—From Domestic Abuse to Political Terror* (New York: Basic Books, 1992), 74.

4. For a look at the "madwoman" in literature, see Sandra Gilbert and Susan Gubar, *Madwoman in the Attic: The Woman Writer and the Nineteeth Century Literary Imagination* (New Haven and London: Yale University Press, 1979). For a look at the "madwoman" as an archetypal figure in women's psychology see Linda Schierse Leonard, *Meeting the Madwoman: An Inner Challenge for Feminine Spirit* (New York: Bantam Books, 1993). For a feminist perspective see Jane Ussher, *Women's Madness: Misogyny or Mental Illness?* (Amherst: The University of Massachusetts Press, 1992).

5. Barbara Ehrenreich and Deirdre English, *For Her Own Good: 150 Years of the Expert's Advice to Women* (New York: Doubleday, 1978), 101.

6. Hill, 149.

7. Charlotte Perkins Gilman, *The Yellow Wallpaper* (New York: The Feminst Press, 1973).

8. Virginia Woolf, *A Room of One's Own* (New York: Harcourt Brace Jovanovich, 1989), 48.

9. Ibid., 49.

10. See Herman, chapters "Terror," "Disconnection," and "Captivity."

11. Carole Spitzack, *Confessing Excess: Women and the Politics of Body Reduction* (New York: State University of New York Press, 1990), 100. For example, Suzanne Fields, writes: "My parents had very different purposes in my life: my mother was to see that I always looked nice, my father was to see what she had accomplished and to admire us both for it." *Like Father, Like Daughter: How Father Shapes the Woman His Daughter Becomes* (Boston: Little Brown & Co., 1983), 173.

12. Herman, 77.

13. John Berger, *Ways of Seeing* (London: British Broadcasting Corporation, 1972), 46.

14. Herman, 79.

15. Juliana Schiesari, *The Gendering of Melancholia: Feminism, Psychoanalysis, and the Symbolics of Loss in Renaissance Literature* (Ithaca, N.Y.: Cornell University Press, 1992), 4.

16. Linda Schierse Leonard, *Witness to the Fire: Creativity and the Veil of Addiction* (Boston: Shambhala, 1989).

17. Louise J. Kaplan, *Female Perversions: The Temptations of Emma Bovary* (New York: Doubleday, 1991), 14.

18. Ibid., 18.

19. Ibid., 1.

20. Susan Bordo, "Material Girl: The Effacements of Postmodern Culture," in *Michigan Quarterly Review* (Fall 1990): 657.

21. Robert J. Stoller, "The Term Perversion," in *Perversions and Near-Perversions in Clinical Practice: New Psychoanalytic Perspectives*, ed. Gerald I. Fogel M.D. and Wayne A. Myers M.D. (New Haven: Yale University Press, 1991), 37.

22. Syvia Plath, *The Collected Poems* (New York: Harper Perennial, 1981), 182.

23. Ibid., 214.

Chapter III: The Awakening

1. Kim Chernin, *Reinventing Eve: Modern Woman in Search of Herself* (New York: Times Books, 1987), 143.

2. Carolyn Heilbrun, *Writing a Woman's Life* (New York: W. W. Norton, 1988), 65.

3. Susan Gubar, "The Blank Page" and the Issues of Female Creativity," in *Feminist Criticism: Essays on Women, Literature and Theory*, ed. Elaine Showalter (New York: Pantheon Books, 1985), 295.

4. Jill Johnston, "Fictions of the Self in the Making," in the *New York Times Book Review*, April 25, 1993, 1. Thanks to William E. Wolf for bringing this article to my attention.

5. Anne Sexton, "Briar Rose (Sleeping Beauty)," in Anne Sexton, *The Complete Poems* (Boston: Houghton Mifflin Company, 1981), 294.

6. Charlotte Perkins Gilman, *The Living of Charlotte Perkins Gilman: An Autobiography* (New York: Harper Colophon Books, 1975), 96.

7. Ibid., 121.

8. See Kat Duff, *The Alchemy of Illness* (New York: Pantheon Books, 1993). Thanks to Mary Leibman for suggesting this book to me.

9. Adrienne Rich, *Of Woman Born* (New York: W. W. Norton & Co., 1976), 85.

10. Sylvia Plath, *Letters Home: Correspondence 1950–1963*, ed. Aurelia Schober Plath (New York: Harper Perennial, 1992), 473.

11. Alice Walker, *Possessing the Secret of Joy* (San Diego: Harcourt Brace and Company, 1992), 106.

12. Anna Ahkmatova, *Anna Ahkmatova: Selected Poems* (London: Penguin Books, 1988), 140.

13. Ibid., 87.

Chapter IV: Unlearning to Not Speak

1. Marge Piercy, *To Be of Use* (Garden City, New York: Doubleday, 1973), 38.

2. Tillie Olsen, "Silences," in *Writing Women's Lives: An Anthology of Autobiographical Narratives by Twentieth Century American Women Writers*, ed. Susan Cahill (New York: Harper Perennial, 1994), 150.

3. Adrienne Rich, *Of Woman Born* (New York: W. W. Norton & Co., 1976), 34.

4. Virginia Woolf, *Three Guineas* (New York: Harvest/Harcourt Brace Jovanovich, 1966), 74.

5. Piercy, 38.

6. Jane Lazarre, *On Loving Men* (New York: Dial Press, 1978), 177.

7. Ibid., 91.

8. Ibid., 98.

9. Ibid.

10. Mary Gordon "The Parable of the Cave or: In Praise of Watercolors," in *The Writer on Her Work*, Vol. 1, ed. Janet Sternburg (New York: W. W. Norton & Co., 1980), 31.

11. Ibid., 32.

12. Ibid.

13. Carol Gilligan, Annie G. Rogers, and Deborah L. Tolman, eds., *Women, Girls and Psychotherapy: Reframing Resistance* (New York: Harrington Park Press, 1991), 1. Although they are talking about adolescent girls and women, the idea that resistance to the pressure of culture to conform is both healthy and political is a radical reframing of what psychology has traditionally viewed as pathological.

14. Lisa Appignanese and John Forrester, *Freud's Women* (New York: Basic Books, 1992), 66.

15. Judith Lewis Herman, *Trauma and Recovery* (New York: Basic Books, 1992), 10.

16. Ibid., 12.

17. Appignanese and Forrester, 68.

18. James Hillman, "On the Necessity of Abnormal Psychology: Anake and Athene," in *Facing the Gods* (Dallas: Spring Publications, 1980), 3.

19. See Charlene Spretnak, *Lost Goddesses of Early Greece: A Collection of Pre-Hellenic Myths* (Boston: Beacon Press, 1984). In her introduction Spretnak outlines the various problems involved in the use of Greek mythology as archetypal patterns for women: "The portraits of the Goddesses in patriarchal mythology are, indeed, patterns of behaviour: they are stories told by men of how women react under patriarchy. As such, they are two steps removed from being natural expressions of the female mode of being" (37).

20. Christine Downing, *The Goddess: Mythological Representations of the Feminine* (New York: Crossroad, 1984), 80.

Chapter V: The Mythic Daughters of Saturn and Their Mortal Sisters

1. Hestia

1. Phyllis Chesler, *Women and Madness* (New York: Avon Books, 1972), xviii.

2. "To Aphrodite," in *Homeric Hymns*, trans. Apostolos N. Athanassakis (Baltimore: The Johns Hopkins University Press, 1976), 48.

3. "Homeric Hymns," in Miriam Robbins Dexter, *Whence the Goddess: A Source Book* (New York: Pergamon Press, 1990), V.21–28, 163.

4. Emily Dickinson, Poem no. 562 in *The Complete Poems of Emily Dickinson*, ed. Thomas H. Johnson (Boston: Little, Brown & Co., 1960), nos. 745, 365.

5. Emily Dickinson, Letter no. 562 in *The Letters of Emily Dickinson*, ed. Thomas Johnson and Theodora Ward, 3 vols. (Cambridge: Harvard University Press, 1958), 617.

6. Stephanie Demetrakopoulos, *Listening to Our Bodies: The Rebirth of Feminine Wisdom* (Boston: Beacon Press, 1979), 55.

7. Sarah B. Pomeroy, *Goddesses, Whores, Wives, and Slaves: Women In Classical Antiquity* (New York: Schocken Books, 1975), 6.

8. For an exploration of Hestia as soul guide see Christine Downing, *Journey Through Menopause: A Personal Rite of Passage* (New York: Crossroad, 1987).

9. Virginia Woolf, *A Haunted House and Other Stories* (New York: Harcourt, Brace and World, 1944), 58–59.

10. Virginia Woolf, *A Room of One's Own* (San Diego, New York, London: Harcourt Brace Jovanovich, 1989), 52.

11. Anne Sexton, "Housewife," in Anne Sexton, *The Complete Poems* (Boston: Houghton Mifflin Co., 1981), 77.

12. John Cody, *After Great Pain: The Inner Life of Emily Dickinson* (Boston: Belknap Press, 1971), 158. Cody, a Freudian analyst, undertook a detailed investigation into the life of Emily Dickinson. Although his psychological interpretation contains a passionate plea to accept that Dickinson suffered mental illness of a severe and lasting kind, one that continually threatened to debilitate and annihilate her, Cody's view of her development as a woman is suffused with misunderstanding and misogyny.

13. Richard B. Sewall, *The Life of Emily Dickinson*, 2 vols. (New York: Farrar, Straus, and Giroux, 1974), 49. Sewall's biography, although definitely not feminist in orientation is, lucid and even-handed.

14. Emily Dickinson, *The Letters* I, L. 65, 161.

15. This incident is noted in Barbara Antonina Clarke Mossberg: *Emily Dickinson: When a Writer Is a Daughter* (Bloomington: Indiana University Press, 1982), 74.

16. Cynthia Griffin Wolff, *Emily Dickinson* (Radcliffe Biography Series, 1988), 63. Although focused on Dickinson's spiritual development, Wolff's biography benefits from a feminist perspective and is most aware of the influences on her development as a woman.

17. Richard Sewall, *The Lyman Letters: New Light on Emily Dickinson and Her Family*

18. Emily Dickinson, *The Letters* II, L. 471, 559.

19. Mossberg, 81.

20. Emily Dickinson, *Letters* I, L. 30, 82.

21. Ibid.

22. Ibid.

23. *Letters* I, L. 36, 97.

24. Emily Dickinson, Poem 1677 in *The Complete Poems of Emily Dickinson*, ed. Thomas H. Johnson (Boston: Little, Brown & Co., 1960), 685.

25. Emily Dickinson, *Letters* II. L. 154, 283–84.

26. *Letters* I, L. 86, 197.

27. Cody, *After Great Pain* , 46.

28. Adrienne Rich, "Vesuvius at Home: The Power of Emily Dickinson," in *On Lies, Secrets, and Silence: Selected Prose 1966–1978* (New York: W. W. Norton & Co., 1979), 158.

29. Ibid., 160.

30. Ibid., 161.

31. Woolf, *A Room of One's Own*, 106.

32. Dickinson, Poem 732 in *Complete Poems*, 359.

33. *Letters*, L.93, 210.

34. Dickinson, Poem 508 in *Complete Poems*, 247.
35. Dickinson, Poem 1072 in *Complete Poems*, 487.
36. Paula Bennett, *My Life a Loaded Gun: Female Creativity and Feminist Poetics* (Boston: Beacon Press, 1986), 82.
37. Ana-Maria Rizzuto, "The Father and the Child's Representation of God: A Developmental Approach," in *Fathers and Their Families* , ed. Stanley H. Cath, Alan Gurwitt, and Linda Gunsberg (Hillsdale, N.J.: The Analytic Presss, 1989). Rizzuto says "Having no sensory experience of God, children are forced to create the representational characteristics of their god out of the most extraordinary being they know: their parents (358). She goes on to say that when the paternal representation seems to prevail in the formation of the God representation "the father was from the very beginning of life the person who literally had taken possession of the child. These individuals show that when the father is an overwhelming figure in the child's life, the God representation is predominanatly made from the paternal representation" (380). Dickinson certainly is a case in point.
38. Mossberg, 115.
39. Emily Dickinson, *Letters* III, L. 891, 817.
40. Joanne Feit Diehl, *Women Poets and the American Sublime* (Bloomington: Indiana University Press, 1990), 29.
41. Dickinson, Poem 528 in *Complete Poems*, 258.
42. Diehl, 29.
43. Ibid., 36.
44. Dickinson, Poem 925 in *Complete Poems*, 435.
45. Diehl, 30.

2. Demeter and Persephone

1. "Hymn to Demeter," in *The Homeric Hymns* (Baltimore: Johns Hopkins University Press, 1976), 1.
2. Sigmund Freud, "Femininity" (1933), SE, 22: 119.
3. H.D., "The Mysteries VI," in *Collected Poems* (New York: New Directions, 1986), 305.
4. *The Homeric Hymns*. I have paraphrased the above-cited myth from this version.
5. Adrienne Rich, *Of Woman Born* (New York: W. W. Norton & Co., 1976), 185.
6. Freud, "Some Psychical Consequences of the Anatomical Distinction Between the Sexes" (1925), SE, 19.
7. Ibid.
8. Freud, "Female Sexuality" (1931), SE 21, 226.
9. Ibid.
10. See Introduction, note 14.
11. Phyllis Chesler, *Women and Madness* (New York: Avon Books, 1972), 195–96.
12. For a major re-visioning of traditional thinking on women's development, see Carol Gilligan, *In a Different Voice: Psychological Theory and Women's Development* (Cambridge: Harvard University Press, 1982). For a re-visioning of mother-daughter relationships, see Elizabeth Debold, Marie Wilson, and Idelisse Malave, *Mother-Daughter Revolution: From Betrayal to Power* (Reading, Mass.: Addison-Wesley, 1993).
13. Kim Chernin, *Reinventing Eve* (New York: Times Books, 1987), 123.
14. Rich, 240.
15. Ibid., 225.

16. C. Kerenyi, *Eleusis: Archetypal Image of Mother and Daughter* (New York: Bollingen Foundation, 1967), 130.

17. Freud, "Femininity" (1933), SE, 22, 135.

18. For biographical material on H.D., I have used the following works: Barbara Guest, *Herself Defined: The Poet H.D. and Her World* (London: Collins, 1985); Susan Stanford Friedman, *Psyche Reborn: The Emergence of H.D.* (Bloomington: The Indiana University Press, 1981); Donna Krolik Hollenberg, *H.D. The Poetics of Childbirth and Creativity* (Boston: Northeastern University Press, 1991).

19. The term "screen husband" refers to the lesbian practice of maintaining an asexual marriage for societal reasons.

20. Guest, 195.

21. H.D., *Notes on Thoughts and Visions* (San Francisco: City Lights Books, 1982), 52.

22. H.D., *Tribute to Freud* (New York: New Directions, 1984), 148–149.

23. Unlike the currently accepted once-a-week mode for psychotherapy, analysis was an extremely concentrated event. The meetings took place every day. H.D. lived in a hotel in Vienna, near Freud's home and office, Berggasse 19, where she spent her days writing and reflecting on the material from the analysis. We have two important documents about that time in H.D.'s life: "Advent," taken from her notebook journals while she was in analysis, and "Writing on the Wall," dedicated "To Sigmund Freud, blameless physician," written in 1944 as a later reflection on the analysis. Both essays have been published together under the title *A Tribute to Freud*.

24. H.D., *Tribute to Freud*, 91.

25. Ibid., 13

26. Ibid., 142.

27. Ibid., 137.

28. Ibid., 116.

29. Ibid., 164.

30. Ibid., 176.

31. Friedman, 26.

32. H.D., *Tribute to Freud*, 33.

33. Ibid., 38.

34. Ibid., 175.

35. Ibid.

36. Ibid., 125.

37. Ibid., 145.

38. Ibid., 177–78.

39. Ibid., 142.

40. Ibid., 117.

41. Ibid., 116.

42. Ibid., 93.

43. Rich, *Of Woman Born*, 220.

44. H.D., *Tribute To Freud*, 13.

45. H.D. "The Master," in H.D., *Collected Poems: 1912–1944* (New York: New Directions Books, 1986), 453.

46. Rachel Blau DuPlessis, " Romantic Thralldom in H.D.," in *Signets: Reading H.D.*, ed. Susan Stanford Friedman and Rachel Blau DuPlessis (Madison: The University of Wisconsin Press, 1990), 406.

47. H.D., *Tribute To Freud*, 136.

48. Adrienne Rich, *Lies, Secrets, and Silences* (New York: W. W. Norton & Co., 1979), 200–1.
49. H.D., "The Master," in *Collected Poems*.
50. H.D., *Tribute to Freud*, 146.
51. H.D., *The Gift* (New York: New Directions, 1982).
52. H.D., *HERmione* (New York: New Directions, 1981), 76.
53. H.D., *Hedylus* (Redding Ridge, Conn.: Black Swan Books, 1980), 124, quoted in Hollenberg.
54. Rich, *Of Woman Born*, 220.
55. H.D., *Collected Poems*, 324.
56. H.D., *Tribute to Freud*, 121.
57. Ibid., 174–75.
58. Friedman, 139.
59. H.D. letter to Brhyer quoted in Hollenberg, 110.
60. Marion Woodman, *The Pregnant Virgin: A Process of Psychological Transformation* (Toronto: Inner City Books, 1985).
61. Ibid., 78.
62. Ibid.
63. H.D., *Collected Poems*, 456.
64. See Hollenberg.
65. H.D., *Collected Poems*, 461.
66. Friedman, 230.
67. Ibid., 112.
68. H.D., *The Gift*, 10.
69. H.D., *Trilogy* (New York: New Directions, 1973), 97–103.
70. H.D., "The Master," in *Collected Poems*.
71. Friedman, ix.

3. Hera

1. "Hymn 12, To Hera," in *Homeric Hymns* (Baltimore: Johns Hopkins University Press, 1976), 59.
2. Freud, "The Taboo of Virginity" (1918), SE, 11: 194.
3. Sylvia Plath, "Stings," in *The Collected Poems*, ed. Ted Hughes (New York: Harper Perennial, 1992), 214.
4. C. Kerenyi, *Zeus and Hera* (Princeton: Princeton University Press, 1975), 92.
5. Jane Ellen Harrison, *Epilegomena to the Study of Greek Religion and Themis* (New Hyde Park: University Books, 1966), 490.
6. Jane Ellen Harrison, *Prolegomena to the Study of Greek Religion* (London: Merlin Press, 1980), 315.
7. Ibid., 316.
8. Harrison, *Epilegomena*, 179.
9. Phyllis Chesler, *Women and Madness* (New York: Avon Books, 1972), 20.
10. Carolyn Heilbrun, *Writing a Woman's Life* (New York: W. W. Norton & Co., 1988), 81.
11. Ibid.
12. Adrienne Rich, "Natural Resources," in *The Dream of a Common Language: Poems 1974–1977* (New York: W. W. Norton & Co., 1978), 62.
13. For the biographical information on Sylvia Plath, I have relied on the following most

recent sources. Although they are not of even quality nor of similar perspective (Plath's biographers seem to be singularly unobjective), each has offered something of value: Paul Alexander, *Rough Magic: A Biography of Sylvia Plath* (New York: Penguin Books, 1992); Steven Gould Axelrod, *Sylvia Plath: The Wound and the Cure of Words* (Baltimore and London: The Johns Hopkins University Press, 1990); Jacqueline Rose, *The Haunting of Sylvia Plath* (Cambridge: Harvard University Press, 1992); Anne Stevenson, *Bitter Fame: A Life of Sylvia Plath* (Boston: Houghton Mifflin Co., 1989). For the difficulty in writing a Plath biography at all, see Janet Malcolm, *Sylvia Plath, The Silent Woman* (New York: Alfred A. Knopf, 1994).

14. Sylvia Plath, *The Journals of Sylvia Plath*, ed. Ted Highes and Frances McCullough (New York: Ballantine Books, 1982), 266.
15. Sylvia Plath, *Letters Home: Correspondence 1950–1963*, ed. Aurelia Schober Plath (New York: HarperCollins, 1975), 32.
16. Adrienne Rich, *Of Woman Born* (New York: W. W. Norton & Co., 1976), 230.
17. Plath, *Letters Home*, 289.
18. Plath, "Full Fathom Five," in *Collected Poems*, 92.
19. Ibid., "Electra on Azalea Path," 116.
20. Plath, *Journals*, 298.
21. Ibid., 223.
22. Plath, *Letters Home*, 314.
23. Plath, "The Colossus," in *Collected Poems*, 129.
24. Adlai Stevenson, 1955 Commencement Address to Smith College, quoted in Axelrod, 35, and in Betty Freidan, *The Feminine Mystique* (New York: Norton & Co., 1974), 60–61. Friedan's book came out in the same year that Sylvia Plath's novel, *The Bell Jar* appeared.
25. Plath, *Letters Home*, 223.
26. Plath, *Journals*, 112–13, and elaborated in *Rough Magic*, 179.
27. Plath, *Letters Home*, 40.
28. Ibid., 233.
29. Ibid., 276.
30. Dalma Heyn, *The Erotic Silence of the American Wife* (New York: Signet, 1992), 65.
31. Plath, *Letters Home*, 297.
32. Virginia Woolf, *A Room of One's Own*, (New York: Harcourt Brace Janovich, 1989), 35.
33. Aurelia Plath, "Introduction," in Sylvia Plath, *Letters Home*, 13.
34. Homer, *The Iliad*, Book XV., trans. E.V. Rieu, Baltimore: Penguin Books, 1954, 271.
35. Plath, *Journals*, 234.
36. It is a chilling fact that in March 1969, Assia Gutmann Wevill, the woman for whom Hughes left Plath, killed herself and their small child by turning on the gas in the oven in her London flat. They had maintained their complicated relationship for almost 10 years. *Rough Magic*, 346.
37. Ted Hughes related the incident to Dido Merwin, recorded in Stevenson, 206, 334.
38. John Bowlby, *Attachment and Loss*, vol. III (New York: Basic Books, 1980).
39. Plath, *Journals*, 310.
40. Plath, *Letters Home*, 450.
41. Sylvia Plath, *The Bell Jar* (New York: Harper & Row, 1972), 27.
42. Plath, *Journals*, 258.
43. Ibid., 295.

44. Plath, *Letters Home*, 466.
45. Plath, Journals, 295.
46. Plath, *Collected Poems*, 222.
47. Jane Lazarre, *On Loving Men* (New York: Dial Press, 1978), 142.
48. Axelrod, 51. Plath's Electra is not the classic kind. Instead of killing the mother to avenge the father's death, Plath is killing the father to avenge her own potential demise.
49. Lynda K. Bundtzen, *Plath's Incarnations: Woman and the Creative Process* (Ann Arbor: The University of Michigan Press, 1988), 159.
50. Plath, *Letters Home*, 468.
51. Plath, *Collected Poems*, 211.
52. Sandra M. Gilbert and Susan Gubar, eds., *Shakespeare's Sisters: Feminist Essays on Women Poets* (Bloomington: Indiana University Press, 1979), 253.
53. Bundtzen, 43.
54. Plath, *Collected Poems*, 255.
55. Ibid., 244.
56. Bundtzen, 33.
57. Peter Orr ed., *The Poet Speaks* (New York: Barnes and Noble, 1966).
58. Plath, *Collected Poems*, 214.
59. Ibid, 206.
60. Margaret Uroff cited in Paula Bennett, *My Life Is a Loaded Gun* (Boston: Beacon Press, 1986), 156.
61. Plath, *Collected Poems*, 231.
62. Ibid., 247.
63. Ibid., 160.
64. Ibid, 272.
65. See Malcolm, *The Silent Woman*. Malcolm's book takes on the daunting process of writing a literary biography by examining Plath and Hughes' relationship, before and after Plath's death, as we have come to know it through the biographers.

4. Aphrodite

1. Aeschylus, *The Danaïdes*. Trans. Ginette Paris in *Pagan Meditations: Aphrodite, Hestia, Artemis* (Dallas: Spring Publications Inc., 1986), 12.
2. Freud, *Civilization and Its Discontents*, trans. James Strachey (New York: W. W. Norton & Co., 1961), 20.
3. Anais Nin, *Incest: From a Journal of Love* (New York: Harcourt Brace Jovanovich, 1992), 178.
4. Noel Riley Fitch, *Anais: The Erotic Life of Anais Nin* (New York: Little, Brown & Co., 1993), 3.
5. Jane Lazarre, *On Loving Men* (New York: Dial Press, 1978), 34.
6. See Dalma Heyn, *The Erotic Silence of the American Wife*. (New York: Signet, 1992), 65.
7. Susan Griffin, "The Uncharted Body" in Robert H. Hopcke, Karin Lofthus Carrington, and Scott Wirth, eds., *Same-Sex Love and the Path to Wholeness* (Boston: Shambala, 1993), 288.
8. See Francis B. Rothluebber, *Nobody Owns Me: A Celibate Woman Finds Her Sexual Power* (San Diego: Luramedia, 1994) for a moving account of one woman's sexual awakening.
9. See Audre Lorde, "Uses of the Erotic: The Erotic as Power," in *Sister Outsider* (Freedom, Calif.: Crossing Press, 1984). Lorde's essay stands as an original and eloquent articulation of the erotic.

10. Ibid., 55.
11. Fitch, 3.
12. Ibid., 37.
13. Nancy Chodorow, *The Reproduction of Mothering: Psychoanalysis and the Sociology of Gender* (Berkeley: University of California Press, 1978), 195.
14. Nin, *Incest*, 45.
15. Phyllis Chesler, *Women and Madness* (New York: Avon Books, 1972), 20.
16. Anais Nin, "Ladders to Fire" in *Cities of the Interior* (Athens: Swallow/Ohio University Press, 1974), 106.
17. Fitch, 6.
18. Ibid.
19. Anais Nin, "Children of the Albatross," in *Cities of the Interior*.
20. Ibid., 132.
21. Ibid 135.
22. Ibid.
23. Ibid., 139.
24. Ibid 140.
25. Ibid.
26. Ibid.
27. Ibid., 142.
28. Ibid., 143.
29. Ibid., 145.
30. Ibid., 146.
31. Ibid., 148.
32. Ibid., 32.
33. Ibid.
34. Nin, *Incest*, 69.
35. Ibid, 79.
36. Ibid.
37. Ibid., 102.
38. Ibid.
39. Ibid., 106.
40. Ibid., 106-7.
41. Ibid, 178.
42. Ibid, 170.
43. Ibid., 132.
44. Ibid., 155.
45. Ibid.
46. Ibid., 205.
47. Ibid., 161.
48. Ibid., 204.
49. Ibid., 206.
50. Ibid., 155.
51. Ibid., 153.
52. Ibid., 152.
53. Ibid., 161.
54. Ibid., 152.
55. Ibid.

56. Ibid.
57. Ibid., 210.
58. Ibid.
59. Ibid., 214.
60. Ibid., 169.
61. Ibid., 221.
62. Ibid., 328.
63. Fitch, 168.
64. Nin, *Incest*, 330.
65. Fitch, 169.
66. Nin, *Incest*, 374.
67. Ibid., 375.
68. Ibid, 381.
69. Ibid.
70. Ibid., 382.
71. Toni Wolff, "Structural Forms of the Feminine Psyche," trans. Paul Watzlawik, Private printing for the Students Association, C. G. Jung Institute, Zurich, July 1956.
72. Nor Hall, *The Moon and the Virgin: Reflections on the Archetypal Feminine* (New York: Harper and Row, 1980).
73. Ibid., 140.

Chapter VI: The Second Gate: The Threshold

1. Gerda Lerner, *The Creation of Patriarchy* "Prospective Immigrants Please Note" (New York: Oxford University Press, 1986), 228.
2. Arnold van Gennep, *The Rites of Passage* (Chicago: Chicago University Press, 1966), 20.
3. Lerner, 227.
4. Morgan Farley, "Her Radiance Everywhere: Poems From a Midlife Awakening" in *Same-Sex Love* (Boston: Shambala, 1993), 51.
5. See Marion Woodman, *Leaving My Father's House: A Journey to Conscious Femininity* (Boston: Shambhala Publications, 1992) for examples of three contemporary women's journeys out of the "Father's House" and into their own lives.

Chapter VII: The Women are Singing

1. Gretel Ehrlich, "River History," in *Sisters of the Earth: Women's Prose and Poetry About Nature*, Lorraine Anderson ed. (New York: Vintage Books, 1991), 114.
2. Margaret Atwood, *Surfacing* (New York: Ballantine Books Edition, 1990), 217.
3. Audre Lorde, "Poetry Is Not a Luxury," in *Sister Outsider* (Freedom, Calif.: Crossing Press, 1984), 36–37.
4. Edward Ardener, "Belief and the Problem of Women," in Shirley Ardener, ed., *Perceiving Women* (New York: John Wiley & Sons, 1975), 33.
5. Catherine Keller, *From a Broken Web: Separation, Sexism, and Self* (Boston: Beacon Press, 1986), 210.
6. For a concise definition of women's culture see Gerder Lerner, *The Creation of Patriarchy* (New York: Oxford University Press, 1986), 242.

7. For a literary criticism using Ardener's model, see Elaine Showalter, *The New Feminist Criticism* (New York: Patheon Books, 1985). My thanks to Professor Joanne Feit Diehl for directing me to Showalter's article, "Feminist Criticism in the Wilderness."

8. Susan Griffin, *Woman and Nature: The Roaring Inside Her* (New York: Harper & Row, 1978), 169.

9. Certainly the immense popularity of Clarissa Pinkola Estes' *Women Who Run with the Wolves: Myths and Stories of the Wild Woman Archetype* (New York: Ballantine Books, 1992) is some indication of women's fascination and hunger for the Wild Mother and her stories.

10. Atwood, *Surfacing*. For an important reading of Atwood's novel see Carol P. Christ, *Diving Deep and Surfacing: Women Writers on Sprirtual Quest* (Boston: Beacon Press, 1980).

11. Atwood, 135.

12. Ibid., 157.

13. Ibid., 200.

14. Stephen Aizenstat Ph.D., *Dreamwork: A Manual of Established and Emerging Methods of Working with Dreams* © August, 1994.

15. Monique Witting, *Les Guerilleres*, trans. David Le Vay (New York: Avon Books, 1971), 112–14.

16. Luce Irigaray, "When Our Lips Speak Together," in *This Sex Which Is Not One*, trans. Catherine Porter (Ithaca, New York: Cornell University Press, 1985), 69–70.

17. Barbara Antonia Clarke Mossberg, *Emily Dickinson: When the Writer is a Daughter* (Bloomington: Indiana University Press, 1982), 39.

18. Thanks to Susan Amons, who curated an art exhibit "Dreams: Poetic Memory," for providing me with a way to think about dreams.

19. Griffin, 175.

20. Thanks to artist Pat Hardy for articulating this process in the catalogue essay for "Dreams: Poetic Memory" an art show at the University of Southern Maine curated by Susan Amons presenting ten women artists who use dreams as the source for their art.

21. Anne Dellenbaugh and Her Wild Song: Wilderness Trips for Women, Box 3111, E. Mere Point Road, Brunswick, Maine 04011.

22. Joan McIntyre, "Mind in the Waters," in *Sisters of the Earth*, 360.

Chapter VIII: The Elemental Daughters of Saturn

1. Anna Ahkmatova, *Selected Poems* (London: Penguin Books, 1988), 21.

2. Clarissa Pinkola Estes, *Women Who Run With the Wolves* (New York: Ballantine Books, 1992), 97.

3. Emily Dickinson, *The Complete Poems of Emily Dickinson*, ed. Thomas H. Johnson (Bosong: Little, Brown & Co., 1960), 173.

4. Sandra Gilbert and Susan Gubar, *The Madwoman in the Attic* (New Haven and London: Yale University Press, 1979), 612.

5. Virginia Woolf, *Three Guineas* (New York: Harvest/Harcourt Brace Janovich, 1966), 36.

6. Griffin, *Woman and Nature: The Roaring Inside Her* (New York: Harper & Row, 1978), 219.

7. Charlene Spretnak, *Lost Goddesses of Early Greece* (Boston: Beacon Press, 1984), 114.

8. Ibid., 117–18.

9. Rich, *Of Woman Born* (New York: W. W. Norton & Co., 1976), 226.

10. Adrienne Rich, "Sibling Mysteries" *The Dream of a Common Language: Poems 1974–1977* (New York: W. W. Norton & Co., 1978), 52.

11. Genevieve Taggard, "Demeter," in *Sisters of the Earth*, ed. Lorraine Anderson (New York: Vintage Books, 1991), 371–72.

12. Wendy Rose, "Naming Power," in *That's What She Said: Contemporary Poetry and Fiction by Native American Women*, ed. Rayna Green (Bloomington: Indiana University Press, 1984), 219.

13. Spretnak, 92.

14. Ibid., 91.

15. Morgan Farley, "Her Radiance Everywhere," in *Same Sex Love and the Path to Wildness*, ed. Robert H. Hopcke, Karin Loftus Carrington, and Scott Wirth (Boston: Shambala, 1993), 66–67.

16. Laura Chester and Sharon Barba eds. Sharon Barba, "A Cycle of Women," in *Rising Tides: 20th Century American Women Poets* (New York: Pocket Books, 1973), 357.

17. Nor Hall, *The Moon and the Virgin* (New York: Harper & Row, 1980), 151.

18. See my chapter "The Mysteries of Creativity" in *Through the Goddess: A Woman's Way of Healing* (New York: Continuum, 1991).

19. *The Exaltation of Inanna*, trans. William W. Hallo and J. J. A. van Dyjk (New Haven: Yale University Press, 1968), lines 146–47.

20. Deena Metzger, "Re-vamping the World: On the Return of the Holy Prostitute," in *Utne Reader* (Aug/Sept 1985): 120.

21. Ibid., 122.

22. Ibid., 121.

23. Ibid., 123.

24. Robert Graves and Raphael Patai, *The Hebrew Myths: The Book of Genesis* (New York: McGraw-Hill, 1966), 65.

25. Elizabeth Cunningham, *The Wild Mother* (New York: Station Hill Press, 1993).

26. Diane di Prima, *Loba* (Berkeley: Wingbow Press, 1978), 116.

27. Monique Wittig, *Les Guerillers*, trans. David Le Vay (New York: Avon Books, 1971), 89.

Chapter IX: The Third Gate: The Return

1. Joy Harjo, "Fire," in *Sisters of the Earth*, ed. Lorraine Anderson (New York: Vintage Books, 1991), 3.

Chapter X: The Women Are Speaking

1. Linda Hogan, "The Women Are Speaking," in *That's What She Said: Contemporary Poetry and Fiction by Native American Women*, ed. Rayna Green (Bloomington: Indiana University Press, 1984), 170.

2. Audre Lorde, "The Master's Tools Will Never Dismantle the Master's House," in *Sister Outsider* (Freedom, Calif.: Crossing Press, 1984), 112.

3. Margaret Atwood, *Surfacing* (New York: Ballantine Books, 1990), 229.

4. Germaine Greer, *Daddy, We Hardly Knew You* (New York: Alfred A. Knopf, 1990).

5. Ibid., 14.

6. Ibid., 21.
7. Ibid., 16.
8. Ibid., 98.
9. Ibid., 130.
10. Ibid., 193.
11. Ibid., 241.
12. Ibid., 246.
13. Ibid.
14. Ibid., 279.
15. Ibid., 311.
16. Ibid., 67.
17. Andrew Samuels, *The Plural Psyche: Personality, Morality and the Father* (London: Routledge, 1989), 82.
18. Sharon Olds, *The Father* (New York: Alfred A. Knopf, 1992).
19. Ibid., 5
20. Ibid., 6.
21. Ibid., 78.
22. Sally Cline, *Women, Passion and Celibacy* (New York: Carol Southern Books, 1993), 245.
23. Dayan, *My Father, His Daughter* (New York: Farrar, Straus and Giroux, 1983), 7.
24. Greer, 20.
25. Dayan, 289.
26. Susan Griffin, *A Chorus of Stones: The Private Life of War* (New York: Doubleday, 1992), 93.
27. Ibid., 8.
28. Diane Wolkstein and Samuel Noah Kramer, *Inanna: Queen of Heaven and Earth* (New York: Harper Colophon, 1983), 147.
29. Ibid., 14.
30. Ibid., 16.
31. Ibid., 150.
32. Ibid., 26.
33. H.D. "The Master," in *Collected Poems* (New York: New Directions, 1986), 451.

Chapter XI: The Daughters of Saturn as Muses

1. Susan Stanford Friedman, *Psyche Reborn: The Emergence of H.D.* (Bloomington: Indiana University Press, 1981), 271.
2. Adrienne Rich, *On Lies, Secrets, and Silences: Selected Prose 1966–1978* (New York: W. W. Norton & Co., 1979), 170.
3. H.D., *Hermetic Definition* (New York: New Directions, 1972), 7.
4. Helène Cixous, *Coming to Writing*, ed. Deborah Jenson (Cambridge: Harvard University Press, 1991).
5. Ibid., 9.
6. Ibid.
7. Ibid., 10.
8. Barbara Kirksey "Hestia: a Background of Psychological Focusing" in *Spring* (Dallas: Spring Publications, 1980), 105–6.

9. May Sarton, *Journal of a Solitude* (New York: W. W. Norton & Co., 1973), 11.

10. Nini Herman, *Too Long a Child: The Mother-Daughter Dyad* (London: Free Association Books, 1989), xvi.

11. Cixous, *Coming to Writing*, 31.

12. Ibid., 36.

13. Ibid., 38.

14. Ibid.

15. Ibid., 41.

16. Ibid., 13.

17. Ibid., 2.

Chapter XII: The Fourth Gate: Possibility

1. Emily Dickinson, *The Complete Poems of Emily Dickinson*, ed. Thomas H. Johnson (Boston: Little, Brown & Co., 1960), 327.

2. H.D. "The Walls Do Not Fall," in *Collected Poems* (New York: New Directions, 1986), 543.

3. Sylvia Plath, "The Elm," *The Collected Poems*, 192.

4. Anais Nin, *Incest: From a Journal of Love* (New York: Harcourt Brace Janovich, 1992), 403.

5. Cixous, *Coming to Writing*, ed. Deborah Johnson (Cambridge: Harvard University Press, 1991), 179.

Bibliography

Aeschylus, *The Danaïdes*. Trans. Ginette Paris. In *Pagan Meditations: Aphrodite, Hestia, Artemis*, 12. Dallas, Texas: Spring Publications, Inc., 1986.

Ahkmatova, Anna. *Anna Ahkmatova: Selected Poems*. Trans. D.H. Thomas. London: Penguin Books, 1988.

Aizenstat, Stephen, Ph.D. "Dreamwork: A Manual of Established and Emerging Methods of Working with Dreams." Unpublished manuscript, 1994.

Alexander, Paul. *Rough Magic: A Biography of Sylvia Plath*. New York: Penguin Books, 1992.

Anderson, Lorraine, ed. *Sisters of the Earth: Women's Prose and Poetry About Nature*. New York: Vintage Books, 1991.

Appignanese, Lisa, and Forrester, John. *Freud's Women*. New York: Basic Books, Inc., 1992.

Ardener, Shirley, ed. *Perceiving Women*. New York: John Wiley & Sons, A Halsted Press Book, 1975.

Athanassakis, Apostolos N., trans. *Homeric Hymns*. Baltimore: Johns Hopkins University Press, 1976.

Atwood, Margaret. *Surfacing*. New York: Ballantine Books, 1990.

Axelrod, Steven Gould. *Sylvia Plath: The Wound & the Cure of Words*. Baltimore and London: John Hopkins University Press, 1990.

Barba, Sharon and Chester, Laura. *Rising Tides: 20th Century American Women Poets*. New York: Pocket Books, 1973.

Benjamin, Jessica. *The Bonds of Love: Psychoanalysis, Feminism, and the Problem of Domination*. New York: Pantheon Books, 1988.

Bennett, Paula. *My Life a Loaded Gun: Female Creativity and Feminist Poetics*. Boston: Beacon Press, 1986.

Berger, John. *Ways of Seeing*. London: British Broadcasting Corporation, 1972.

Bettelheim, Bruno. *The Uses of Enchantment: The Meaning and Importance of Fairy Tales*. New York: Vintage Books, 1977.

Boose, Linda E., and Flowers, Betty S. *Daughters and Fathers*. Baltimore and London: Johns Hopkins University Press, 1989.

Bordo, Susan. "Material Girl: The Effacements of Postmodern Culture." *Michigan Quarterly Review* (Fall 1990).

Bowlby, John. *Attachment and Loss*. Vol. III. New York: Basic Books, Inc., 1980.

Bundtzen, Lynda K. *Plath's Incarnations: Woman and the Creative Process*. Ann Arbor: The University of Michigan Press, 1988.

Carrington, Karin Lofthus; Hopcke, Robert H.; and Wirth, Scott, eds. *Same-Sex Love and the Path to Wholeness*. Boston: Shambhala Publications, 1993.

Cahill, Susan, ed. *Writing Women's Lives: An Anthology of Autobiographical Narratives by Twentieth Century American Women Writers*. New York: Harper Perennial, 1994.

Cath, Stanley H.; Gurwitt, Alan; and Ross, John, eds. *Father and Child: Developmental and Clinical Perspectives*. Boston: Little, Brown & Co., 1982.

Cath, Stanley H.; Gurwitt, Alan; and Gunsberg, Linda, eds. *Fathers and Their Families*. Hillsdale, New Jersey: The Analytic Press, 1989.

Chernin, Kim. *Reinventing Eve: Modern Woman in Search of Herself*. New York: Times Books, 1987.

Chesler, Phyllis. *Women and Madness*. New York: Avon Books, 1972.

Chodorow, Nancy. *The Reproduction of Mothering: Psychoanalysis and the Sociology of Gender*. Berkeley: University of California Press, 1978.

Cixous, Helène. *Coming to Writing and Other Essays*. Ed. Deborah Jensen. Cambridge, Massachusetts: Harvard University Press, 1991.

Cline, Sally. *Women, Passion and Celibacy*. New York: Carol Southern Books, 1993.

Cody, John. *After Great Pain: The Inner Life of Emily Dickinson*. Boston: Belknap Press of Harvard University Press, 1971.

Christ, Carol P. *Diving Deep and Surfacing: Woman Writers on Spiritual Quest*. Boston: Beacon Press, 1980.

Cunningham, Elizabeth. *The Wild Mother*. New York: Station Hill Press, 1993.

Dayan, Yael. *My Father, His Daughter*. New York: Farrar, Straus & Giroux, 1983.

Demetrakopoulos, Stephanie. *Listening to Our Bodies: The Rebirth of Feminine Wisdom*. Boston: Beacon Press, 1979.

Dexter, Miriam Robbins, *Whence the Goddess: A Source Book*. New York: Pergamon Press, 1990.

Dickinson, Emily. *The Letters of Emily Dickinson*. 3 vols. Ed. Thomas H. Johnson and Theodore Ward. Cambridge, Massachusetts: Harvard University Press, 1958.

———. *The Complete Poems of Emily Dickinson*. Ed. Thomas H. Johnson. Boston: Little, Brown & Co., 1960.

Diehl, Joanne Feit. *Women Poets and the American Sublime*. Bloomington: Indiana University Press, 1990.

di Prima, Diane. *Loba*. Berkeley: Wingbow Press, 1978.

Downing, Christine. *The Goddess: Mythological Representations of the Feminine*. New York: Crossroad, 1984.

Duff, Kat. *The Alchemy of Illness*. New York: Pantheon Books, 1993.

Ehrenreich, Barbara and English, Deidre. *For Her Own Good: 150 Years of the Experts Advice to Women*. New York: Doubleday, 1978.

Estes, Clarissa Pinkola. *Women Who Run With the Wolves: Myths and Stories of the Wild Woman Archetype*. New York: Ballantine Books, 1992.

Fields, Susan. *Like Father, Like Daughter: How Father Shapes the Woman His Daughter Becomes*. Boston: Little, Brown & Co., 1983.

Fitch, Noel Riley. *Anais: The Erotic Life of Anais Nin*. New York: Little, Brown & Co., 1993.

Fogel, Gerald I., M.D., and Myers, Wayne A., M.D., eds. *Perversions and Near Perversions in Clinical Practice: New Psychoanalytic Perspectives*. New Haven: Yale University Press, 1991.

Freud, Sigmund. *Civilizations and Its Discontents*. (1930). Standard Edition (SE), 21. London: Hogarth Press, 1953.

———. "The Dissolution of the Oedipus Complex." (1924b). SE, 19. London: Hogarth Press, 1953.

———. "Female Sexuality." (1931a). SE, 21. London: Hogarth Press, 1953.

———. "Femininity." (1933). SE, 22. London: Hogarth Press, 1953.

———. "Some Psychical Consequences of the Anatomical Distinction Between the Sexes." (1925). SE, 19. London: Hogarth Press, 1953.

———. *Studies on Hysteria*. (1893–1895). SE, 2. London: Hogarth Press, 1953.

———. "The Taboo of Virginity." (1918). SE, 11. London: Hogarth Press, 1953.

Friedan, Betty. *The Feminine Mystique*. New York: W. W. Norton & Co., 1974.

Friedman, Susan Stanford, and DuPlessis, Rachael Blau Eds. *Signets: Reading H.D.* Madison: The University of Wisconsin Press, 1990.

Gilbert, Sandra M. and Gubar, Susan, eds. *Madwoman in the Attic: The Woman Writer and the Nineteenth Century Imagination*. New Haven: Yale University Press, 1979.

Gilbert, Sandra M. and Gubar, Susan, eds. *Shakespeare's Sisters: Feminist Essays on Women Poets*. Bloomington: Indiana University Press, 1979.

Gilligan, Carol; Rogers, Annie G.; and Tolman, Deborah L., eds. *Women, Girls and Psychotherapy: Reframing Resistance*. New York: Harrington Park Press, 1991.

Gilman, Charlotte Perkins. *The Living of Charlotte Perkins Gilman: An Autobiography*. New York: Harper & Row, 1975.

———. *The Yellow Wallpaper*. New York: The Feminist Press at the City University of New York, 1973.

Graves, Robert, and Patai, Raphael. *The Hebrew Myths: The Book of Genesis*. New York: McGraw Hill, 1966.

Green, Rayna, ed. *That's What She Said: Contemporary Poetry and Fiction by Native American Women*. Bloomington: Indiana University Press, 1984.

Greer, Germaine. *Daddy We Hardly Knew You*. New York: Alfred A. Knopf, 1990.

Griffin, Susan. *A Chorus of Stones: The Private Life of War*. New York: Doubleday, 1992.

———. *Woman and Nature: The Roaring Inside Her*. New York: Harper & Row, 1978.

Guest, Barbara. *Herself Defined: The Poet H.D. and Her World*. London: Collins, 1985.

Hall, Nor. *The Moon and the Virgin: Reflections on the Archetypal Feminine*. New York: Harper & Row, 1980.

Hallo, William W., and van Dyjk, J. J. A., trans. *The Exaltation of Inanna*. New Haven: Yale University Press, 1968.

Harrison, Jane Ellen. *Epilegomena to the Study of Greek Religion and Themis*. New Hyde Park, New York: University Books, 1966.

———. *Prolegomena to the Study of Greek Religion*. London: Merlin Press, 1980.

H.D. *Collected Poems*. Ed. Louis L. Martz. New York: New Directions, 1986.

———. *Hedylus*. Redding Ridge, Connecticut: Black Swan Books, 1980.

———. *Hermetic Definition*. New York: New Directions, 1972.

———. *HERmione*. New York: New Directions, 1981.

———. *The Gift*. New York: New Directions, 1982.

———. *Notes on Thoughts and Visions*. San Francisco: City Lights Books, 1982.

———. *Tribute to Freud*. New York: New Directions, 1984.

———. *Trilogy*. New York: New Directions, 1973.

Heilbrun, Carolyn. *Writing a Woman's Life*. New York: W. W. Norton & Co., 1988.

Herman, Judith Lewis, M.D. *Trauma and Recovery: The Aftermath of Violence—From Domestic Abuse to Political Terror*. New York: Basic Books, Inc., 1992.

Herman, Nini. *Too Long a Child: The Mother-Daughter Dyad*. London: Free Association Books, 1989.

Heyn, Dalma. *The Erotic Silence of the American Wife*. New York: Signet, 1992.

Hill, Mary. *Charlotte Perkins Gilman: The Making of a Radical Feminist 1860–1896*. Philadelphia: Temple University Press, 1980.

Hillman, James, ed. *Facing the Gods*. Dallas: Spring Publications, Inc., 1980.

Hollenberg, Donna Krolik. *H.D.: The Poetics of Childbirth and Creativity*. Boston: Northeastern University Press, 1991.

Irigaray, Luce. *This Sex Which is Not One*. Trans. Catherine Porter. Ithaca, New York: Cornell University Press, 1985.

Johnston, Jill. "Fictions of the Self in the Making." In the *New York Times Book Review*, April 25, 1993.

Jones, Suzanne W., ed. *Writing the Woman Artist: Essays on Poetics, Politics, and Portraiture*. Philadelphia: University of Pennsylvania Press, 1991.

Juhasz, Suzanne, ed. *Feminist Critics Read Emily Dickinson*. Bloomington: Indiana University Press, 1983.

————. *The Undiscovered Continent: Emily Dickinson and the Space of the Mind*. Bloomington: Indiana University Press, 1983.

Kaplan, Lousie J. *Female Perversions: The Temptations of Emma Bovary*. New York: Doubleday, 1991.

Kashak, Ellen. *Engendered Lives: A New Psychology of Women's Experience*. New York: Basic Books, Inc., 1992.

Keller, Catherine. *From a Broken Web: Separation, Sexism, and Self*. Boston: Beacon Press, 1986.

Kerenyi, C. *Eleusis: Archetypal Image of Mother and Daughter*. New York: Bollingen Foundation, 1967.

————. *Zeus and Hera*. Princeton University Press, 1975.

Kilbansky, Raymond; Panofsky, Erwin; and Saxl, Fritz. *Saturn and Melancholy: Studies in the History of Natural Philosophy, Religion, and Art*. New York: Basic Books, Inc., 1964.

Kirksey, Barbara. "Hestia: A Background of Psychological Focusing." In *Spring*. Dallas: Spring Publications, 1980.

Kramer, Samuel Noah and Wolkstein, Diane. *Inanna: Queen of Heaven and Earth*. New York: Harper Collins, 1983.

Lattimore, Richard, trans. *Hesiod*. Ann Arbor: University of Michigan Press, 1973.

Lazarre, Jane. *On Loving Men*. New York: The Dial Press, 1978.

Leonard, Linda Schierse. *Meeting the Madwoman: An Inner Challenge for Feminine Spirit*. New York: Bantam Books, 1993.

————. *Witness to the Fire: Creativity and the Veil of Addiction*. Boston: Shambhala Publications, 1989.

————. *The Wounded Woman: Healing the Father Daughter Relationship*. Boston: Shambhala, 1982.

Lerner, Gerda. *The Creation of Patriarchy*. New York: Oxford University Press, 1986.

Levin, David Michael, ed. *Pathologies of the Modern Self: Postmodern Studies on Narcissism, Schizophrenia, and Depression*. New York: New York University Press, 1987.

Lorde, Audre. *Sister Outsider*. Freedom, California: The Crossing Press, 1984.

Malcolm, Janet. *The Silent Woman: Sylvia Plath and Ted Hughes.* New York: Alfred A. Knopf, 1994.

May, Rollo. *The Courage to Create.* New York: Bantam Books, 1975.

Metzger, Deena. "Re-vamping the World: On the Return of the Holy Prostitute." In *Utne Reader* (August/September 1985).

Mitchell, Juliet. *Psychoanalysis and Feminism: Freud, Rich, Laing and Women.* New York: Vintage Books Edition, 1975.

Mossberg, Barbara Antonia Clarke. *Emily Dickinson: When a Writer is a Daughter.* Bloomington: Indiana University Press, 1982.

Nin, Anais. *Cities of the Interior.* Athens: Swallow/Ohio University Press, 1974.

————. *Incest: From a Journal of Love.* New York: Harcourt Brace Jovanovich, 1992.

Olds, Sharon. *The Father.* New York: Alfred A. Knopf, 1992.

————. *"Saturn" From the Gold Cell.* New York: Alfred A. Knopf, 1991.

Orr, Peter, ed. *The Poet Speaks.* New York: Barnes and Noble, 1966.

Piercy, Marge. *To Be of Use.* Garden City, New York: Doubleday & Co., Inc., 1973.

Plath, Sylvia. *The Bell Jar.* New York: Harper & Row, 1972.

————. *The Collected Poems.* Ed. Ted Hughes. New York: The First Harper Perennial Edition, 1981.

————. *The Journals of Sylvia Plath.* Ed. Ted Hughes and Frances McCullough. New York: Ballantine Books, 1982.

————. *Letters Home: Correspondence 1950–1963.* Ed. Aurelia Schober Plath. New York: Harper Perennial, 1992.

Pomeroy, Sarah B. *Goddesses, Whores, Wives, and Slaves: Women in Classical Antiquity.* New York: Schocken Books, 1975.

Reis, Patricia. *Through the Goddess: A Woman's Way of Healing.* New York: Continuum, 1991.

Rich, Adrienne. *Blood, Bread and Poetry: Selected Prose 1979–1985.* New York: W. W. Norton & Co., 1986.

————. *The Dream of a Common Language: Poems 1974–1977.* New York: W. W. Norton & Co., 1978.

————. *The Fact of a Doorframe: Poems Selected and New 1950–1984.* New York: W. W. Norton & Co., 1984.

————. *Of Woman Born: Motherhood as Experience and Institution.* W. W. Norton & Co., 1976.

————. *On Lies, Secrets, and Silence: Selected Prose 1966–1978.* New York: W. W. Norton & Co., 1979.

————. *Your Native Land, Your Life: Poems.* New York: W. W. Norton & Co., 1993.

Rieu, E.V., trans. *The Illiad.* Penguin Books, 1954.

Rose, Jacqueline. *The Haunting of Sylvia Plath.* Cambridge: Harvard University Press, 1992.

Rushton, Patricia. *Women's Courage to Create: The Relationship of Trauma to Creativity.* Unpublished Master's Thesis, Pacifica Graduate Institute: Santa Barbara, California, 1993.

Samuels, Andrew. *The Plural Psyche: Personality, Morality and the Father.* London: Routledge, 1989.

Sarton, May. *Journal of Solitude.* New York: W. W. Norton & Co., 1973.

Schiesari, Julianna. *The Gendering of Melancholia: Feminism, Psychoanalysis, and the Symbolics of Loss in Renaissance Literature.* Ithaca: Cornell University Press, 1992.

Sewall, Richard B. *The Life of Emily Dickinson*. Vol. I and Vol. II. New York: Farrar, Straus, & Giroux, 1974.

———. *The Lyman Letters: New Light on Emily Dickinson and Her Family*. Amherst, Massachusetts: University of Massachusetts Press, 1965.

Sexton, Anne. *The Complete Poems*. Boston: Houghton Mifflin Company, 1981.

Showalter, Elaine, ed. *Feminist Criticism: Essays on Women, Literature and Theory*. New York: Pantheon Books, 1985.

Spitzack, Carole. *Confessing Excess: Women and the Politics of Body Reduction*. New York: State University of New York, 1990.

Spretnak, Charlene. *Lost Goddesses of Early Greece: A Collection of Pre-Hellenic Myths*. Boston: Beacon Press, 1984.

Sternburg, Janet, ed. *The Writer on Her Work*. Vol. 1. New York: W. W. Norton & Co., 1980.

Stevenson, Anne. *Bitter Fame: A Life of Sylvia Plath*. Boston: Houghton Mifflin Co., 1989.

Tessman, Lora Heims. "Fathers and Daughters: Early Tones, Later Echoes." In *Father and Child: Developmental and Clinical Practices*. Ed. Stanley H. Cath, Alan Gurwitt, John Ross. Boston: Little, Brown & Co., 1982.

Ussher, Jane. *Women's Madness: Mysogony or Mental Illness?* Amherst: The University of Massachusetts Press, 1992.

van Gennep, Arnold. *The Rites of Passage*. Chicago: Chicago University Press, 1966.

Walker, Alice. *Possessing the Secret of Joy*. San Diego: Harcourt, Brace & Co., 1992.

Witting, Monique. *Les Guerillas*. Trans. David Le Vay. New York: Avon Books, 1971.

Woodman, Marion. *Leaving my Father's House: A Journey to Conscious Femininity*. Boston: Shambala Press, 1992.

———. *The Pregnant Virgin: A Process of Psychological Transformation*. Toronto: Inner City Books, 1985.

Wolff, Cynthia Griffin. *Emily Dickinson*. Reading, Massachusetts: Radcliff Biography Series, Addison-Wesley Publishing Company, 1988.

Wolff, Toni. *Structural Forms of the Feminine Psyche*. Trans. Paul Watzlawik. Private printing for the Students Association, C. G. Jung Institute. Zurich, July 1956.

Woolf, Virginia. *A Haunted House and Other Stories*. New York: Harcourt, Brace and World, 1944.

———. *A Room of One's Own*. New York: Harcourt Brace Jovanovich, 1989.

———. *Three Guineas*. New York: The Dial Press, 1978.

Young-Bruehl, Elisabeth. *Freud on Women: A Reader*. New York: W. W. Norton & Co., 1990.

Copyright Acknowledgments

Illustration and Plate Credits

The author and publisher wish to thank the custodians of the works of art and photographs for supplying them and granting permission to use them:

Art on the cover is by Sudie Rakusin, 3315 Arthur Minnis Road, Hillsborough, North Carolina 27278.

1. Photograph opposite the Preface: from the author.
2. *Vestal Virgin* reprinted with permission from the Louvre.
3. *Emily Dickinson* reprinted by permission from the Special Collections of Amherst College Library.
4. *The Honorable Edward Dickinson* reprinted by permission from the Jones Library, Amherst, Massachusetts.
5. *Demeter and Kore* Greek Stone Relief. Eleusis. 6th century B.C. reprinted by permission from Alinari Art Resource, N.Y.
6. *H.D. and Frances Perdita* reprinted by permission of The Beinecke Rare Book and Manuscript Library, Yale University Library.
7. *Professor Charles Leander Doolittle* reprinted by permission of The Beinecke Rare Book and Manuscript Library, Yale University Library.
8. *The Holy Marriage of Zeus and Hera* wooden relief from the Heraeon on Samos, c. 620 B.C.E. Published in Karl Schefold, *Myth and Legend in Greek Art*, New York: Harry N. Abrams, 1966, Plate 39.
9. *Sylvia Plath and Ted Hughes* reprinted by permission of Lilly Library, Indiana University, Bloomington, Indiana.
10. *Otto Plath at the Blackboard 1930.* Copyright © 1975. Reprinted with permission from the Estate of Aurelia Schober Plath. All rights reserved. Photo first appeared in *Letters Home*.
11. *Reclining Woman* Babylon, Parthian period. Reprinted by permission of the Louvre.
12. *Anais Nin* from *A Journal of Love: Incest—The Unexpurgated Diary of Anais Nin 1932–1934.* Copyright © 1992 by The Anais Nin Trust (Rupert Pole, Trustee). Reprinted by permission, courtesy of Gunther Stuhlmann, author's representative.
13. *Joaquin Nin* from *A Journal of Love: Incest—The Unexpurgated Diary of Anais Nin 1932–1934.* Copyright © 1992 by The Anais Nin Trust (Rupert Pole, Trustee). Reprinted by permission, courtesy of Gunther Stuhlmann, author's representative.

Index